P9-CQP-259

IF YOU CAN SEE IT
YOU CAN BE IT

Also by Jeff Henderson

Cooked:
My Journey from the Streets to the Stove

Chef Jeff Cooks:
In the Kitchen with
America's Inspirational New Culinary Star

America I AM Pass It Down Cookbook:
Over 130 Soul-Filled Recipes

Please visit the distributor of SmileyBooks: Hay House USA: **www.hayhouse.com**®;
Hay House Australia: **www.hayhouse.com.au**; Hay House UK: **www.hayhouse.co.uk**;
Hay House South Africa: **www.hayhouse.co.za**; Hay House India: **www.hayhouse.co.in**

IF YOU CAN SEE IT
YOU CAN
BE IT

12 Street-Smart Recipes
for Success

Chef Jeff Henderson

SMILEYBOOKS

Distributed by Hay House, Inc.
Carlsbad, California • New York City
London • Sydney • Johannesburg
Vancouver • Hong Kong • New Delhi

SUSTAINABLE FORESTRY INITIATIVE

Certified Chain of Custody
Promoting Sustainable Forestry
www.sfiprogram.org
SFI-01268

SFI label applies to the text stock

*This book is dedicated to my wife, Stacy
and our children Jamar, Jeffery Jr.,
Noel, Troy, Nicholas, and Grace*

Contents

Author's Note

Some names in this book have been changed to protect the privacy of those who graciously consented to share their experiences and life stories. I am grateful for their willingness to participate.

part 1

The Basics

chapter 1

Permission to Dream

> *Every great dream begins with a dreamer.*
> *Always remember, you have within you the strength,*
> *the patience, and the passion to reach for*
> *the stars to change the world.*
> — Harriet Tubman

No matter what stage I'm on, what detention center I visit, or what book signing I attend, someone will always ask: "Jeff, how did you do it, man?"

After all, I could easily have been a statistic. I could have fallen back into a trap with some of my boys in the 'hood doing the same ole hustle the same ole way. I could still be in the joint—or I could be dead.

People want to know how a youngster from poverty who failed his way through public school, got caught up in the '80s crack epidemic, got indicted and sent to federal prison, then didn't hit the streets again until he was 32 wound up working for five-star hotels. They want to know how he became the author of four books, a celebrity chef, a top inspirational speaker, and finally a mentor-coach who travels the world teaching and preaching about the power we have within us to transform our lives. In short, they want to know how I changed my own life.

The answer is simple: I made a choice to change. To go from being one of the "have-nots" to being one of the "haves." I decided that I wanted more from my life, and I found the way to get it. Though I had wise and unexpected mentors along the way, I still had to find my own way.

Here's where you just got lucky. Too often I didn't have anyone to show me the way up, but I'm here to show you how, right now. I didn't always take the fastest or the easiest route, but because real life became my boss and teacher, I can offer you a road map and some life-saving shortcuts—i.e., the fast pass to real freedom.

When I was first locked up, I felt my life was over. Done. Finished. I blamed everyone but myself for my imprisonment —my mother who raised me, my father, the police who arrested me, the informant who testified against me, the prosecutor who prosecuted me, the judge who sentenced me, anyone I could think of. When the reality sank in of the many years I would have to endure alongside 1,500 other men, I felt uncertain of myself and very alone, isolated from those who I thought would never leave me no matter what. Sometimes when I would awaken in the night, it all seemed like a dream. Thoughts of escape crept into my thinking at times—even thoughts of death.

Change will not come if we wait
for some other person or some other time . . .
We are the change that we seek.

— President Barack Obama

The first cubicle I was housed in was a stone's throw away from the Pacific Ocean, where large rocks bordered the miles of barbed-wire fence on the prison perimeter. Just hearing the water crashing up on those rocks helped keep me sane. It kept me thinking about the outside world every night. It helped ease the bitterness I had toward some of the women and homeboys in my life.

Just a few years earlier, it seemed as if I had it all—the house on the hill, the Mercedes, the Rolex, the cash, the respect. I'd started selling weed in high school, and I liked the money and the status that came with it—girls liked me, guys wanted to be cool with me. Then I moved into selling crack cocaine, and by the time I was 19, I was a millionaire. I treated it like a business: I never took the drugs I sold, and I never took part in the violence that plagued life on the streets where I lived and worked. But after five years my illegal business caught up with me. When I look back now, I guess I always knew my bad choices were going to take me down, I just didn't know when or how.

I started serving my prison sentence, at the age of 24, at Terminal Island, the medium-security federal correctional institution in San Pedro, California. I spent the first few years in Terminal Island's turn-of-the-century concrete-jungle North Yard. This highly restricted area was the place where mostly young, hardheaded Black and Latino homeboys; low-level members of drug cartels; heroin, crack, and meth junkies; and foot soldiers of the Aryan Brotherhood served their time.

It was also where I started to see some things more clearly for the very first time. On long summer nights I walked the prison track, in conversation with men from all over the world, from different gang sets, and with different religious beliefs. It was the old-timers, though, and the lifers, who walked miles each evening after chow, who helped me grasp reality in a whole new way.

Thanks to a few wise old heads who introduced me to books on history, self-improvement, and business and drilled down on me with some serious one-on-one real-life coaching, seeds of a more promising future outside the prison walls were sown in my soul. I began to see how narrow-minded my worldview was back in the neighborhood. And as I started to open my mind, my outlook on life started to change.

Things shifted even more when, as a first-time nonviolent offender who showed potential for rehabilitation, I was transferred after a few years to the less-restrictive South Yard—a section of the prison nestled under tall palm trees, with green rolling lawns and the best ocean view of the entire complex. This was where the Wall Street elite, Black intellectuals, corporate CEOs, top-tier counterfeiters, Colombian drug lords and street-level kingpins, Mafia godfathers, and other nonviolent white-collar crooks enjoyed the perks of "Club Fed."

My transformation took off after my relocation to the South Yard, through thought-provoking conversations and solid schooling in Black and White history, politics, race, religion, and a particular brand of street-smart economic realities. Over time I began to better understand how this game called life really works. Gradually, my bitterness softened, and those seeds of personal transformation started to take root.

Another turning point came when I started working in the prison kitchen. I learned to cook, and I realized that I liked it, and people started to say that my food was good. Food, after all, is one of the most important things in your life when you're locked up. I started to think that maybe I could flip this skill into a job on the outside.

After about three and a half years at Terminal Island, my security level dropped, and I became eligible for transfer to a low-security prison. I went first to Nellis, in Las Vegas, then was transferred to FPC Sheridan in Oregon. It took Alan Hershman, a part-time sheepherder and drug rehab instructor at Sheridan, to put the last piece into place—to get me to really stop justifying and accept the fact that I was the only one responsible for my choices and my crime. Something clicked in Hershman's class when I had to write a 55-page memoir exploring my criminal past and a 5-page strategic action plan detailing my future as a former felon. Looking back gave me a crucial perspective on where I'd been and how I'd gotten to where I was, and looking ahead showed me that there was something worthwhile where I was going.

In other words, I had finally learned how to dream again.

Now, I hope you're not reading this book in prison—though if you are, I'm really happy to offer you a helping hand to turn your life around the way I did. The thing is, mental prisons are as confining as physical ones. Both hold you in tiny, restricted, uninspiring spaces where your fate is in someone else's hands. And in both cases, your journey to freedom begins the day you decide to change your mind.

I'm going to show you how to launch your journey, if you're ready to take the first step—and you won't have to spend 20 years finding your way in the dark, like I did. I'm going to shine a light in the darkness and show you the way to live your dream. Because you don't have any time to waste.

Your Time Is Now

Society has a way of convincing the dismissed and the disadvantaged that they don't even have a right to dream. The fact is, it's hard to believe in dreaming when life has stomped the dreams right out of you. Happy childhood memories can get real blurred if you were raised in a home where physical or verbal abuse or alcohol or drug abuse was the norm. Losing a good job, failing in business, or descending into an addiction—no matter what kind—can also smother your ability to dream.

If you've been chronically unemployed or underemployed, if you've got a job but don't quite fit in with the status quo, or if you've been branded as someone with "issues"—co-workers, family, and even friends may be quick to hate on you for even daring to say the word *dream*—that is, if you even have the guts to share your life's ambitions with them.

I hear you, I feel you. I've been there. I know what it's like to be scarred by generational poverty or cursed by circumstantial poverty, to have lost your way because a parent rolled out on the family, to climb a few steps up the ladder of success only to slide back down, or to be denied simply because you made poor choices in life and now you're permanently certified as "less than."

Do not wait; the time will never be just right.

— Napoleon Hill

I know what life is like for the have-nots, however they got to where they are. Some of these individuals are stuck in the worst situations you can imagine and still they're willing to do whatever it takes to change their circumstances. Then you've got the other folks, the ones who aren't thinking about changing. They blame and make excuses, the way I used to. They're living the lives of victims. But remember, they have the potential to change their lives, too. All they need is for one spark of hope to catch fire inside them—and that can inspire them to act on their potential. This book is a way to ignite that spark.

If you're ready and willing to take action now—this book is for you. It doesn't matter if you were raised in a trailer park in the cornfields of Nebraska, a housing project on the South Side of Chicago, a barrio in East L.A., one of the nation's urban 'hoods, or a dysfunctional home in the 'burbs—I'm giving you permission to dream, and I want you to dream big. You could almost say you have an obligation to dream when you think of the ones who went before you and paved the way.

Former slaves didn't have the luxury of saying, "No, I can't," because they'd spent generations in bondage. Millions of immigrants who arrived on America's shores penniless, uneducated, speaking foreign languages, and unprepared for prejudices didn't have the option of turning back. Slaves and immigrants had one powerful thing in common—a *dream*. They were seduced, inspired, and driven by America's powerful dream of freedom and the promise of a better life for their loved ones.

There's one thing we need to get straight—and I'm not being heartless, I'm just keepin' it real. Whatever hole you're in, you have to climb out of it yourself. No one is going to rescue you— but you. I'll say it again: you have permission to dream, and to make your dreams come true. And I want you to start right here, right now, right where you are. I want you to realize that you have the potential to go where you want to go in life, and that now is the time to plan your trip to success. Don't settle for anything less.

I don't care if you're White, Black, Asian, or Latino; if you've been fired, laid off, long-term unemployed or underemployed, on welfare, or locked up; or if you're a single mom or dad—you got the right stuff to get yours. You've just got to learn how to spin your dream into reality—and I'm gonna show you exactly what I mean.

Get Your Hustle On

Back in the day, things were pretty simple. You had a dream, you worked hard, you got a good shot to make it happen. But today, access to the American dream is no longer guaranteed. Getting straight A's in school—not enough. Getting a college degree—not enough. Even working your behind off—not enough.

Back then, anyone with a pretty good idea and a decent amount of drive had a fighting chance to carve out a place in the world—the classic American-dream success story. But that isn't enough anymore. The paths that many of our parents and grandparents walked to find success have largely disappeared. To succeed today, you need to be a new breed of American dreamer. You need to be what I call a "hustlepreneur."

To hustle means to work strategically toward success when the odds are stacked against you.

— Supreme Understanding

The words *hustle* and *hustler* have gotten a bad rap. When we hear them, most of us think of scams or something shady or illegal. Dictionary definitions of *hustler* include "streetwalker," "wheeler-dealer," and, as *Merriam-Webster* puts it, "unscrupulous person who knows how to circumvent difficulties." Now, I'm not saying these definitions are wrong. I'm saying they're limited. In the words of author Supreme Understanding, the core definition is simple: "To hustle means to work strategically toward success when the odds are stacked against you."

Now, maybe you're asking, what are hustlepreneurs? They're successful entrepreneurs, solopreneurs, or strivers in any lane who have beaten those outsized odds to make something new of their lives. That might sound like some kind of a riddle, but it's really just the truth about the world we live in today. A hustlepreneur is someone who dreams big—and eats, sleeps, and breathes his or her dream until it becomes reality.

A hustlepreneur is what you need to become in order to make *your* dream of success a reality, no matter what your dream may be, and that's what I'm going to help you become in the course of this book. Stay with me—we'll get there! I'm going to guide you every step of the way in the chapters ahead. But first let's take a closer look at the traits of this uniquely motivated, highly skilled individual who's found a way to beat the odds.

If we take the negative stain away from hustlin', we see all kinds of people who provide for their families and support their communities using the core skills of the hustlepreneur. The mother in the projects who cooks and sells soul food out of her apartment to make a few extra dollars is a hustlepreneur. The father who works a 9-to-5 gig, then turns around and works odd jobs from fixing cars to doing minor home repair, is a hustlepreneur. The Latino mom and dad who work seven days a week cleaning people's houses so their kids can go to college—they're hustlepreneurs. These people know how to make it happen against all the odds. And they make the time to figure out how to overcome obstacles and challenges—big and small.

Yes, there are destructive "hustler" types out there—pimps, drug dealers, con men, and destroyers who exploit the weak for personal gain. But when you examine these traits without prejudice, you see that people with a positive hustle do a lot of the same things and possess a lot of the same traits that successful mainstream businesspeople do.

Hustlepreneurs aren't afraid to be first in line to try something new. They are creative problem solvers who never flinch at a no. They understand how to provide what people want and need and turn it into a revenue stream. They understand the concept of supply and demand and actually get pumped up instead of depressed by new market trends. They identify weak competitors and relieve them of their misery. They are always on alert and ready to outdo the competition. The very best hustlepreneurs—on the block or in the boardroom—are visionary, persuasive, and charismatic. Their "brand" is so powerful that people want to follow where they lead.

There are a lot of books on how to become successful on bookshelves out there. In this book, I'm giving you a new definition—I'm showing you the road map to success for the 21st century. When just an idea won't get you there, and just an education won't get you there, and even hard work still isn't enough, this is the road less traveled that you need to take to reach your dream.

A Hustlepreneurs' Hall of Fame

I said that the hustlepreneur is the new breed of American dreamer, and that's true, now that more of us have the odds stacked against us than ever before. But it's also true that the street-smart skills that will take you down the hustlepreneur's road go way back in our history; they've just gone by different names over the years. Just think of Madame C. J. Walker, or Henry Ford, or John H. Johnson, or the late Reginald Lewis, who built TLC Beatrice International, or former basketball great turned business mogul Magic Johnson, or Sara Blakely, creator of Spanx.

There's something about oppression, restrictions, and being told, "No, you can't," that makes the hustlepreneur want to say, "Just watch me!" When Black slaves were freed but still faced discrimination, they rose to the challenge by creating schools for their children and businesses that offered the products and services that Whites refused to sell them.

The challenges of segregation inspired some enterprising Black hustlepreneurs to build thriving communities such as "Black Wall Street" in Greenwood, Oklahoma—one of 20th-century America's wealthiest and most successful African American communities.

Hustlepreneurship cuts across lines of race and nationality. Irish, Italian, Jewish, and other European immigrants came to this country in the 19th and 20th centuries with nothing more than the clothes on their backs and a dream. Most didn't whine; they said, "Watch me," and went to work.

Andrew Carnegie, the "father of American steel," immigrated as a child with his parents in 1848, and before constructing his first steel mill in the mid-1870s, he worked in factories and spent time as a messenger boy, learning the hustle that would lift him to greatness. Since that time, new waves of immigrants—Asian, East Indian, Latino, African, and more—have used that same hustlepreneur spirit to beat the odds stacked against them and stake claims in areas where older generations of immigrant businesspeople have moved out and moved on. They've taken that sliver of opportunity and started import shops, grocers, dry cleaners, nail salons, and other small businesses in tough inner-city neighborhoods. And although some immigrant groups are sometimes criticized for dominating the business scene in low-income neighborhoods, their struggle, their skills, and their eye for opportunity should not be dismissed—all are part of the strong and sturdy hustlepreneur thread that is sewn into the fabric of American life.

To be ambitious is to be great in mind and soul.

— Marcus Garvey

Now, maybe you're saying, hold up—what do last century's immigrants have to do with me right now? The point is that America has always been a nation of hustlepreneurs. But their special brand of hustle is more crucial than ever to succeed in today's global economy. So let's take a look at a couple of people living an ordinary life in our world today who found the hustle that made their dreams come true.

When Tina Jackson got pregnant at the age of 17, before she even finished high school, any dreams she might have had seemed far away. Tina grew up in Houston, Texas, living back and forth between her divorced parents—both from the South, uneducated and from generations of poverty. Called "TJ" by her friends, she was always a smart girl academically; she had a sense of direction growing up. At the same time, Tina was schooled early in life about crime, drugs, and gang life from her younger brother—who eventually became a drug dealer—and her baby's father, a charismatic two-bit street hustler named Bank. It was tough for her after their breakup; she had to leave her father's house before the baby was born, so she went back to her mother, and went on welfare to support her daughter.

But though Tina let her circumstances hold her back for many years, she was always aware of her surroundings and the direction she wanted go in life. She finally decided to follow her dream to become a hairstylist. She earned her certificate at a local cosmetology school, then used her skills in negotiating and persuasion to get hired in an upscale salon downtown, away from the environment that for many years held her and so many others back.

Today Tina is working full time. She just bought her first home, and in her spare time she has taken up interior design and is turning it into a successful side business.

Keme Henderson took a different hustlepreneur path. At 37, Keme had a master's degree in social work with $100,000 in student loan debt and a job that wasn't making a dent in paying off her loans. Now, Keme loves to bake, and her friends kept telling her that her cookies and cheesecakes were good enough to sell. But the idea seemed too far-fetched—until she dug deep into her reserves of guts and passion and opened Somethin' Sweet, her own bakery operating out of her home.

With basically no start-up money, Keme put her hustling skills into action. "I'd load my cookies in my car on Saturday mornings and go from beauty shop to barbershop, to meeting people at gas stations, at their homes, at churches and businesses, and I'd hustle cookies and cheesecakes all day. I've also done cold calling to larger businesses, asking if I could drop off samples."

At one point, Keme knew only the negative definition of a hustler. "I always hated the word, sounded like it had to be illegal." Now, she says, "They could put my picture in the dictionary next to the word *hustlepreneur,* and I'd be perfectly okay with that."

Your Journey Starts Here

True hustlepreneurship means that you're aiming to operate at the top of your game, because you can see yourself as a success and you won't give up until you've reached the point where you can be a success. In this book, I'm going to walk you through all the steps you need to take to become a certified hustlepreneur. I'm going to show you how to drill down to the core of your dream—whether you can already see it or you don't know where to start. And whether you're from the mean streets or from Main Street, I'm going to give you a street-smart advantage that will put you in the fast lane to making your dream a reality.

I'm in the human transformation, potential, and upliftment business, so today I work hard to help others find their God-given gifts so they can make better choices in their lives. And that's the first step on your journey of transformation. It took me years and years of my life to put these pieces of my personal life puzzle into place—but like I said before, you don't have that kind of time to waste. So I've found some great resources to speed you on your way.

In the next chapter, I'm going to give you access to a couple of amazing tools that most people don't know about or never get access to—mirrors where you'll see your true self and your real strengths reflected in a whole new light. After that, I'll help you get a real clear picture of where you've been and where you want to go. And I'm gonna walk you through a creative, thought-provoking process that will help you hone right in on *your* American dream and figure out how to jump-start it, starting right now.

Once you've got your dream in your sights, I'm going to show you how to translate it into a vision, a set of goals, and an action plan to make it happen. Then I'll introduce you to Chef Jeff's 12 Street-Smart Recipes for Success. Each of these is like a secret ingredient that you can choose to use to create a unique recipe that's all your own, just the way you'd adjust a dish to your personal taste. I'll offer some stories of real people—some famous, some not—that show these street-smart strategies in action. And I'll give you a set of "Street-Smart Challenges" in each chapter to help you put your new skills to work.

You're going to be writing a bunch of stuff down in the exercises ahead, so before you do anything else, get yourself a yellow legal tablet or blank book. This will become your See It, Be It journal, and you'll use it in a bunch of ways as we go forward. Doesn't have to be anything fancy, though it can be if you want. You can create your journal on your laptop as well—whatever suits you best.

Chef Jeff's Recipe for Success

How do you learn to cook? By following recipes, right? You start by working with recipes that other people have developed, refined, and perfected. As you learn the techniques—knife skills, measuring standards, cooking processes—and start to understand how different ingredients and flavors work together, you reach a point where you don't need to work off of someone else's recipe anymore; you can step into the kitchen and come up with the bomb creative dishes of your own.

So I'm going to start by giving you my basic recipe for success that you can work with as a model while you build your success formula. We are in the kitchen of unlimited possibilities, and it won't be long before you have what you need to create your own recipe, based on your unique strengths, essence, and vision.

When I was 12 years old, I had a dream of one day owning a house on a hill with a white picket fence for me and my family and my mother, who never seemed to have the time to dream anything for herself. I mixed my childhood dream with the poor ingredients of a street hustler: bad choices, crime, and wealth at other people's expense, and I went to prison at 24. My time there changed the way I viewed myself and the world, and I started to stock my pantry with better ingredients. I got the chance for some real *self-discovery* and began to understand myself better than I ever had.

We've removed the ceiling above our dreams.
There are no more impossible dreams.

— Jesse Jackson

After my release in 1996, my new dream was to become a successful chef and never to return to prison again. I got into some serious *no-limits dreaming* as I drilled down on my new hopes for my life. I turned my dream into a crystal-clear *vision,* a set of precise *goals,* and a bulletproof *action plan* to make it a reality. Then I executed my plan with a new set of secret ingredients— the *street smarts* that I'd developed over the course of my life—to become the person who's talking to you right now.

Are you ready to get cookin'?

Chef Jeff's Recipe for Success

Yield:
What you put into it is what you'll get out of it

Ingredients:

- A whole lot of **self-discovery** to reveal the unique qualities that make you

- Tons of **limitless dreaming** to help you see where you want to go

- A generous quantity of **vision** to get your dream heated up

- Just the right amount of your own secret ingredients—the **street smarts** that you choose and add to make this recipe your own

Method:
Combine all ingredients in the large container of your mind and **mix well!** You'll have to decide for yourself, based on your circumstances and the unique qualities of yourself, exactly what technique you're going to use to cook up this standout dish. Is it going to be baked or broiled? Grilled or fried to perfection? Whatever you decide, now you've put your **goals** and your **action plan** in the mix. And your recipe for success won't be the same as anyone else's.

If your recipe's not coming out right, don't get frustrated and don't give up. Go back to the work table and learn the lessons of life from your mistakes. Change up your approach a bit. Tweak the proportions of your life ingredients—use a bit more of this and a little less of that—or just rethink your method of preparation and come up with a new action plan. Get out of your comfort zone and take another look at the secret ingredients that may be missing from your mental mix.

There's a line I love—something that Benjamin Jealous, head of the NAACP, used to describe what the NAACP does. He said that it "dreams bold dreams and then turns them into reality." That's exactly what we're going to do together in the pages ahead. I want you to dream your boldest, biggest dream. I want you to see it so clearly you can almost touch it and taste it. Then I want you to turn it into reality using your unique recipe for success, based on the essence of who you are.

Now, I know you can do this. I've given you my basic recipe, and I'll walk you through every step in the pages ahead as you learn to make it your own. I know that if you can see it, you can be it—so get ready to get yours!

chapter 2

Know Thyself

> *If I didn't define myself for myself,*
> *I would be crunched into other people's*
> *fantasies for me and eaten alive.*
> — Audre Lorde

I've often said that my arrest in 1988 was truly a rescue and my imprisonment actually saved my life. This revelation, of course, came years after I stood in a San Diego courtroom in 1989, numbed to the bones as Chief Judge Gordon Thompson sent me away to the big house: over a decade of my life was to be served.

I felt hopeless as I glimpsed the emotional faces of my family in the gallery. I believed that my life was over. Who could have imagined that a new beginning was in the future for me, and that a better life was about to begin right on the South Yard of Terminal Island? Who would have guessed that a few streetwise fellow inmates would be the teachers and counselors who would hold up a mirror for me to take a hard look at my life and direct me on the path of discovering who I really was?

Please understand that I would never wish my past life on anyone. My goal is to help you avoid wasted years of lockdown, whether in a mental prison or a physical one. It took me decades to find a mirror that would give me a clear reflection of who I truly was, but I'm going to give you the fast pass. I want to get you to a place where you can really see your dreams because you have the power that comes from knowing *who you are*—your true strengths, your real personality, and your natural gifts.

> **It's time to look yourself in the eye and discover your true self.**

I say it right on the cover of this book: *if you can see it, you can be it.* Now it's time to look yourself in the eye and discover your true self. Self-awareness will help you *be you* more effectively because when you see value in yourself, you can communicate better, make better decisions, and stop wasting time. The more you know about yourself, the easier it will be to make decisions that allow you to express the full range of who you are. And no matter what stage of life you're in, self-knowledge can be the difference between going around on a merry-go-round repeating the same mistakes or playing to your greatest strengths. But until you have that knowledge, all the wishing and hoping in the world won't make your dreams come true.

Dream the Right Dream

For the past six years, I've been a part of Disney's Dreamers Academy with television and radio talk show host, best-selling author, and comedian Steve Harvey. This mentoring program was created by Disney and Steve to help disadvantaged teens prepare for real-world careers and life in general. I once listened to Harvey tell the challenged youth how he became a successful entertainer, author, and philanthropist by discovering his gifts.

Before performing stand-up comedy for the first time in 1985, Harvey worked as an insurance salesman, a car assembler at Ford Motor Company, and a postal worker. He even tried professional boxing. Like most who have achieved success, Harvey did what he had to do to survive. But the one thing that lifted him out of dead-end jobs was a laserlike focus on his true and extraordinary gift—making people laugh.

This self-knowledge was the launchpad that helped rocket Harvey into the stratosphere of superstardom. There isn't a soul on earth who can snatch Steve's dream or derail his life's quest because he's so deeply in tune with what comes naturally to him that he can now branch out into all sorts of enterprises—game shows, talk shows, books, and movies. He's rolling with a limitless mind machine and ready to tackle whatever his unshackled, creative self comes up with for him. He's always ready to be in the game because he *knows who he is*.

When I talk to my own children about their future, that's exactly how I put it to them: they have to know themselves before they can dream the dream that's right for them. Some of us are so quick to send our kids off to college and put ourselves or them deep in debt—but are they going for what they were born to do or are they going to please others? I tell my children I won't bankroll their college until I feel they've figured out their greatest strengths and their academic weakness. You want to become a newscaster? Well, if you're an introvert and you don't like to talk, you're not going to be on television delivering no news to no one. You want to work in book publishing? Well, if you can't sit still long enough to read a book, that's not gonna work for you.

Like Steve Harvey's, my own dreams are rooted in the DNA of who I am. Don't get me wrong, I can still miss a step here and there and have setbacks, but they won't break my stride. Why? Because I'm in that space now where the inner me and the outer me understand each other and work in sync like a bicycle chain and the wheel sprocket. My deep self-understanding, self-development, and commitment to who I am have opened doors for me in the culinary and communication arenas, including book publishing, motivational speaking, and education. This is how I became Chef Jeff Henderson.

Know Thyself to Be Thyself

Way, way back in the day, I mean back in the B.C. times, the Greeks built a temple of knowledge, wisdom, and prophecy dedicated to the Greek god Apollo. The Temple of Apollo at Delphi is one of the most famous shrines in the world. Among its ruins, carved onto the rocky surface of its outer temple, a great truth is still visible that, translated into English, reads:

"Man, know thyself."

In other words, people have gotten this message for thousands of years. So I'd say it's about time for you to ask the same question: *Do you really know yourself?* I'm not talking about the way you think other people see you—like your mama who tells you you're the best of the best because she loves you, or the shady girlfriend or boyfriend who makes you feel like you're never good enough. I'm talking about you on the *inside,* my friend. I'm asking if you can see the strengths, weaknesses, and ways of thinking, being, and behaving that are uniquely yours. The core essences that can help you turn your dreams into reality.

Who are you, really? What do you bring to the table that no one else can offer? Can you answer these questions for real? If not, don't trip; we'll get there, stay the course with me. And don't be surprised if you feel uncertain right now. The truth is that we don't always see ourselves clearly or objectively, the way we really are. Lots of times the picture is clouded by judgments, both good and bad—our own and other people's, too. It's clouded by how we wish we could be, or how we're afraid we're not good enough, or what one person said about us yesterday, or what some other person wants from us tomorrow.

So how do you get a clear look in that mirror that's going to show you your real self? It's not the same as looking in the bathroom mirror, where you can see if you need a shave or a haircut or a few more hours of sleep. But the good news is there are tools you can use to sharpen your vision—and we're going to open up that box in just a few minutes and pull out two powerful self-tests designed to show you *you* in a whole new light.

You never find yourself until you face the truth.

— Pearl Bailey

None of this happened for me overnight; there was no magic wand, no single "aha" moment. I struggled with self-discovery on the streets and while in prison and learned how to face the realities about myself. In fact, for me, "Man, know thyself" is an ongoing process of *discovery and rediscovery* even to this day. It's an amazing adventure that I'm going to share with you right now. Without a doubt, once you really become in tune with your unique personality, character strengths, and special abilities and learn how to parlay those traits into your dreams, you can become unstoppable if only you really see yourself in that position. And if you got a knot in your stomach when you read the word *test* a minute ago, chill out—it's not nearly as hard as you think.

Tests and Detests

As a kid, I never did well with tests in school. I was so fidgety, I couldn't sit still for five minutes. My mind was always racing as I tried to figure out stuff. When I sat down to take school tests, I felt confined and nervous, always looking around shadily. I liked multiple-choice tests more than others because I could just guess at the answers, as wrong as they were; it was like rolling dice and hoping to score at least a C.

About 18 months into my prison sentence, I worked up the courage to take an aptitude test. It was a requirement of the GED course I had decided to take, thanks to the encouragement of a few educated inmates. The test was a letdown in some respects and a boost up in others. I scored low in English and math, but I scored pretty well in history. It was a sign that my newfound interest in politics, world and American history, and the different cultures that the seasoned prisoners shared with me was starting to pay off.

For the first time in my life, a test was a good thing, because I learned about my weaknesses in basic education. I had a real yardstick, one that wasn't personal; no one was judging me. It was like reading your gas gauge to confirm how much gas is in your tank. You don't decide your car is bad because the tank is low; you just need to know if you can make it to your destination. I needed to know my strengths and weaknesses if I ever hoped to achieve my dreams.

It took me close to three years to earn my GED because I failed the test over and over. But I became less intimidated and more determined each time because, for the first time, I was able to connect test taking and the value of education with the act of self-discovery.

Many of you feel the same way about taking tests as I did at first—and there's a reason so many of us have come to hate or fear tests of all kinds. The standardized testing that was the norm for schools when I was growing up—the same kind you probably had to take, too—it's just not designed to zone in on students' individual strengths; it was created to test millions of kids across the board, except I think they forgot to weigh in on the disadvantaged mindset. For the most part, standardized tests don't measure your intelligence or even how much you've learned; they just measure how well you take tests. But if you don't pass these tests at an early age, you get labeled as a low achiever. And once that happens, you naturally get the idea that tests are not for you.

But the tests you're going to use in the pages ahead aren't tests you can pass or fail. They're designed to focus on your strengths and who you are. This is information you can't afford to sleep on. Even organizations like the NFL are getting hip to these tests. In place of the short, basic intelligence test they've given to prospective players for decades—with unrevealing questions on subjects like arithmetic—the league has shifted to a new psychological assessment designed to measure players' motivation, mental toughness, and passion: the qualities they need to succeed on the field.

So let's stop fearing these tests. It's time to up your game for real. After all, life is all about tests—tests of our will, our faith, and our ability to hang on during hard times. Tests, like life, can be an adventure in their own right, if we cultivate the right attitude—and my attitude is that this exploration of your character strengths and hidden abilities can be the first step in changing your life once and for all.

Know Thy Strengths: The Values in Action (VIA) Inventory

Maybe you're wondering how any test can measure everybody? After all, most of us like to think of ourselves as complicated, one-of-a kind individuals. And in many ways that's true. There's no other you; everyone's DNA is unique. No one else has had your exact upbringing or personal experiences with individuals and circumstances. But on another level—as different as we all are—we also all have a lot in common. And science can prove it.

Check this out. Back in 2000, 55 top scientists set out to explore the characteristics that human beings have been using to create, strive, and thrive since the beginning of time. They studied the writings and teachings of philosophers, religious leaders, and other great thinkers across centuries and cultures. Out of all this research, they found six universal qualities that they drilled down even further into 24 key character strengths. And they dreamed up—you got it—a test, called the Values in Action Inventory of Strengths (VIA for short).

Now, some of you are probably thinking, *What the heck is a Values in Action Inventory of Strengths?* Stay with me now! Developed at the VIA Institute in Cincinnati, the scientifically validated survey, which you can take for free online, is designed to help people know themselves so they can put their unique characteristics to good use. The mission of the VIA Institute is "to strengthen the world," says psychologist Dr. Ryan M. Niemiec, VIA's education director. "It's to educate people to tap into their strengths, to create their best life but also to improve the lives of others."

The VIA Survey works like this: it gives you 120 statements to either agree or disagree with: things like "I find the world a very interesting place" and "I never quit a task before it is done." Then it analyzes your answers and tells you which of those 24 character strengths are the very strongest in you—a groundbreaking opportunity for insight. "For the first time in history, there is this formal classification of what the wisest philosophers and theologians and educators throughout time have had to say about what's best in human beings," explains Dr. Niemiec. "It's fascinating for people to apply that to themselves and see that these are positive characteristics that they have, that they can work on, that they can express to other people." Get ready, because the test can be an eye-opener: "Some people react with surprise" when they learn their strengths, Dr. Niemiec says. "They're kind of shocked in a positive way."

These are the 24 strengths that VIA tests:

VIA Classification of Character Strengths

Appreciation of Beauty and Excellence: You notice and appreciate beauty, excellence, and/or skilled performance in all domains of life, from nature to art, to mathematics, to science, to everyday experience.

Bravery: You are a courageous person who does not shrink from threat, challenge, difficulty, or pain. You speak up for what is right even if there is opposition. You act on your convictions.

Creativity: Your ability to think of new ways to do things is a crucial part of who you are. You are never content with doing something the conventional way if a better way is possible.

Curiosity: You are curious about everything. You are always asking questions, and you find all subjects fascinating. You like exploration and discovery.

Fairness: Treating all people fairly is one of your abiding principles. You do not let your personal feelings bias your decisions about other people. You give everyone a chance.

Forgiveness: You forgive those who have done you wrong. You always give people a second chance. Your guiding principle is mercy, not revenge.

Gratitude: You are aware of the good things that happen to you, and you never take them for granted. Your friends and family members know that you are a grateful person because you always take the time to express your thanks.

Honesty: You are an honest person, not only because you speak the truth but also because you live your life in a genuine and authentic way. You are down-to-earth and unpretentious; you are a "real" person.

Hope: You expect the best in the future, and you work to achieve it. You believe that the future is something you can control.

Humility: You do not seek the spotlight, preferring to let your accomplishments speak for themselves. You do not regard yourself as special, and others recognize and value your modesty.

Humor: You like to laugh and tease. Making others smile is important to you. You try to see the light side of all situations.

Judgment: Thinking things through and examining them from all sides are important aspects of who you are. You do not jump to conclusions, and you rely only on solid evidence to make your decisions. You are able to change your mind.

Kindness: You are kind and generous to others, and you are never too busy to do a favor. You enjoy doing good deeds for others, even if you do not know them well.

Leadership: You excel at the tasks of leadership, encouraging a group to get things done and preserving harmony within the group by making everyone feel included. You do a good job organizing activities and seeing that they happen.

Love: You value close relationships with others, in particular those in which sharing and caring are reciprocated. The people to whom you feel most close also feel most close to you.

Love of Learning: You love learning new things, whether in a class or on your own. You have always loved school, reading, and museums; anywhere and everywhere you see an opportunity to learn.

Perseverance: You work hard to finish what you start. No matter the project, you "get it out the door" in timely fashion. You do not get distracted when you work, and you take satisfaction in completing tasks.

Perspective: Although you may not think of yourself as wise, your friends do. They value your perspective on matters and turn to you for advice. You have a way of looking at the world that makes sense to others and yourself.

Prudence: You are a careful person, and your choices are consistently prudent ones. You do not say or do things that you might later regret.

Self-Regulation: You self-consciously regulate what you feel and what you do. You are a disciplined person. You are in control of your appetites and your emotions, not vice versa.

Social Intelligence: You are aware of the motives and feelings of other people. You know what to do to fit in with different social situations, and you know what to do to put others at ease.

Spirituality: You have strong and coherent beliefs about the higher purpose and meaning of the universe. You know where you fit in the larger scheme. Your beliefs shape your actions and are a source of comfort to you.

Teamwork: You excel as a member of a group. You are a loyal and dedicated teammate, you always do your share, and you work hard for the success of your group.

Zest: Regardless of what you do, you approach it with excitement and energy. You never do anything halfway or halfheartedly. For you, life is an adventure.

More than 2 million people around the world have taken the VIA Survey, and I want even more people who've been downsized, dismissed, disregarded, and slapped around by life to take this game-changing test. Those of us from the world of "have-nots" or "lost-a-lots" live in environments where people too often focus on what's wrong with us—our lack of money, education, or status. We *need* more positive affirmation of what's right with us.

If you're thinking that a test like this can't tell you anything about yourself you don't already know, you will be surprised, my friend. If I'd been asked to list my greatest strengths before I took the VIA Survey, most likely I would have said "my ability to influence and inspire people, build relationships, and find my way around obstacles." After taking the VIA Survey and having the answers scientifically assessed and ranked, I discovered that my three leading character strengths are actually "appreciation of beauty and excellence," "gratitude," and "zest." It's like I said before: we just don't always see clearly in that mirror of self, and that's why it's so important to get a straight-up view. Not that I'm saying the test knew me better than I knew me; in fact, when I thought about the strengths the VIA Survey showed me, I realized they all reflected steps on the path I'd taken to become who I am today.

What you'll discover will be wonderful.
What you'll discover will be yourself.

— Alan Alda

Looking at my first character strength—"appreciation of beauty and excellence"—took me back to my early years in L.A., when I'd ride the school bus through neighborhoods full of elegant cribs and dream that someday one of those could be mine. This strength explains why the ocean view, the palm trees, and the manicured lawns at Terminal Island's South Yard prison facility moved me to dream bigger than ever about life's possibilities.

And yes, I am extremely grateful. When we were kids, my grandmother and my mother taught my sister and me always to be grateful for what we had. Thanking people and showing gratitude for what people have given and shared with me is in my DNA. This book and the knowledge I'm sharing on how to become who you were meant to be are a direct reflection of that gratitude. And after a decade in the joint, locked up on an island, nearly forgotten under restrictive rules and surrounded by concrete, barbed wire, and gun towers, I remain extremely grateful for little things like sitting on a soft sofa with a remote control in my hand or going for a walk with my family on the beach whenever I feel like it and even going to the bathroom with no one watching.

My third strongest character trait is "zest," and life for me, indeed, has always been an adventure. I've never used illegal drugs or narcotics. Never needed them to feel bigger than life. I can see now that I was always high on what life offered; I didn't need an external crutch because I had zest for life.

It's a cliché, but as a kid, and even today, I am the early bird getting that worm! I wake up at 4:30 A.M. every day, focused on being successful—which means mastering what I do best, no matter what road I must travel to get there.

Zest is still with me every day, too. When I love to do something, when I'm excited about knocking out a goal that I'm passionate about, I go hard at it, full of everything I got. When I set out to become a chef, I was a beast—I made the decision to zone out everything that had nothing to do with chefdom. I had no life balance; at times I neglected my family, which I'm not proud of, but I wanted success that bad. I was never late, I was the first to work, I asked questions, I studied the most talented cooks on the hot line, and then I turned my focus on the top chefs in the business, duplicating the strong traits that made them the best and most respected in the food world. Besides creating the best-tasting food I could make, it was also about the beauty of the food, how it was served, and the final presentation of the dish—that's what brought the ultimate appreciation to me as a chef.

Today, when I'm not in the kitchen cooking or serving up hope in prisons and alternative high schools, I'm taking the stage for some of the world's biggest brands: UBS, American Express, and Bank of America. The energy and excitement I bring to my corporate audiences have established me as a presenter who connects corporations to the stories of everyday Americans. Having the ability to do this and the blessing to serve the have-nots—these I truly believe are my greatest strengths and one day my legacy.

And what does knowing my strengths mean for me? It means that whenever I'm doing business, whether I'm preparing for a speech or making a new career move, I can make decisions that build on my greatest assets. I pass up projects or ideas that don't connect me to my signature strengths and brand. Things that are less than excellent or don't fuel my zest for living or satisfy my need to have things around me that have a lot of visual appeal, great style, or natural beauty don't stay for long in my world.

It also means that I can find new ways to develop and reinforce those strengths. If you can see it, you can be it, or, to put it another way, when you know it, you can grow it! Dr. Niemiec at the VIA Institute puts it this way: "When people see their strengths, they start to identify and see themselves in that way. 'Oh, I'm the creative, curious person' or 'I'm the fair, kind' or 'the spiritually creative person. . . .' Then they begin to shift their identity and how they see themselves." Once you have your gifts in focus, not only will you see yourself more clearly, you're going to start drawing people to you who also see your special gifts and talents.

Finding the Strongest You

The mission of the VIA Institute is to strengthen the world with people who have found their strengths and use them to create their best life and the best life for others. If you're ready to become one of them, let's get started!

There are more advanced VIA reports available for a reasonable cost and even coaching on ways to apply them in real life, but let's start with the free VIA Survey online where you will receive immediate results listing your strengths in rank order at no cost. You can use your computer, tablet, or smartphone—and you'll be investing 20 minutes in you instead of updating your Facebook page or reading the latest celebrity gossip.

To start, go to www.chefjeffseeitbeit.com and click on the link to the VIA Survey. That'll take you to the Website of the VIA Institute, where you'll click on the "Get Your Free Profile" tab. You will be asked to create an account with a username and password. After you've registered and logged in, you'll be directed to the page where you will take the VIA Survey. If you're not real computer savvy, just ask a friend to sit with you and look over your shoulder while you go through the steps. (Just don't ask your friend to give you the answers—it's not that kind of test!) You never know, your friend might be interested in taking the VIA Survey as well. You can also visit the book Website and watch a short video where I'll walk you through the process.

As I said, the survey is made up of 120 questions—each one a statement that you rate on a scale from "very much like me" to "very much unlike me." Answer all the questions, then click "Submit" and you're done.

You'll see three options for viewing your results. If you choose the free VIA Me! Character Strengths Profile, you'll immediately be directed to a report that ranks your 24 strengths in order from strongest to not-so-strong. Think about that for a second. The VIA Me! profile *doesn't measure weaknesses*. You will only see your highest "signature" strengths, middle strengths, and then lesser strengths. If you choose one of the more in-depth reports for a modest fee, you'll see a link to download your report.

All the reports come with an explanation of each strength, and I want you to read about all 24. After you've done that, zoom in on your top five strengths. Mine are: *Appreciation of Beauty and Excellence, Gratitude, Zest, Creativity,* and *Hope.* What are yours?

List your five top signature character strengths in your See It, Be It journal.

1. _____

2. _____

3. _____

4. _____

5. _____

Owning Your Strengths

This is great information, but it's still sort of general—just a set of words. You're the only one who can connect the dots and zero in on how these newly discovered qualities show up in your life.

So find a quiet place to kick back, open up your See It, Be It journal, and start thinking about what you've just written down. Do you recognize these strengths in yourself? Did any of them surprise you? Did they get you to look at your familiar qualities in a new way?

Gene, 49, now has a stable job and the makings of a career as a catering manager at a gourmet shop, but he's also cycled in and out of prison. "This last stay has really made me start thinking clearer," he says. "For the first time in my life I can say that I am happy with the way my life is going." And his VIA results are helping him to grow even stronger: "I am learning more and more about myself every day."

When Gene took the VIA test, here's what showed up as his top five signature strengths:

1. Teamwork

2. Kindness

3. Gratitude

4. Appreciation of Beauty and Excellence

5. Leadership

Now, what do you do with this information? Let's say your top strength is "fairness." What have you done recently—or even a while back—that represents your being fair? Maybe you could have taken credit for someone else's idea at work, but you didn't. Or maybe you stepped in and helped a couple of friends resolve a beef they couldn't fix. Maybe, when you were a kid, it upset you when someone got in trouble for something he didn't do. Chances are you'll find yourself coming up with plenty of examples. If you're stuck, though, you can use the VIA report to jump-start you with ideas of "fairness" in action. Or ask someone who knows you well, someone you can trust, to tell you the truth: "Do you think of me as fair? Why do you think that?"

When you've thought over your top five strengths, take your journal and write a short summary of each one. Make sure to write in full sentences, in the first person. When you say "I"—*I am this, I do this*—you step into those strengths and own them. And having this information in writing can remind you that you were born this way. These are traits you've always used, instinctively, even before you knew them by name.

Here's what this looked like for Gene:

Gene's Top Five
VIA Signature Strengths

My Top Character Strength: *Teamwork*

I am a team player. I like being in a group or club and getting things done.

My Second Character Strength: *Kindness*

I am a very kind person. I tend to put others' feelings in front of mine.

My Third Character Strength: *Gratitude*

I am very grateful for everything I have in my life. I am a very blessed person. I am now realizing that.

My Fourth Character Strength: *Appreciation of Beauty and Excellence*

I love to look at things of beauty. Even when I am out walking, I tend to stop and smell the roses. There are so many beautiful things around me I don't want to miss.

My Fifth Character Strength: *Leadership*

I am a strong leader. I will do what it takes to get the task done.

Let's look at another example. Ursula, 40, is a single mother who's recently relocated from the urban North to the urban South and been "hustling" for a year. She supports her five-year-old with a string of freelance jobs from office temping to proofreading to being a virtual assistant for busy entrepreneurs. Her VIA test revealed these top five signature strengths:

1. Love of Learning
2. Spirituality
3. Curiosity
4. Hope
5. Appreciation of Beauty and Excellence

This list didn't entirely surprise her—it just shed a new light on what she thought she already knew. "I definitely see all of these characteristics in me," she said. "What's new is thinking of these as *strengths*. That excites me!"

Here's what Ursula wrote when she reflected on how her top five strengths show up in her life.

Ursula's Top Five VIA Signature Strengths

My Top Character Strength: *Love of Learning*

Love of learning means that I love learning things for learning's sake. Something I have said to myself as long as I could remember is "Not a day goes by that I don't learn something new." And for the most part this is very true. No matter how mundane, I do learn something new every day. I've just embarked on a new study and ordered books aplenty from Amazon.

My Second Character Strength: *Spirituality*

My spirituality is listed as number two, and I think it would be more of a tie with number 1. My spirituality is what informs me. I have always relied on my connection to Source, though I've called it many names. It has been this more than anything that has given my life the most meaning.

My Third Character Strength: *Curiosity*

Curiosity. To me, this has what has driven both my quest for learning and spirituality, an "openness to experience." I can think of many things I've experienced because I wanted to see what would happen. I think that would definitely qualify as curiosity!

My Fourth Character Strength: *Hope*

Again, I never would have looked at this as a strength, but it seems that for many periods all I had was hope. Hope that things would be different/better. My hope is different now, it tends more toward optimism. I no longer hope that things will be different/better, but I just know they will.

My Fifth Character Strength: *Appreciation of Beauty and Excellence*

I love this! My fifth strength is appreciation of beauty and excellence. Nothing inspires greatness in me more than seeing things "done with high quality" and "performed with excellence." I LIVE for this. I *can* and *do* appreciate this aspect of me, and am thrilled that it can be considered a strength!

Now, write about your own signature strengths in your See It, Be It journal.

My Top Character Strength:

_____

_____

My Second Character Strength:

_____

_____

My Third Character Strength:

_____

_____

My Fourth Character Strength:

_____

_____

My Fifth Character Strength:

_____

_____

Okay, you've seen how your character strengths show up in your life. Let's go a step further and look at how they've actually served you, in real, specific ways. When has your fairness helped you out? Has your spirituality shored you up when times got tough? Has your honesty worked to your advantage? Be as specific as you can and complete the following statements (or write them out fresh in your journal).

My top character strength

was useful when . . .

My second character strength

was useful when . . .

My third character strength

was useful when . . .

My fourth character strength

was useful when . . .

My fifth character strength

was useful when . . .

In case you're wondering if it's possible to apply your results in your life in a realistic way, listen to Amsa Herut, age 23—a recent college grad working her first job as a broadcast associate for a TV station—who's contemplating her future. Amsa Herut finds herself drawn to both law school and the study of literature. "I'm confused about what career path I really want to pursue," she said. "I took the test in hopes of gaining some clarity. I definitely can see how these traits play out in my life—the test offered me a lot of insight."

By now, your mirror should be reflecting you a new, realistic picture of the "strongest you." I hope you're really seeing—and feeling—your greatest gifts. But knowing your strengths takes you only so far. What do I mean? Well, you don't just sit in a closet and treasure your gifts. You use them in the world, and the way you do that is another part of you that's unique to you. How you relate to other people, how you operate in most situations— things like this make up your *personality,* and that's the part of the picture we'll move on to now.

The Enneagram: What's Your Number?

I admit I was really satisfied that I got this "know thyself" stuff down cold after studying my VIA Survey results. But one of my downest mentors, Jack, challenged me to take the road less traveled and roll toward another level of self-discovery. Jack persuaded me that if I was truly committed, I should look at myself through another lens as well. And that's when he turned me on to the Enneagram.

I know, I know, the word *enneagram* sounds totally from space. At least it sounded that way to me the first time I heard it. But it turns out the word is actually just a stand in for the "number nine." The Enneagram—why don't we make it cool, let's call it the E-gram—is a self-awareness test that breaks down all the ways people think and act into nine types that go back at least as far as the "know thyself" oracle at Delphi.

*Knowledge of the self is the mother
of all knowledge.*

— Khalil Gibran

Now, I'm not talking about "types" like the superficial stereo-types we build up around race or class or walk of life. I'm talking about a much deeper way of seeing ourselves. Russ Hudson, co-founder of the Enneagram Institute in Stone Ridge, New York, and co-author of *The Wisdom of the Enneagram, Personality Types, Understanding the Enneagram,* and *Discovering Your Personality Types* helped to translate this contemporary yet centuries-old tradition for me: "The Enneagram acts as a kind of 'mirror' to reveal features of our personality that normally are invisible to us," he said. "It offers an amazing map of human consciousness and helps us raise our awareness of who we are and how we function in daily life."

There it is again, the mirror we've been looking into. Our reflection in the E-gram shows us what's driving us when we're on "cruise control"—and it shows us what happens to our automatic reactions and patterns when something in our lives takes us off course. We need balance in order to live our best lives, and the E-gram not only helps us achieve this balance, it helps us to maintain it by showing us how our personalities function in real life from the unhealthiest (highly stressed) to the healthiest (stress-free) levels.

Your straight-no-chaser E-gram profile helps you become aware of how you think about yourself, why you think that way, how you act when you're stressed or tripping out, how you act when you're feeling good, and how you affect the people around you. It reveals what happens when you forget key parts of yourself because you've developed a one-track mind or your blind side has tossed your glasses out of the window. Discovering, digesting, and integrating your E-gram number into your everyday life can not only help you right your course when you're off track, its wisdom can also save you from making a lot of big mistakes. As Russ Hudson emphasizes, "The Enneagram is about learning to be more aware and awake to how we handle the things that life throws at us."

Here's how the Enneagram groups what seems like the vast range of motivations, attitudes, fears, and desires into nine basic personality types:

The Nine Types in Brief

Type One: The Reformer

The principled, idealistic type. Ones are conscientious and ethical, with a strong sense of right and wrong. They are teachers, crusaders, and advocates for change: always striving to improve things, but afraid of making a mistake. Well-organized, orderly, and fastidious, they try to maintain high standards, but can slip into being critical and perfectionistic. They typically have problems with resentment and impatience.

At their Best: wise, discerning, realistic, and noble. Can be morally heroic.

Type Two: The Helper

The caring, interpersonal type. Twos are empathetic, sincere, and warm-hearted. They are friendly, generous, and self-sacrificing, but can also be sentimental, flattering, and people-pleasing. They are well-meaning and driven to be close to others, but can slip into doing things for others in order to be needed. They typically have problems with possessiveness and with acknowledging their own needs.

At their Best: unselfish and altruistic, they have unconditional love for others.

Type Three: The Achiever

The adaptable, success-oriented type. Threes are self-assured, attractive, and charming. Ambitious, competent, and energetic, they can also be status-conscious and highly driven for advancement. They are diplomatic and poised, but can also be overly concerned with their image and what others think of them. They typically have problems with workaholism and competitiveness.

At their Best: self-accepting, authentic, everything they seem to be—role models who inspire others.

Type Four: The Individualist

The introspective, romantic type. Fours are self-aware, sensitive, and reserved. They are emotionally honest, creative, and personal, but can also be moody and self-conscious. Withholding themselves from others due to feeling vulnerable and defective, they can also feel disdainful and exempt from ordinary ways of living. They typically have problems with melancholy, self-indulgence, and self-pity.

At their Best: inspired and highly creative, they are able to renew themselves and transform their experiences.

Type Five: The Investigator

The perceptive, cerebral type. Fives are alert, insightful, and curious. They are able to concentrate and focus on developing complex ideas and skills. Independent, innovative, and inventive, they can also become preoccupied with their thoughts and imaginary constructs. They become detached, yet high-strung and intense. They typically have problems with eccentricity, nihilism, and isolation.

At their Best: visionary pioneers, often ahead of their time, and able to see the world in an entirely new way.

Type Six: The Loyalist

The committed, security-oriented type. Sixes are reliable, hard-working, responsible, and trustworthy. Excellent "troubleshooters," they foresee problems and foster cooperation, but can also become defensive, evasive, and anxious—running on stress while complaining about it. They can be cautious and indecisive, but also reactive, defiant, and rebellious. They typically have problems with self-doubt and suspicion.

At their Best: internally stable and self-reliant, courageously championing themselves and others.

Type Seven: The Enthusiast

The busy, productive type. Sevens are extroverted, optimistic, versatile, and spontaneous. Playful, high-spirited, and practical, they can also misapply their many talents, becoming over-extended, scattered, and undisciplined. They constantly seek new and exciting experiences, but can become distracted and exhausted by staying on the go. They typically have problems with impatience and impulsiveness.

At their Best: they focus their talents on worthwhile goals, becoming appreciative, joyous, and satisfied.

Type Eight: The Challenger

The powerful, aggressive type. Eights are self-confident, strong, and assertive. Protective, resourceful, straight-talking, and decisive, but can also be egocentric and domineering. Eights feel they must control their environment, especially people, sometimes becoming confrontational and intimidating. Eights typically have problems with their tempers and with allowing themselves to be vulnerable.

At their Best: self-mastering, they use their strength to improve others' lives, becoming heroic, magnanimous, and inspiring.

Type Nine: The Peacemaker

The easygoing, self-effacing type. Nines are accepting, trusting, and stable. They are usually grounded, supportive, and often creative, but can also be too willing to go along with others to keep the peace. They want everything to go smoothly and be without conflict, but they can also tend to be complacent and emotionally distant, simplifying problems and ignoring anything upsetting. They typically have problems with inertia and stubbornness.

At their Best: indomitable and all-embracing, they are able to bring people together and heal conflicts.

Just as we all possess all 24 of the VIA strengths in varying degrees, each one of us embodies some degree of each E-gram type. We're simply defined by the one we use most often and most naturally. Each type expresses its qualities in a variety of ways—through progressive stages from healthy to unhealthy—so an E-gram quality that made you a superstar on Monday could take you down for the count on Wednesday. That's why it's so important to know the full range of your E-gram type tendencies.

To use some familiar examples, Oprah Winfrey, Michael Jordan, and Tour de France cyclist Lance Armstrong are all "high achiever" Enneagram Type Threes, says Russ Hudson. At their best, Threes possess very similar traits. They are competitive, creative, driven, and ambitious. "But Lance Armstrong is in the situation he's in right now because he wasn't aware of some of his Three tendencies and they got the better of him," Hudson explains. Being reckless, being too competitive, cutting corners to win at all costs—these are genuinely unhealthy Three characteristics.

When I received my own E-gram profile, I was characterized as a Type Six, which makes me the Loyalist—a self-reliant, hard-working, responsible, and trustworthy type of guy; a good troubleshooter who has strong organizational skills and knows how to build community. On the downside, my type also tends to be defensive, evasive, cautious, and indecisive. When stressed, Sixes battle with self-doubt and suspicion.

As much as I hated to admit it, I recognized many of these reflections in the E-gram mirror. As the street and drug game seduced me during my teen years, my suspicion of people around me grew. Everyone was suspect in terms of trying to undermine me or jack me for my cash-cow hustle. *Trust* was not a word in my vocabulary. Paranoia was what kept me alive, helped me survive the streets, prison, and corporate America. But it hurt relationships and blocked opportunities, too. Later on, suspicion slowed my professional progress to become a top chef, as did self-doubt—my fear of executive-chef responsibilities, managerial tasks, and financial reports. Raised in poverty, introduced to street life young, and exposed to prison, I allowed suspicion to become a defense against anyone I did not trust. It's a common thinking process for most people, and it sure played a part in my journey to chefdom. People looked at me differently because of my past and the fact that I never attended culinary school. In my past life, I had cast quick judgments on people; when someone in the kitchens came off as a challenge, my guard came up and I quickly determined him as someone I had to keep an eye on.

Thankfully, my wife stepped in and helped me reset my confidence buttons. "Are you going to let fear of food menus and biased-people challenges destroy your dream? You managed crews of people on the streets and in prison kitchens," she said. "If other chefs you admire, who never even graduated from high school, are on top, you can get to the top, too. Now apply for the chef position so we can get that money! I'm going to help you face down your fears."

Bam! Stacy created my Excel spreadsheets for the kitchen, spell-checked all my menus and e-mails, taught me Microsoft Word and Excel, and helped me learn difficult French cooking terms. She let me take the extra family cash to buy more tools of my trade. Stacy provided the perspective that I needed to balance my stressed-out Six tendencies so I could be the best Loyalist I could be.

Discovering Your True Type

I dealt with my E-gram number head-on and you can, too, because you can't lose. We can't be truly strong unless we know our weaknesses. Even Superman had to face his fears. If he didn't know what Kryptonite was, where it came from, or who had a lump of it ready to toss in his face, he was a dead man.

Truth is powerful and it prevails.

— Sojourner Truth

So, are you ready to discover your own super-self-knowledge— so you can face the Kryptonite in your own life? Knowing what your Kryptonite is—that's more than half the battle.

The Scientifically validated Riso-Hudson Enneagram Type Indicator (RHETI) offered by the Enneagram Institute is available online, just like the VIA Survey—and like the VIA Survey, it consists of a series of statements you'll either agree with or disagree with. The difference is that the E-gram gives you pairs of statements and asks you to choose the one that's more true of you. Don't worry if sometimes it's hard to choose—if you're saying, "But both of those things are true!" or "Neither of those sounds right!" You're not alone. "When I first took the test, I was a bit overwhelmed by having to choose between two options," said Audre, 25. If one statement feels just a little bit truer than the other, a little more like you, that's the one to pick.

As much as possible, try to answer the questions without thinking about how you "should" respond or how you'd like to see yourself. Audre struggled a bit with this: "I was focused on things that I know I'm changing. So I told myself, 'Don't think about what you should do, respond with what you actually do—how you would normally behave.'"

There are a number of free Enneagram questionnaires available online, but I chose the free RHETI Sampler offered by the Enneagram Institute, because the RHETI is acknowledged "gold standard" in Enneagram-based personality tests. You'll find a link to the RHETI Sampler at www.chefjeffseeitbeit.com. And if you decide you want to dig even deeper, there's a more comprehensive test available for a small fee.

After completing the questionnaire, just like the VIA Survey, you'll get a report that tells you your most likely type: "The Helper/Type 2," "The Enthusiast/Type 7," etc. You will also receive definitions of all nine personality-type categories. Look up your definition by number. Here's how it looked for Ursula, whom you met before:

Type Three: The Achiever

The adaptable, success-oriented type. Threes are self-assured, attractive, and charming. Ambitious, competent, and energetic, they can also be status-conscious and highly driven for advancement. They are diplomatic and poised, but can also be overly concerned with their image and what others think of them. They typically have problems with workaholism and competitiveness. At their Best: self-accepting, authentic, everything they seem to be—role models who inspire others.

Write your E-gram type number in your journal. Then write out the definition you've found—with one important difference: *write it with "I."* Own it—it's you!

Ursula wrote:

Type Three: The Achiever

I am the adaptable, success-oriented type. *I am* self-assured, attractive, and charming. Ambitious, competent, and energetic, *I* can also be status-conscious and highly driven for advancement. *I am* diplomatic and poised but can also be overly concerned with *my* image and what others think of *me. I* sometimes have problems with workaholism and competitiveness.

At *my* Best: *I am* self-accepting, authentic, everything *I* seem to be—a role model who inspires others.

Now, take some time to think more deeply about how your profile fits you, just like you did after you took the VIA Survey. Do you see yourself clearly as your E-gram type? Do you think other people see you that way? Phoenix, age 40, found her results so on point that she posted her results on Facebook: "I got so many messages from friends saying, 'Why did it take you so long to see, or hear, or believe what we've been telling you for years?'"

If your top two results are closely tied or aren't making sense to you, it's recommended that you let a few weeks pass and then take the test again. "I was one of those people who had to take the Enneagram test twice because I was constantly going back and forth between who I am right now and who I desire to be," said Audre. "But when I finally got my number, it definitely made sense, both the positive and the negative things about my Type Nine. I realized that I could use this as an opportunity to have a more three-dimensional view of myself."

Like Audre, ask yourself if you're expressing your type's best characteristics or the ones on the downside. If you're a Type Three like Ursula, are you living on the higher end of life, unselfish and compassionate, or are you out of balance with your Achiever characteristics, always striving to impress others or constantly self-promoting? Identify three instances where you functioned like your type at its best, and when these characteristics contributed to your success or happiness in your life. Then think of three times when your type's characteristics under stress led you to do things that weren't so right for you—when your type tripped you up or got in the way of your success or happiness. Write down these examples in your See It, Be It journal.

Here's how this exercise looked for Ursula:

I functioned well as a Type Three Achiever when . . .
The "goal-oriented, ambitious, organized, diplomatic, charming, and image conscious" aspects of Three made it possible for me to have success in business. I had success in the career that I left and when I landed in a completely unexpected field I continued to excel. I have just completed

my B.A. (after many years without a final degree), I'm looking forward to reflecting and building on these traits in my next job.

My Type Three Achiever tendencies caused problems for me when . . .
The competitive aspect of my nature has driven people away and turned them off; I have felt very alone because of this. Being "appropriate" instead of "sincere" has backfired on me and has had me labeled as "fake." Not deadly, but definitely not a shining moment.

Putting the Pieces Together

Okay, so you've done some pretty interesting personal detective work by this point. You've investigated your personality with the help of the E-gram. What's really interesting is to see how this fits with what you've already discovered about yourself through the VIA Survey! After all, you can have a picture in two separate pieces, and maybe they're both nice to look at, but it's only when you put them together that you see the whole picture.

Still with me? Go back to the place in your journal where you wrote about your five signature VIA strengths. Read those through again. Now think about what you've just learned about your E-gram type. How do your core strengths line up with your personality? Maybe there's a natural fit—like a Two (Helper) whose strengths include "love" and "kindness." Or maybe the pairings aren't so obvious—like a Helper who's strong in "perspective" and "prudence."

*Knowing yourself
is the beginning of all wisdom.*

—Aristotle

Or maybe you're even noticing some ways your strengths and your personality play out against each other. For instance, Creativity, my "ability to think of new ways to do things," is my fourth strength, according to the VIA Survey. But the E-gram reminds me that, as a Six, the Loyalist, I can be defensive and my self-doubt can rise at times—and that can make it hard for me to follow through on creative ideas. Just knowing these two things about myself gives me more room to balance out whatever comes at me. It helps me keep my behavior and decisions in check and notice when or how I might be getting in my own way. Wherever your self-discovery leads you, trust that you can make sense of it. After all, you know yourself!

Now you have a good sense of your signature character strengths and personality-type traits. You know what makes you tick and what kinds of motivations are likely to drive your decisions. You're armed with information that many people never get, and that most of your competitors surely don't have.

The Me in the Mirror

Remember that song Michael Jackson sang back in the day, about making a difference for good in the world? *I'm starting with the man in the mirror. . . .* That's where we all start, and that's where you are right now. So turn to a new page in your See It, Be It journal and write at the top: "The Me in the Mirror."

Now take a deep breath and think back over all the "know thyself" work you've done so far.

What are the most important discoveries about you that have come to light? Maybe they're things you know now that you didn't know before. Maybe they're things you thought about yourself that you now can confirm. Maybe you've connected the dots between your VIA strengths and your E-gram type traits.

Spend some time reflecting on the qualities of your self-portrait, what you've learned, and what the experience was like. Then take 15 minutes to write about it in your journal—whatever it meant for you. "I've never really done anything like this before," wrote Max, 40, who works in technology for financial firms. "This turned out to be one of those life-changing experiences—

one of the few times that I've ever been able to truly articulate how my brain and my personality work.

"My Enneagram number is Type Nine, The Peacemaker. In my VIA profile, my number one attribute is 'humor.' And I apply humor to as many conversations as I can possibly have because I'm a person who talks a whole lot. I try to apply humor everywhere I go, and I'm going to try to figure out how to get paid to do it, but in the meantime it's been a wonderful experience in getting an open door into understanding my own brain, my own soul, my own person, and being able to share that with others in a way they can understand."

For Max, the testing provided a deep "aha" moment. Ursula said it "wasn't so much of an 'aha' as it was a positive affirmation." Which was it for you? Here's what a few others had to say.

The Me in the Mirror

John:

Perseverance: This is one of top 5 VIA strengths. Now I see how this can help me achieve anything I set my mind to. It's my secret fifth gear. When folks around me start to drop out, now I know that's my time to rev up. Developing my natural gift of perseverance and marrying it to my E-gram Type Three, the Achiever, is gonna give me mad skills!

Lourdes:

Fairness and Spirituality: These VIA strengths make me laugh because my friends in high school used to call me "The Golden Rule" girl. But it's important to me to "do unto others as you would have them do unto you." Being fair is a part of who I am, and now I can see that as a positive value and not a weakness. You don't have to be all "rachet" like the Basketball Wives to make your way in the world. These tests remind me that it's cool to "do you"!

Vanessa:

Love and The Helper: My top VIA character strength is "love." Dang! I love being thought of as a good friend and a kind and caring person, but my E-gram Type Two busted me. Sometimes I get so carried away helping everybody else that I sacrifice myself, even when nobody has asked me to help. Then I get mad and hurt. This is a good thing to think about. Big Mama always used to say, "Don't let your kindness be your weakness." Because of this test, I really "got it!" now.

Know Thyself, Love Thyself

When you look at your reflection in the mirror of self-knowledge, it's my best hope that you like what you see. This is no time to be hiding your light under a bushel! If you truly want success, you must know yourself first of all, and you must take a huge step farther and *believe in yourself*. Most important, you must *love* yourself. I know this may sound like some way-out stuff if you're coming from a neighborhood where everyone is down on you to the point that you get down on yourself, or a place where you doubt your abilities to do well for yourself. But I'm here to tell you that lack of self-esteem can kill your dream—and I'm proof that you can learn to love you.

When I first went to prison, most of us who came from generational poverty, 'hood life, and lifelong social trauma knew little to nothing about ourselves or our real culture. But when the elder Black men I respected in prison called me "son" and "brother," I started to feel good in my own skin.

*Self-esteem means
knowing you are the dream.*

— Oprah Winfrey

Phoenix's Story

I am a mother of a five-year-old and I've been married for eight years. I work full time as an executive assistant and have a small handmade-jewelry business, which is my passion. I'm hoping to be able to utilize what I've learned about myself through this experience in both my personal and professional growth, and to also use it for powering myself forward in my professional life.

Do I need to follow my passion for the jewelry side 100 percent? Should I just do it part time? Am I just supposed to be in the corporate business world? At this moment, I don't really know anything and I feel like I am spinning out of control. I'm trying to calm down and get some direction, refocus my energy, and figure out not only what I need to be doing but what is really going to make me happy.

One of the things that I have been struck by is how taking these tests is showing me the things that other people have seen in me all along but I haven't been able to recognize or take ownership of.

My top five character strengths were an "appreciation of beauty and excellence," "humor," "judgment," "creativity," and "social intelligence." And those traits did not surprise me at all. I was a bit surprised by my Enneagram number, which was Type Six—The Loyalist—because there's so much wonderful stuff going on with that type. It also helped me see that I'm not necessarily crazy because there are so many conflicting things about my personality that I have a problem with at times. But the E-gram helped me see that all of these things are part of who I am. And it helped me come to a new acceptance of all that I am instead of fighting tooth and nail with people about who I am—who I really am versus who they think I am.

It didn't start in the kitchen, even though that was the launchpad where my career took off later on. Years before I discovered food, I discovered me, in books that portrayed powerful, smart Black men as well as women. Black men other than drug dealers, street hustlers, and players. I read about Malcolm X's transformation from street smart to book smart; I read about Sojourner Truth leading a people out of slavery; I read about a Black man who worked in the lab with Thomas Edison when electricity was discovered. These portraits of Black people in Black history began to change the way I saw life, the way I saw the world, and they began to change the way I saw myself. When I looked in the mirror, I began to see and understand that I came from a tradition and bloodline of extraordinary men and women who had accomplished great things against impossible odds. They had done it by giving their great gifts to other people—sharing knowledge and wisdom, or a new identity, or a road to freedom. They could accomplish these feats because, no matter what they had to face in their lives, they knew their value and their worth. They loved the "me" that they saw in the mirror.

That's the same reflection I want to hold up for you right now. You must love who you are no matter what life has dealt you. You can first learn how to love yourself by understanding the amazing gifts that you have to offer yourself and the rest of the world— and if you've stayed with me this far, you should be starting to see that picture emerge in living color. You know your greatness comes from what you have to give, and now you know exactly what that is.

Self-discovery, my friend, is a lifelong journey. That's why I make it my business to study, reflect, and gain new experiences every day. That's why I remain deeply grateful that I have been blessed with the tools that I have shared in this chapter. The VIA Survey and the Enneagram test were additional tools that allowed me to look in the mirror and discover my signature strengths, personality traits, and ways of seeing and being Chef Jeff—that I might have never come to know.

I appreciate you for hanging with me throughout this chapter. As you know, I'm a guy who takes pride in empowering individuals and building community by holding the mirror steady so you can see yourself more clearly and grow to your full potential. Because I know and believe that, armed with self-knowledge, we can not only change ourselves, we can help to change the world!

chapter 3

Picture-Power

> *Every great dream begins with a dreamer.*
> *Always remember, you have within you*
> *the strength, the patience, and the passion*
> *to reach for the stars to change the world.*
> — Harriet Tubman

The picture calmed me, lifted me up, made me feel good about my new relationship; somehow, as I held it in my hand, it seemed to make my future more real. In the photo, a beautiful, successful-looking, elegantly dressed Black couple enjoyed an evening out at a high-end white-tablecloth restaurant. Happiness, security, and romance were all over their faces.

I slowly tore the photo from the seam of the *Essence* magazine. Then I folded it gently, tucked it in an envelope with a love letter, and addressed it to my "new girl," Stacy, the lady who would one day become my wife and the mother of our five children.

This practice had become a ritual that lifted me far beyond the confines of my present life, an 8-by-12-foot jammed cubicle in the federal prison where I was serving my time for conspiracy to distribute a controlled substance. Every time I mailed a photo to Stacy, the picture of my future came a little more clear.

Not much more than a decade after I sat in my cubicle cutting out those pictures, Stacy and I were living those dreams. We were that happy, loving, successful couple dining at white-tablecloth restaurants. In fact, by that time, I was employed as the first African American executive chef at Las Vegas's renowned Bellagio Hotel. Two years later, I was celebrating the release of my memoir, *Cooked: From the Streets to the Stove, from Cocaine to Foie Gras,* which became a *New York Times* bestseller.

Before moving forward, you need to ask yourself an important question: Are you really ready to discover your dreams and turn them into reality? If not, put this book down until you're ready to make a bulletproof commitment. Neither one of us has time to waste with some pipe dream. But if you're serious about transforming your life, about unlocking that prison door of your mind that's blocking you from what the world has to offer, then you have to accept the fact that it's time for a change *and* that *only you can change you.*

You've already taken the first step toward success. Are you ready to take the next one? It's time to move forward and parlay what you've learned about yourself to reconnect with the spirit of your deep possibilities. Get ready for the ride. You are about to unleash your amazing inner abilities—in a space where dreams are born and reborn and driven by images and words. Your passport to a new life gets stamped with a technique I like to call "picture-power."

> How do you make the impossible possible and **turn your dreams into your reality?**

The Power of a Dream

Successful people around the world—"the haves"—know that dreams are powerful and create wealth. They give you the ability to defy reality, to do the unthinkable, and to go places that no one—other than you—can imagine. Dreams help us rise above past and present circumstances. Dr. Martin Luther King, Jr., transformed a nation with a revolutionary dream. Nelson Mandela, who served 27 years in prison for fighting the oppressive injustices of apartheid, never stopped dreaming of freedom and liberation for his people—and he became the first Black president of a democratic South Africa.

How do you make the impossible possible and turn your dreams into your reality? First and foremost, you have to be able to *see it.* And you have to keep it locked in your mind's eye—because if you're not consciously picturing what you do want, your mind is unconsciously filled with images of whatever happens to be there, and those may be things you *don't* want. Unlocking the door where your dreams are stashed starts with opening your mind so there's space for new possibilities, then filling it with pictures of the people, places, and things that you truly want to be a part of your daily life.

The practice of looking through magazines and selecting pictures of things I desired or wanted to come true is actually linked to a long-standing tradition. Back in the day, our wise ones used metaphysics—the study of philosophical, scientific, and spiritual principles that don't necessarily mix with "physical reality"—to unleash the unknown and unused parts of our brains. The technique was first introduced by a teacher named Catherine Ponder; she called it "treasure mapping," and in the decades since it's evolved into something called a "dream board" or "vision board"—a practice you may even have heard of, as it's taken off in recent years. Ultimately, putting pictures on paper engages your imagination—and your imagination is always stronger than your will. Our rational minds don't always drive the car; at times our subconscious mind is at the wheel.

When I was in prison, I had no knowledge of these concepts. I just knew that I couldn't leave the prison yard unless I transcended it—and pictures were my escape to the outside world. With old issues of *National Geographic,* I could travel the world and see myself going to Africa. With *Ebony* and *Essence,* I could see positive images of Black people that showed me there had to be another way to get on top—and if others had found it, so could I. *Robb Report* and *Businessweek* fed my natural love of business and entrepreneurship. I was fascinated by the pictures and stories of how people in power truly ran the world.

A few months before I was released, I was given an article in *USA Today* about America's top Black chefs. By this time I'd already learned to cook in the prison kitchen and become the head inmate baker, and I'd been praised for the passion in the food we served. Other inmates kept telling me, "Jeff, you should consider becoming a chef." Now I was holding that possibility right in my hand, looking at those three top Black chefs standing there in their crisp white chef coats: Ethiopian-born chef Marcus Samuelsson, Patrick Clark, and Robert Gadsby, who was about to open a 77-seat restaurant in Los Angeles.

I mean I was holding that photo in awe—and at that moment I was able to see myself one day among them. I saw myself as a real chef, not a hash slinger in a local dive, but an executive chef running kitchens just like I did in federal prison. I saw myself cooking in some of the West Coast's finest restaurants, on the hot line sautéing, seasoning, and plating the food on fine china. I could feel the kitchen pressure; the chef calling orders, critiquing, and praising. Just the thought of tasting the ingredients I'd never seen as a child and learning the knife skills the pros used gave my dream power, color, and substance.

Like I said, I didn't know I'd tapped into a time-honored practice as I lay in my bunk tearing out photos and picturing the life I wanted after my release. But the one thing I knew for sure was that the pictures gave me a clear sense of purpose and direction. They brought back the feelings of unlimited possibilities that I had as a little boy.

No-Limits Dreaming

When you are a youngster, nothing seems impossible. Ask kids what they want to be in life and they won't hesitate to say, with unflinching optimism, computer programmer, doctor, teacher, football or basketball player, or big-time rapper. Children can come up with big-time make-believes and escapades at a moment's notice because they are huge dreamers.

As a little homeboy, I was a fearless young dreamer, doing most of my fantasizing on the yellow school bus that carried my sister and me every morning from our place in South Central L.A. to a school in the suburbs of Culver City. I would always rush past my big sister Junell to get the seat next to the window for the best views of L.A. Looking out that window was my escape from the frustration we lived in, if only for just a few moments.

Through my Coke bottle–thick Clark Kent glasses, I stared down fine neighborhoods and cream-of-the-crop communities that were foreign to me—big stucco houses with three-car garages attached, long brick driveways, and green manicured lawns. Sometimes I'd see fathers and mothers in corporate suits climbing into brand-new luxury cars, surely headed for those big-time downtown gigs. Sometimes, their kids were in tow, with smiling faces, books tucked under their arms and colorful old-school metal lunch boxes in their hands, no doubt stuffed with top-dollar brand-name snacks, like iced Honey Buns and Hostess Twinkies. I didn't know for sure what was in those boxes, but I knew they ate better lunches than the school-issued, cellophane-wrapped no-brand free lunches served at the "poor kids" school.

> *The poor man is not he who is without a cent,*
> *but he who is without a dream.*
>
> — Harry Kemp

Those early-morning visual fairy tales were mind-blowing. Just a school bus away, I could see it with my eyes and feel it in my soul, but I couldn't touch that life. It was a gated fantasy in reality—but in the space of my imagination, it was a totally different story. In my mind, I could be rich and own a real house that wasn't connected to another house or surrounded by concrete like those in poor neighborhoods across America.

I longed for the picture-perfect American dream I gazed at every day through my school-bus window. I saw myself one day with a family of my own, with a fenced-in backyard where my kids could play safely. There was a swimming pool with an old-school diving board, too. With my mind's eye, I saw the swing hanging from my very own avocado tree, just like the one my granddaddy built for his grandchildren. In my future home, everyone had his or her own bedroom, no sharing. There was a basketball rim with red, white, and blue netting hanging above the garage door out back, and there were two cars in the driveway.

I wasn't dreaming just for myself. I dreamed for my mother, because she didn't seem to have any time for dreaming. Life for my mom was an obstacle course. She was a single mom working two low-wage jobs and struggling to keep my sister and me fed and clothed. As her only son, I felt the great pressure of making her life better; I felt the burden of fulfilling her dreams like they were my responsibility. I loved my mom, and as far as I was concerned she *was* my responsibility. She deserved the best life had to offer, and, as her son, I had no doubt that I'd get it for her.

I was such a dreamer as a kid that I even saw myself *inside* the house of my dreams. I could see my mother and my sister cooking in our spacious kitchen on a six-burner stove, with a fancy double-door refrigerator, like the ones I saw on TV, filled to the brim with lots of choices for breakfast, lunch, and dinner. My dream was very specific. I even saw the laundry room with a spanking-new Maytag washer and dryer for my mother, with no coin slots. In my dream, Mother didn't have to lug our dirty clothes to the old, crowded neighborhood Laundromat where she'd have to wait in line for hours to drop her hard-earned change into broken-down washing machines.

I want to stop here for a moment. This is real important. My childhood dreams didn't include ways to *get* nice things; they were just filled *with* nice things. Like so many other kids, I had no limits to what I could imagine. Now, if I ask adults to tell me where they want to be, where they want to live, or what kind of material stuff they'd like to have, say, five years from now, they can't even answer before they start calculating how much all of those things are gonna cost. And that takes them straight to a place of fear: "What kind of job would I need to live that large? Can I afford it? Will I be able to hold on to it? Do I even deserve it?" Their logical minds kick in, that part of the brain that specializes in creating, recognizing, and enforcing limited thinking—what I call the "No, you can'ts." Kids just don't think like that. They're no-limits dreamers.

And that's the space of limitless possibility I want to put you back into, starting now. We need to get that creative, limitless mind cracking, the part that operates far beyond the "No, you can'ts" and runs right over self-inflicted mental roadblocks.

Today, I want you to start by reconnecting to your earliest

dreams by making a playdate with your limitless inner child. Think hard and give honest answers to the following questions.

When I was a kid . . .

I spent hours

_____

_____

I was the happiest or most excited when

_____

_____

My biggest heroes or heroines were

_____

_____

I dreamed of having

_____

_____

I dreamed of doing

_____

_____

I dreamed of being

_____

_____

When I was an adolescent . . .

I spent hours

_____

_____

I was the happiest or most excited when

_____

_____

My biggest heroes or heroines were

_____

_____

I dreamed of having

_____

_____

I dreamed of doing

_____

_____

I dreamed of being

_____

_____

Don't underestimate the power of the child's imagination! "When was the last time you pretended?" Ursula said about this part of our "know thyself" process. "When was the last time you actually let yourself imagine again—like a little kid? I have a five-year-old, and he's really good at pretending; he gets mad at me if I won't agree to be in his submarine when we're in the car. If I resist, it's 'Mommy, this is a submarine!' For him, it's deadly serious. I have to take a page from that book."

Now that you've reconnected with your limitless childhood dreams, it's time to put your adult self in that same no-limits space and focus on the dreams you're having for your life today. Don't let yourself slip into an adult's limited thinking—don't worry about how you could ever possibly get these things. Allow yourself to dream, and dream big! And remember, your dreams aren't just idle wishes: they're the things you are truly passionate about experiencing, achieving, and having in your life. Picture-power is going to be your passport to success in all areas of your life, because it literally allows you to see what you want to be.

Hello to the Future

Ready to put on your 3-D glasses and take a look at those dreams up close? Then let's get started. We're about to shift our focus from words to pictures, and pictures have an incredible power to change your mind—so hang on!

3-D Future You

1.   Start with a piece of poster board, the kind you can get at Staples or Office Depot or most stationery stores. I like the kind that's 36 by 48 inches and folds up into thirds—because that way it stands up by itself *and* you can easily fold it away to keep it private. This is the launchpad where the 3-D Future You will take shape and take off!

2.   Draw a circle right in the center of your board. Inside the circle, write down your five VIA signature strengths and whichever key words from your E-gram type description speak to you most right now. These words reflect who you are—the solid core you can build your dreams around. If you prefer, you can use the "no excuses" method: take an 8½ x 11 spiral notebook and devote separate pages to certain ideas or areas of your life. Just be sure to put your VIA and E-gram core

at the center of each page, and make sure there's at least one page that directly reflects your vision for success in your life.

3. Now is the fun part! Start looking in magazines, newspapers, online, and even in your family album to find photos, pictures, words, captions, poems—anything from anywhere that best represents you, what you want to be and have, or any symbols of success or special things that spark your imagination.

   Aim high. Don't settle for ordinary. This is the time for the extraordinary you to be revealed in any or all of the following areas: health, wealth, work, relationships, personal growth, and so on. Take these extraordinary images and paste them on your poster board to create your 3-D Future You collage.

   Feel free to include images of any role models you admire. It doesn't matter if they're famous or not. In fact, if they *are* famous, make sure you're including them because they represent a quality you want to have—not just because you're drawn to the glamour of their lives.

   For example: You may choose the words or images of people like Hillary Clinton or Jay-Z, Warren Buffett or Oprah Winfrey, Sonia Sotomayor or Michelle Obama. Or maybe your inspiration is closer to home, like your pastor, your parents, or your grandparents.

   Before attaching any individuals to your collage, ask yourself what it is you like about them. Are they great leaders? Savvy businesspeople? Outstanding artists or philanthropists? Quiet world changers who built your community? What aspect of their character or achievements inspires or motivates you? Add pictures of these people and descriptions of the inspirational thoughts and feelings they bring up in you.

Don't worry if you don't fill up all the space on that big board. *Do* make sure all the images you use are detailed and reflect what you *really* want. If an important part of your definition of success is having your dream job, don't just paste a picture of a person in a suit on your paper. Lay out the specifics of your dream. Are you searching for a corner office in a skyscraper? What does your desk look like? What's the view out that 40th-story window? Or do you want a laid-back, creative workspace full of original local art? The details are important, so do the work to find what really represents your dream come true.

4.   You're getting closer to seeing your dream. Now take some time to *feel* it, too. Imagine yourself enjoying your dream come true, and try to call up the emotions that come with it. Find the words that match your feelings and add them to your collage, either by cutting them out of a magazine or newspaper or by writing them on your board. Create clear, heart-touching *emotional* pictures to go with the visuals. If you *see it* and *feel it,* and really own that you deserve your dream, that's what gives you the power to *be it.*

If you want to view a some good online examples of *3-D You* picture-power collages, including one that I made myself, visit www.chefjeffseeitbeit.com. If you're still feeling uncertain about how to do this, or you're wondering whether it's worth it, listen to what Ursula, who's done this kind of work before, has to say: "Any time I've ever done a type of vision board, everything that I put on that board has manifested. There's some kind of incredible alchemy involved in this process."

The know thyself-ers I worked with found this exercise revealing and challenging, too. "The bottom line for me is my concern that I may be 'dreaming too big,'" said Audre. "I look at some of the things that I put on my board and say, 'Who are you to want that?' The challenge is not to psych myself out and to allow myself to have these big dreams."

Max agreed: "One of the things that makes this exercise both eye-opening and difficult is realizing that I've never been at a point in my life when I could allow myself to visualize the future. We've all found ways to make certain dreams real, but the challenge is learning how to harness your long-distance vision." Amsa Herut's concern was more about whether her picture-power rang true: "Am I really creating a vision for what I want to do? Or creating a vision for what I'm telling myself I want to do?"

If you're feeling any uncertainty of your own, know that you're not alone—then do your best to quiet those fears of "dreaming too big." There's no such thing!

Good-bye to the Past

As you looked for positive, powerful images and words that move and inspire you about your future, did you also experience some old memories or pictures from your past? Surprising flashbacks or remembered conversations can bring back old thoughts, attitudes, or behaviors that compromised or derailed your past dreams.

The most important thing to remember is that the past and future can't exist in the same space. So something's got to go. I let my past go 20 years ago. How about you? To manifest your future dreams, you have to let go of everything that no longer serves you.

Old issues and hurts can sabotage your success—they're dream crushers. Good memories are worth keeping, but the ones that still sting need to be acknowledged and then released. You can't afford to let ancient history undermine your future. So be strong. Don't sweep your past under the rug or deny that the dead ends and detours ever happened. You have to face your setbacks and mistakes, fears and failures, habitual stumbling blocks and choices that don't get you where you want to go—that's the only way you can break free and get on with your 3-D Future You game plan. You can gauge the power of the past by how much upset,

> **The past and future can't exist in the same space.**

74

anger, or frustration it can still provoke in you. Your feelings are real, and it's time to deal with them *now*.

Earlier in this chapter, you created your **3-D Future You** collage, so now you're ready to tackle past experiences that left you feeling stuck or powerless. It's time to create the **3-D Past You** collage. Select pictures and words that reflect your past experiences or behaviors that stressed you out or tested you, decisions that put your dreams on lockdown, anything that's part of the **3-D Past You.**

You can get some ideas by looking back at the work you did in Chapter 2. The strengths at the bottom on the list on your VIA results and the negative qualities of your E-gram type can give you a helpful window into the patterns that seem to hold you back. The reason why this process is important is that, if you don't pay attention to your self-sabotaging patterns and consciously release them, the subconscious mind tends to keep replaying those old broken records. These habits and patterns don't serve you well, and they can even get in between you and your dreams. So now's the perfect time to let them go.

3-D Past You

1. Start just the way you did before, with a piece of poster board or a notebook. Gather pictures and words that represent behaviors, experiences, and situations that blocked your dreams. Things that make you feel frustrated, angry, ashamed, depressed, or worthless. These are the parts of the past that still give you grief.

   Flip through each picture and word and remember the story that each one reveals and why it triggers you. Maybe you'll notice some connections between the parts of your past you're dealing with here and the aspects of your personality that can trip you up, as noted in the E-gram. Be courageous and look at these experiences and behaviors head-on, even if it's uncomfortable.

2. Paste or attach these images and words to your poster board to create your 3-D Past You collage. Once

you've done this, reflect on the parts of your past it shows. They've gotten you this far, but they cannot take Future You any further. It's time to thank them for the lessons and *let them go.* You may even want to speak these words out loud: "Thank you for bringing me to where I am today. I am ready to move on, and I release you now."

3. Once you've reviewed and released 3-D Past You—*this is important*—create your own ritual for letting go. You can file your collage away in a private place and take a look at it every month, or three or six months or a year from now, to see how far you have come. The most important thing to affirm is that the past is gone, my friend.

Practice Builds Power

When you're finished, turn back to 3-D Future You and take a good look at the picture-power collage that you've created. Every word your eyes land on and every image you see should remind you of something good you've achieved that you'll continue to build on or something that you want to achieve but haven't quite reached yet.

It's time to claim your future today, right here, right now. You've created a display that spotlights your dreams in living color. Now hang it, or place it in a spot that catches your eye and ignites your imagination every day. Display your dreams with confidence and know that the universe is paying attention.

If you don't want anyone to see it, that's fine—your 3-D Future You is your business. But if you do want to share it, make sure you show it to someone you trust, someone who'll be able to see what you see in your future and won't hate on you for daring to dream too big.

This picture-power work is the real deal. It isn't magic; it's a disciplined process that really works. And I'm speaking from my own experience, too. The life I live today is a direct reflection of the art of picture-power. Remember that *USA Today* article I mentioned, about the top Black chefs, including Chef Gadsby? The mental image it created for me, of myself cooking in a top-of-the-line kitchen, stuck with me, and upon my release from prison on October 2, 1996, I was determined to get in at Gadsby's. It took a month of persuasion and appealing to the chef himself before he finally gave in and hired me as a dishwasher in his kitchen. Because I could see it, I now had the chance to be it. The opportunity was a game changer, and I never looked back.

To this day, I rely on the picture-power process to keep me in touch with my true essence and my ever-evolving future self as I discover new passions and new opportunities. Today, right now, I see myself in the near future with my own restaurant, more TV shows, and more success in my business ventures. My brain plays the scenes over and over in the movies of the life I see myself and my family living—and you can do the same with your very own scenes of you, living your own version of the American dream.

Dream On

Congratulations! You have just activated your limitless mind. The universe is on notice that a new you—3-D Future You—is in charge. You've honestly looked at what aspects of your past may be blocking your growth, and you've made a commitment to keep those sabotaging forces out of your life. You now know what you want and why you want it, and you're prepared to use these road signs on your path to success and fulfillment.

So where do you go from here? We started this chapter by talking about the power of dreams, those inspiring images that help us rise above our past and present circumstances and set our sights on the future. The next step now that you've tapped into your own picture-power is to take your dreams for your life and put them into equally powerful words.

You can start by letting your picture-power marinate for three days.

Owning Your Dreams

Day One: Sit down, record the date in your See It, Be It journal, and take a good look at your 3-D Future You collage.

What jumps out at you—what words or images grab your attention first and most strongly? Make some notes so you'll remember your thoughts.

Day Two: Sit down, record the date, and examine your collage again. What stands out for you now? Are they the same words or pictures as yesterday or something different? Make some notes about how you're seeing things today.

Day Three: Sit down, record the date, and review your picture-power collage one more time. Pay attention to the area or areas of your life where your dreams are really popping off that paper (or board or wall). Ask yourself: "Out of all the dreams shown here, which one(s) really spark(s) my spirit with the most passion?"

What you're doing here is lasering in on what's most important to you—the core of your dreams of success. Now it's time to go one step further and *write it down*.

Look at your life in every aspect—health, wealth, work, relationships, personal development—and decide what's most important to you. What is jumping out of your picture-power collage as the piece of the puzzle you can no longer live without? Don't play yourself short. Don't worry about what seems realistic or what the haters say you'll never achieve. This is *no-limits* dreaming!

If you don't like the way the world is, you change it.

— Marion Wright Edelman

This is the point in our process where you've really nailed your ability to *see it*—so we're going to translate your dream into a concrete *vision*. Here's what it might look like if I wrote down the vision I'm seeing for my life right now that's rooted in the big dreams reflected on my picture-power board:

Jeff's Vision

I am chef-owner of a successful restaurant that gets rave reviews and lots of repeat customers. I have a highly rated cooking show on TV that viewers love, with more ideas in the pipeline. All of my business ventures are succeeding and my family is well provided for.

Go ahead and write your own vision in your See It, Be It journal now.

My Vision

_____

_____

_____

_____

_____

_____

_____

_____

How Your Vision Becomes Real

Are you ready to turn your vision into a reality? I hope you are, though we still have a bunch of work to do. If you've followed the steps I've outlined and understand the words I've shared, your journey has begun. You have looked at who you are, what you really want to be, and how you will choose to live your life.

Your dreams are within reach. So don't just talk about it . . . BE ABOUT IT! It's time to commit to getting your mind right so you can get your game tight. It's time to grow some backbone, get disciplined, and get ready for sacrifice and some hard, hard work.

Quiet that skeptical mind; ignore the disbelievers. This is your moment to make your vision real, and the chapters ahead will give you the tools you need.

So read on, my friend, and remember—*if you can see it, you can be it!*

chapter 4

From Vision to Action

> *The big secret in life is that there is no big secret.*
> *Whatever your goal, you can get there*
> *if you're willing to work.*
> — Oprah Winfrey

For me, almost everything starts in the kitchen. It's the place where I get organized, prepared, and ready to execute my dishes. The ingredients, utensils, gadgets, and instructions have to be prioritized, prepped, and put in their proper place so I can start making magic.

Let's say we're going to cook my signature crispy fried chicken. The basic ingredients are chicken, flour, salt, onion powder, some oil, and a frying pan. A very close friend by the name of Friendly Womack, Jr., my mentor and former head inmate cook in the prison kitchen during the 1990s, taught me a whole new way to prepare this dish. The chicken gets layered with seasonings two times: the chicken is seasoned, the flour gets spiced up, then it's all tossed together and dropped into fry baskets with bubbling hot canola oil. In the end, you don't just have fried chicken; you have the original Friendly Fried Chicken.

Friendly and I took the basics, added select seasonings, purposeful preparation, and a few secret ingredients, and here we have created a special and story-driven dish. It's something like what we're doing in this book. We are in the kitchen of unlimited possibilities, working on the process of cooking up the ultimate dish, which is you.

Putting Your Vision into Action

When you get right down to it, being successful in your life is a lot like being successful in the kitchen—and realizing the vision you wrote down for yourself in the last chapter really is a lot like preparing a great meal. Good food doesn't fall out of the sky, and neither will your success!

Let's say you want to make a meal for family and friends that they will never forget. That's your **vision**. How are you going to get from here to there? You have to start breaking it down: first of all, what are you going to cook? You decide on a few dishes that will go together well and please the people you're feeding. These are the specific **goals** you need to meet to make your vision a reality. Now you need to break it down some more. For each one of those dishes, you need to follow the steps in the recipe. You gather your ingredients, measure them out, and identify the right cooking method—is your dish baked or broiled? cooked on a grill, in a pot, or in the oven? Then you time it and watch it carefully until it's done to perfection. These steps are the **action plan** that gets you to your goal.

> Trying to realize your vision without goals and an action plan is like trying to cook without heat.

Trying to realize your vision without goals and an action plan is like trying to cook without heat. Doesn't matter if it's Friendly Fried Chicken, pan-seared diver scallops, or the career of your dreams: breaking down the accomplishment of your vision into steps keeps you from getting overwhelmed and guarantees that you have a solid map for getting where you want to go.

So that's what we're going to do in this chapter: come up with the goals and the action plan that will get you where you want to go. I'm going to break it down for you with some straightforward advice on how to turn your vision into a set of practical steps that will help you achieve your success. You've done the work to develop your vision for your life—that means you can *see* it. Here's where you find the steps you need to take to *be it*.

The Power of a Plan

I learned the power of making a plan—and even more important, writing it down—while I was still in prison. Prior to my release, along with the 55-page memoir I mentioned, I had to write what wound up being a 5-page strategic action plan. I wrote out where I planned to stay when I got out; how I planned to find a job; how I would develop and maintain relationships; how I planned to avoid criminal relapse and the wrong crowd; how I'd identify the people I *did* want to have around me; how I'd work with my probation officer to keep her off my back, and how I planned to transition to life outside prison. Alan Hershman, who led the class where we did these assignments, did a lot of research for inmates to help us fill in the blanks. He'd pull stuff off the Internet, like the *USA Today* article on successful Black chefs and a list of hotels for me to contact in my area of release.

When he first gave me the assignment, I struggled, because I had never written anything down in detail like that before. I always kept stuff in my head. This time I had to put it on paper. And even though it was difficult, it made all the difference. When you write down your goals and your plan, it focuses your attention on what's important. It makes you accountable for what you're trying to accomplish. And it helps you remember what you've set out to do. It's the difference between going shopping without a shopping list—wandering around the grocery store relying on your memory, getting distracted by things you don't need, and going home without some key ingredient—or shopping with a detailed list and having exactly what you need to cook that dinner when you get home.

Ninety percent of Americans don't have any written goals. Shocking! Is it any wonder that they can't bring their vision to life? It's not enough to be a go-getter—you've got to be a goal-getter. I want to challenge you to become a 10-percenter and write down your goals so you can turn your vision for success into reality now. Not someday, but NOW!

I can only guess what you're thinking right now: *But Jeff, I don't have time to sit down and write a bunch of goals!* Or *I don't have to write this stuff down—I already know what I want to accomplish, it's all in my head.* Or maybe *I don't even know where to begin.*

You're going to come up with a bunch of reasons why you don't want to do this, or why you don't need to. But I'm here to tell you that you *can* do it, and you *do* need to, or the success you're reaching for is going to stay far out of reach. To think of it another way, writing down your goals is like signing a check: you can fill in the recipient and the amount, but it's not legit until you sign it, just like your goals aren't legit on the success track until you write them down. I still write down my goals, even today, right in my smartphone.

So I want you to promise yourself that when you finish reading this chapter—before you go to bed tonight—you're going to sign that success check. You're going to have the heart to put pen to paper (or fingers to keyboard) and put your goals and your action plan in writing. And if you don't know where to start, don't worry—I'm gonna break it down for you right now.

Setting Your Long-Term Goals

Before you do anything else, I want you to take out your See It, Be It journal and reread the vision for your life that you wrote down at the end of the last chapter. Imagine it becoming a reality —really feel the excitement of living that no-limits life. Now, what has to happen to get you there? What are the specific goals you need to reach?

---

*The future belongs to
those who prepare for it today.*

— Malcolm X

Let's say your vision is to be financially secure and working at a job you love to do. Depending on where you're starting from, you might need to choose the occupation you want to work in where you can earn enough to get that security, gain some experience in that field, or earn a training certificate or an associate's or bachelor's degree.

Or, if your vision is to own that house on the hill with the white picket fence (or the deluxe apartment in the sky), your goals might include paying off your credit-card debt, building up your credit rating, choosing the area where you want to live, and saving up the down payment for that dream home. For me, when I was working toward the vision of becoming a top-notch chef at one of L.A.'s top restaurants, one of my long-term goals on the way there was to be in charge of a kitchen of my own. Do you hear what I'm saying?

Think of five big things you know you'll have to accomplish to get your vision off the ground. I want you to make them **positive** statements, not negative—you're talking about what to do, not what *not* to do. So instead of "stop bumping heads with my co-workers," try "find constructive ways to talk through issues with co-workers." I also want you to make your goals **specific,** you know, straight to the point, just the way I asked you to make your vision detailed and complete, because if your goals are too broad, they can't be measured—and you need to be able to measure your progress in order to stay focused and motivated. Use dates, times, and amounts whenever you write down your goals. If you plan to own your own home "someday," chances are that someday will always stay just a little ways off in the future. So don't write "get my business to be profitable"; write "have my business making a 15 percent profit annually by December 31, 2014." Instead of "get my college degree," write "complete my unfinished bachelor's degree by December 2016."

My Long-Term Goals

1. _____

2. _____

3. _____

4. _____

5. _____

Now take a look at your list and ask yourself two questions: "Which of these things is most important to me?" and "Is there one thing I have to do first before I can move on to the other goals?" To use the examples above, it's going to be hard to raise your credit rating unless you pay off your credit-card debt first, and you can't start college if you still need your GED. So take a mo-

> Read your list of long-term goals every day, and visualize them as though you've already achieved them.

ment to put your long-term goals in order, either by importance to you or by what it makes sense to accomplish first.

Now write your goals in the priority you've given them in your See It, Be It journal:

My Prioritized Long-Term Goals

1. _____

2. _____

3. _____

4. _____

5. _____

Now you've got a list of goals that are positive, on point, and prioritized. By writing them down, you've given them power, as I've said—but don't stop there. Make a commitment to yourself to read your list of long-term goals every day, and visualize them as though you've already achieved them: see yourself holding that diploma in your hand or at the celebration for your promotion at your job. Really feel the excitement and sense of satisfaction that goes along with each achievement. When you do this, you're powering up your subconscious mind by telling your brain to think of your vision as though it's already real. Remember, the brain doesn't know the difference between what you imagine, if it's backed by intense emotion, and what is real. And when your subconscious is engaged, you're harnessing a huge amount of manifestation power in the service of your vision.

Setting Your Short-Term Goals

What you have in front of you now is the big motor that's going to put your vision in drive. How are you going to start it up? The goals on this list are still pretty big—so now we're going to break them down into smaller pieces.

Take the first long-term goal on the list you've made. What do you need to do to make this a reality? If your first long-term goal is to complete your unfinished bachelor's degree within two years, you might need to enroll at a school, transfer your credits, or apply for a student loan. These are your short-term goals. They should be positive and precise as well: "Enroll in school in time for the fall semester," "Submit student loan application by August 1."

Write your first set of short-term goals in your See It, Be It journal.

My Short-Term Goals

1. _____

2. _____

3. _____

4. _____

5. _____

Your long-term goals aren't likely to change once you've put them in place—they're connected directly to your long-term vision for your life. Your short-term goals, however, are going to evolve as you progress. Make it a point to look at your short-term goals once a week to make sure they're on track and, when you achieve one, put something new in its place.

Okay, hope you're with me so far, but maybe you're still wondering what this process looks like in real life. So let's look at an example.

Martin's Story

Martin Lewis is a graphic designer who got laid off from a good job at a marketing firm. With jobs so hard to come by, he decided to do his own thing. But being in charge of your own business is no joke, and Martin is still in the process of trying to make it work.

Martin is an E-gram Type Nine—the Peacemaker—so he's easygoing and trusting but has to guard against "going along to get along." His top five VIA strengths are "love," "fairness," "gratitude," "kindness," and "teamwork"; "perseverance" and "self-regulation" are way down the list of lesser strengths, so he knows he has his work cut out for him if he's going to make a success of running his own business. His picture-power collage shows an airy workspace with lots of natural light, pictures of well-dressed people in meeting rooms (the clients he hopes to meet), the logo of a prestigious design award, and a home with a view of the ocean. Here's how he puts his vision into words:

Martin's Vision

I am a cutting-edge freelance designer with a steady stream of clients. My business is profitable enough to let me enjoy this lifestyle now and save for retirement later. I have the work flexibility and financial freedom to live in a place I love.

That's the vision—and Martin needs long-term goals to get him there. Here's what those goals look like:

Martin's Long-Term Goals

1. Make my business break even—so my income covers all my expenses—within one year

2. Put a marketing plan in place by the end of this year

3. Find 10 lucrative new clients within 18 months

4. Build my business so that it turns a 20 percent profit within two years

5. Expand by hiring at least one employee within three years

As you see, all of these goals are positive—Martin isn't setting a goal to "stop my income from falling short of my expenses"! He's turned it around so the focus is on what he does want, not what he doesn't. They're all on point—he can pin them down to numbers (10 new clients, 20 percent profit) and time frames (one year, two years). And he's put them in order of their priority: it doesn't make good business sense to hire an employee before the business starts breaking even.

Now Martin has to break it down. Starting with the first long-term goal on his list—"Make my business break even within one year"—here's how he drills down to the short-term goals that will get him there.

Martin's Long-Term Goal

Make my business break even within one year

Martin's Short-Term Goals

1. Review last year's profit-and-loss records

2. Connect with five successful people in my field over the next two months to talk about their road to success, fee structures, and "breaking even"

3. Increase my rates by 10 percent for new clients, start-
    ing now

4. Increase my rates for all my clients within three months

5. Set up a new system to track time spent on projects by
    the end of August

6. Reduce expenses in my home office (utility bills, etc.)
    by 10 percent within six months

If you've gotten to this point—where you can imagine walking in Martin's vision, in his long-term and short-term goal "shoes"— you're doing great! You're beginning to see your vision more clearly. And now I'm going to ask you to break your short-term goals down just one more time, into really bite-sized pieces.

Your Action Plan

If you're baking a cake, you don't just throw a bunch of flour and eggs in a cake pan and hope you end up with a cake. You gather and measure your ingredients, preheat the oven, oil the cake pan up, combine ingredients just the way the recipe says, pour the batter into the pan, and bake it for the right amount of time. Once you've gone through these steps, *then* you have the desired cake you set out to make.

Each of your short-term goals is supported by a set of or-dered steps. This is your action plan: what you can do right now to complete your short-term goals, which gets you on track toward your long-term goals, which move you toward the life vision that's keeping you going. And it's like I said at the start of this chapter: trying to achieve your vision without laying out these steps is like trying to bake that cake without a recipe. Your chances of success are slim to none.

To put it another way, a goal without an action plan is nothing more than a wish. So let's keep on breaking it down. You prob-ably can't get your enrollment in a college degree program final-ized this week or even this month, but you can read up on schools in your area and go to open houses, or find out how to apply online. You can't land a new job by tomorrow, but you can send an e-mail to a former boss or co-worker telling her that you're looking and asking her to serve as a reference.

Take a look at the first goal on your list. What can you realistically do in the next month to move closer to it? What can you do in the next week? These are the do-it-right-now steps that move you along your path to your vision of how you see your new life. Write them down.

My Action Plan for the Month

1. _____

2. _____

3. _____

4. _____

5. _____

My Action Plan for the Week

1. _____

2. _____

3. _____

4. _____

5. _____

Now, your action plan isn't the same as a to-do list you might make (and need to make!) to remind you of your focused tasks each day—like "do laundry" or "pay bills." To keep it real, lots of the items on your to-do list will naturally grow out of your action plan—that means you're putting more of your time, energy, and money toward your vision. But your action plan is bigger than a list of daily "to dos." And just like your short-term goals, it will evolve as you knock out some steps and move on to others. Look it over every day: post a copy in the bathroom, keep a copy on the dashboard of your car, save it as a PDF file on your smartphone—the way I do—to take ownership of where you are and map out what you're going to do next. Check things off as you get them done so that you have that sense of accomplishment.

> *There are no unreasonable goals,*
> *only unreasonable deadlines.*
>
> — Brian Tracy

If you don't get something done within the time you planned to, don't beat yourself up, just decide you will get it done. As leadership and achievement expert Brian Tracy says, "There are no unreasonable goals, only unreasonable deadlines." If you've set a deadline for yourself that turns out to be unreasonable, just change it up and go from there.

What's most important is that you're doing something every day to *make it happen!* It's like that wise old head Isaac Newton said—once you're in motion you tend to stay in motion. So now's your time to get moving!

Breaking It Down

When we last saw Martin, he had a list of goals he could reach in the short term to get him closer to his goals for the long term. The next step is to turn these short-term goals into an action plan for right now—this week, this month. So Martin breaks it down again, piece by piece. Here's what his action plan looks like:

Martin's Action Plan for the Month

1. Research and read four articles on successful graphic designers

2.   Find former colleagues on LinkedIn and schedule phone or in-person meetings

3.   Join professional organizations to make new connections

4.   Notify current clients of my 10 percent rate increase

5.   Determine how I will solicit new client business

6.   Post new client rates on my Website

7.   Research time-tracking software to find the best system for me

8.   Identify four cost-cutting measures for my home office (utility bills, etc.) that will reduce expenses by 10 percent within six months

Martin's Action Plan for the Week

1.   Read two articles on successful graphic designers

2.   Invite one former colleague, former supervisor, or client prospect out for coffee

3.   Send a quote to New Client X for her project, using higher rate

4.   Send an e-mail to Old Clients Y and Z explaining that their next projects will be subject to higher rate

5.   Sign up for free trial of time-tracking software

6.   Change all the lightbulbs in my office

Let's give it up to Martin for building an action plan to meet the long-term and short-term goals he has set for himself. He'll keep on updating the action plan as he accomplishes one thing after another, and he'll evaluate his short-term goals every month to make sure they still support his long-term goals. Seems simple enough when you really break it down, doesn't it?

Well, you're so right—it is simple. But that doesn't mean it's easy every step of the way. So let me set you up with another strategy from the Chef Jeff playbook—a bulletproof technique to keep you moving forward when things get a little bumpy.

Bumps in the Road

In that Pre-Release Plan, Alan Hershman didn't stop at asking us to map out what we were going to do—he made us focus on what we *weren't* going to do as well. He'd seen lots of people go in and out of the system, and he knew that any of us could relapse at any time. He wanted us to write out how we, as released felons—especially those with addiction or anger issues—would avoid falling into the same traps again with the wrong crowd. We had to be specific and purposeful about how we'd avoid the obstacles that were bound to be in our way.

You may not face challenges quite like these—I hope you don't! Still, it's natural that on your road to making your vision a reality, you're going to hit some bumps here and there. When that happens—when things don't go the way you want them to or the way you've planned them—it's easy to blame the things, people, or circumstances around you. But the truth is that most of the obstacles that stand between you and your goals aren't coming from somewhere else—they're coming from inside you. Now don't get discouraged! You can bust a move around a lot of these roadblocks if you just see them coming. So what we're going to do now is take a look at some of the stuff that might get in your way down the road.

> **Most of the obstacles that stand between you and your goals are inside you.**

Take a look back at what you've learned about yourself so far in this book. From the VIA test, you know your signature strengths, and you know which strengths aren't so well developed in you. From the E-gram, you know how you function when you're at your best, and you know how you can get when your unconscious tendencies hijack your best intentions because you're stressed or afraid. And from the 3-D Past You collage you made in the last chapter, you have insight into some of the stuff that's tried to take you out when you stopped paying attention to what you were doing.

Based on all that you know now, what are some of the roadblocks you're likely to face in getting where you're trying to go in life? And what inner strengths are you going to tap to overcome them? For example, maybe you know you're liable to get stopped in your tracks if you hit criticism (even constructive criticism) from someone whose opinion you value. Well, if you remember from your E-gram (or your experience) that you tend to be a people pleaser, but one of your signature strengths is bravery, maybe you can find the guts to do what you need to do even if that person looking over your shoulder doesn't agree. Or if you sometimes find yourself spinning your wheels when self-doubt starts to creep in, you can make it a point to go back to your VIA results and remind yourself of all the strengths you possess.

Spend a few minutes writing in your See It, Be It journal:

Challenges I May Face:

_____

_____

_____

_____

What I Can Do about Them:

_____

_____

_____

_____

As you're working on your monthly and weekly action plans, look back at these challenges anytime you hit a bump and you'll remind yourself that you have what it takes to make a conscious decision to get past it. Remember, within every setback is an opportunity—to grow, to change, to learn to use your strengths in new ways.

Inside the War Room

Now, I know what you may be thinking. It's hard as hell to set goals and create an action plan if you have a demanding, high-stress job or if you're working two jobs just to get by. You're not among the fortunate few who have high-six-figure gigs with paid vacations and time off for reflection and prioritizing. If you're unemployed or work a low-wage gig, survival is a 24/7 thing; relaxing is a luxury. I get it. But just because it's harder to plan when you're poor or stressed by circumstances doesn't mean you're excused from this responsibility.

Mapping out my daily action plan is still a major part of my daily program. To this day, I rise at 4:30 every morning—the time I had to wake up in prison to report for kitchen duty. I start my day in the "war room," a room in my home that's completely mine, with a picture window. There's no messing around in my war room. It's my mental gym, the place where I exercise my mind, sharpen my intellectual skills, and plan my action steps. Every morning, I go over the to-do list that I've prepared the evening before. I look over my "stickies," the big ones I've taped to my wall and others that I've stored on my iPhone. At the end of my day, I write down what I accomplished that day and make notes about what has to get done the next day. I look at my action plan and my long- and short-term goals and think and plan big for the future. I start and end every day in the war room.

> **Create your own "war room," where you can get your mind right and your plans tight.**

Create your own war room. It doesn't have to be a real room; just find a space that's yours and yours alone, a spot where you can get your mind right and your plans tight. Every evening, review your goals and your action plan, and make a realistic list of things you need to do the next day. And take a few minutes before closing your eyes to chart your progress (or setbacks) in your See It, Be It journal.

Now you're rolling! Your vision is in motion—and it's up to you to keep it moving. Nobody else can do it for you. Only you can make this happen.

So keep reading—because in the next chapter, I'm gonna introduce you to strategies that will help you work your plan more effectively and speed you faster than you ever thought possible toward your vision for your life.

The Hustlepreneur

Growing up in South Central L.A., I got my early education in street smarts right in my family. Stories passed down about my great-grandfather—a photographer, a sharp-dressing salesman who hustled snapping pictures in pool halls and nightclubs in Mobile, Alabama—laid the groundwork for my street-smart inheritance. I still have his prized huge green Polaroid Land Camera in my possession, and a photograph of him in a dapper black-and-white zebra-print single-breasted suit with matching tie and wing-tip shoes, sporting a pair of black-framed glasses.

His son, my grandfather, Charles Henderson, Sr., was just like his father. He adopted his work ethic and fashion sense—I have a photo of him in a shiny sharkskin suit, black shirt, silver tie, and black fedora. He loved the finer things in life, and when life didn't provide easy access to his dreams, he found a way to make them happen using the tools of the hustlepreneur. When I was growing up, my grandfather wasn't asking me if I had done my homework, he was taking me out to work with him in the janitorial business he'd started after he got tired of doing nickel-and-dime jobs for other people's bottom lines. Granddaddy had no problems convincing owners of places such as Baskin-Robbins Ice Cream, the Laundry Land Laundromats, and the Jewish bakeries and delicatessens on Wilshire Boulevard that he could provide

> **Street-smart people know how the world works and how it can work for them.**

expert service at reasonable prices. To this day, I owe him a huge debt of gratitude. He was the one who taught me how to work hard and be detailed; he had me cleaning toilets; changing fluorescent lightbulbs; waxing, stripping, and buffing floors at 12 years old.

My father wasn't a flashy dude like my great-grandfather or my grandfather, but he, too, made his way in life based on street smarts rather than book smarts: without formal education or the ability to read or write too well, he started his own photography business with a $100 investment and a Pentax K1000 camera and kept it going for more than 30 years. He was sort of an introvert—quiet and very laid-back—but super street smart, which proves that extroverts don't have a lock on those skills. Together, these men planted the street-smart seeds that would eventually blossom and help me become business minded just like them, overcome the negatives of my past, and transition into a productive life.

The Street-Smart Advantage

In life, there are street-smart people and there are book-smart people. Book-smart people may have the top-notch educations, but many have no idea how to apply what they've learned in the real world effectively. Street-smart people are the opposite: without formal education, they know what's going on, how the world works, and how they can make it work for them in their own unique way.

To no surprise, I ran into a whole lot of street-smart dudes in the joint. They had their own change-making hustles and bartering systems. Inmates found creative ways to make money, from braiding hair to shining shoes to writing love letters for men who couldn't write. Even the deep-pocket Wall Street boys I met on the South Yard spread the money around, paying top dollar for inmate-catered ramen noodle dishes and black-market goods that occasionally showed up on the yard—fine imported cigars, hygiene products, high-end walking shoes. Even jailhouse lawyers got paid for filing appeals for inmates who thought they had a chance to get life sentences up off their backs. Hell, in prison, I jumped on the food hustle myself: fried and baked chicken were at a premium on the North and South Yards. Kitchen inmates ate better and were allowed unofficial "no look" passes by some kitchen guards. Sometimes the guards even allowed high per-formers on the kitchen crew to slip out the side door of the dining hall and sell or trade hard-boiled eggs, onions, bananas, and other in-demand ingredients to fellow prisoners. Especially for the ones who got no support from family members on the outside, it was all about survival.

There in prison, one Wall Street guy I became cool with said to me, "Jeff, you're a smart guy." No one had ever told me that before. He said, "When you were on the street, you had all the traits of success and all the skills of a legitimate businessman. You just had a bad product." So when I went straight—I just changed the product. It wasn't drugs anymore; my product was me.

Those of us who have excelled in the street smarts face the same challenges as employees in corporate America. We, too, have to market and sell ourselves to get hired or start a business. Many street-smart people, however, have a competitive edge over some book-smart people. We are able to adapt, go with the flow, and make tough decisions on the fly. We have a survival gene; by necessity we're closer to the ground and have our fin-gers on the deeper pulses of society, and we quickly tune in to the environment and people around us. And of course, it's not always either/or: book smarts and street smarts can go hand in hand.

When you're street smart, you know your way around, you know how to handle yourself in tough situations, and you're able to "read" people well. Street-smart kids know how to keep them-selves safer—whether they're walking to school, riding the bus with bullies and thugs, hanging out on the street corners, or riding their bikes around the neighborhood with a sharp eye out for danger. They are master communicators who use their words and body language to make that bully choose a different victim or influence other kids to step up or back down. Street-smart folks aren't just tough. They're working with a very special set of tools. These are skills that range from having a deep awareness of themselves and their surroundings to employing savvy techniques for competing or collaborating with the people around them to being a "knowledge-jacker"—those who seek out and absorb game-changing information wherever they can find it. I'm talking about the unique tool kit of the hustlepreneur, and it's packed with the skills not taught in a classroom that can accelerate your journey on the road to success in whatever you're doing.

From the Mean Streets to Main Street

A while back, I read the eye-opening research of Bill McCarthy, associate professor of sociology at the University of Toronto, and John Hagan, a professor at Northwestern University. McCarthy and Hagan used their research on juvenile crime—reported in their book *Mean Streets: Youth Crime and Homelessness*—to shed light on what it takes to succeed. The professors concluded that people who succeed in the criminal world possess many of the same characteristics and attributes that successful people in the business world do. What's different is the environment in which they express their talents.

The professors interviewed about 500 youth whose average age was between 19 and 20. Many were involved in some type of criminal activity. McCarthy and Hagan's research revealed that the young people who worked outside the law—on the street—were making more money each day (about $101 in 1992) than their peers who were working legit but low-wage jobs, like those in fast-food joints, earning about $37 a day at the time of the study.

Drawing on theories about what helps people do well in traditional businesses, McCarthy and Hagan concluded that youth in the criminal world actually use the same strategies and character traits to succeed as prosperous people in the legit business world. Among other similarities, they noted how people who are the most successful in what they do have a strong desire to succeed, and they usually specialize in one enterprise, be it selling stocks or selling stolen cars for parts. Both groups are risk takers; both are willing to work with and manage other people; and most important, both successful criminals and successful CEOs are extremely competent—they know how to execute the task at hand and get the job done with the least amount of effort. Both, in their own way, have the skills necessary for success.

> *Don't sit down and wait for the opportunities to come. Get up and make them!*
>
> — Madame C. J. Walker

Now, don't get this twisted—I'm not at all suggesting that you become a criminal to get your dream off the ground. What McCarthy and Hagan observed were desperate young people trying to survive. These youths misused their incredible talents because they had no understanding of the riches that they possessed inside. They had no real answer to the magic question: "Who am I?" But you do. You're ahead of the game. And you can use your street smarts to succeed in the best possible way.

In this chapter I'm going to show you how the same skills and strategies can guarantee success on both the main streets and the mean streets if you can develop the right mind-set. These are the skills of the hustlepreneur that we touched on in Chapter 1—the same ones Tina Jackson used to talk her way into the job she wanted and Keme Henderson used to build her cookie business from scratch. They're also the skills passed down to me from my father and his father and his father before him. Great-granddaddy had the street-smart gift of gab. Granddaddy made his way with his street-smart principles of persuasion and successful competition. And my dad had the classic street-smart skills of humility and adaptation—like a chameleon, he could fit in everywhere he went.

Like I said, street smarts are what make up the must-have tool kit that every hustlepreneur rolls with. In fact, it's what defines hustlepreneurs and sets them apart from everyone else out there struggling to come up. Hustlepreneurs are the individuals who've replicated my recipes for success to the very best of their ability: they know who they are, they know what they want, they've figured out how they're going to get there, and they have reached a level of consistent execution of street-smart strategies that will get them to the top quicker than they ever thought possible.

And you're on your way to becoming one of them! You've done the work of self-discovery. You've trained your eye on a clear and inspiring vision for your life. And you've established goals and developed an action plan to get you there. Now it's time for your advanced training course.

The Hustlepreneur

When I met Rodney, he was serving time for slinging drugs, like me—but that wasn't the whole story of his roots. Rod's mother, Betty Gene, was a hustlepreneur who bought and resold secondhand goods on the streets of L.A. This was her day job, so she would often take the young Rod to work with her, passing down the skills she used to make money so she could take care of her family—survival traits that ranged from expertly negotiating prices to competing successfully on the male-dominated streets. For a few years Rod refined those skills as a drug dealer, but when he got out of prison, he used what he'd learned to launch a plumbing business in L.A., operating with a few trucks and a crew of guys who needed a second chance in life. He was able to use his hustlepreneur skills, along with his charismatic personality and his extraordinary drive, to carve out his version of a legit American dream.

Now, you might be asking, why wasn't it enough for Rod to be just an entrepreneur—a plumber going into business for himself? It's like we saw in Chapter 1: today it takes hustlepreneurship to beat the odds, and you can bet that there were some odds stacked against Rod. Being an entrepreneur may have worked in a different time, in the old economy, but in the new economy you need to be a hustlepreneur, and I don't care if you're on Wall Street or in East Oakland. In a market where college students are graduating with an average of $35,000 in student debt—

sometimes way more, reaching seven figures after graduate or professional school—and with no jobs on the horizon, you need to go beyond the old ways of thinking.

Hustlepreneurs are masters of the street-smart strategies that give them an edge in this new world—the extraordinary ones have some book smarts, too—and their skills can be applied by anyone who is committed to achieving lifelong success. Now, don't be thinking that this level of success comes automatically because you're reading this book; lots of work must be done. There are hundreds of street-smart rappers who wind up broke after one or two club hits. And we hear, read about, and see the negative exploits of the "street-smart fools" on the evening news almost every night. These are really ego-driven fakers who use false bravado as a veil to cover insecurities and straight-up ignorance.

The point is, having street smarts without a road map and the right mind-set is like being a man lost in the desert with a bucket of ice. He's cool for the moment, but soon his salvation will melt away.

True hustlepreneurs have that unique map. Not only do they see opportunities when others don't, they're able to move in and excel through innovation and masterful execution. They are the ones who make a way when there seems to be no way. They have self-issued Ph.D.'s in "street-ology," from courses not taught in traditional curriculums—hard-knock lessons learned through experiences and the daily fight for survival since childhood. Those who live by the law of hustle go at everything with intensity. They are the determined and creative people who refuse to wait for others to make their dreams come true.

> As our world keeps changing, **it will be the hustlepreneurs who will lead the way.**

Domingo Diaz had to flee Cuba in 1966 after Fidel Castro came to power. He came to America and found a job in Atlanta, scrubbing and mopping floors as a janitor. Realizing that other

Cubans in his neighborhood couldn't find their favorite foods in their local grocery stores, Diaz scraped together enough money to start a small bodega where he and his son sold the things that Cubans in the neighborhood desired. Within ten years, the Diaz family added four more stores to their portfolio. Today, Diaz Foods is a corporation with almost 400 employees and annual sales of about $200 million, specializing in transporting and distributing Hispanic food to restaurants and grocery stores in almost 30 states.

Diaz is a classic example of the hustlepreneur. They are game changers, always challenging, bending, and re-creating rules to accomplish their goals and to make themselves stand out among the competition. And their mentality is key to surviving and thriving in a world of economic chaos and instability. As our world keeps changing, it will be the hustlepreneurs who will lead the way with insight, imagination, hard work, and exceptional, experience-based execution—in other words, *with street smarts*.

Portrait of a Hustlepreneur

Life, in the late 1970s, wasn't easy for Anthony Jay Mahavorick. At age 17, the Glendora High School grad was living in the back of his car after his mother kicked him out of their lower-middle-class crib, partly because he had issues with the succession of stepfathers who had entered his life. Later, Mahavorick found a tiny 400-square-foot low-rent California apartment with so few amenities he had to wash dishes in the bathtub.

The youngster survived on dreams, picturing himself one day wealthy, living in a mansion and respected by millions. Today, Mahavorick—known worldwide as Tony Robbins, master motivator, sought-after public speaker, and author of best-selling self-help books—is living his dreams large.

"I hustled and hustled and hustled," Robbins said in a 1991 interview with the *Los Angeles Times*. He began his career promoting seminars for the great motivational godfather Jim Rohn and working with other speakers as well—the perfect environment for a rising knowledge-jacker who knew how to learn from everyone and everything around him. As a mentor, Rohn taught Robbins that material goods won't guarantee happiness or success—effectively a lesson in street-smart humility. "What we do with the things we have makes the biggest difference in the quality of life," Robbins says, recalling Rohn's advice.

Robbins created his own opportunity and pursued his vision, goals, and action plans with passion. He has mastered the power of persuasion; he is someone who recognized a human need and filled it with gusto. And today, Robbins is an industry unto himself. The multimillionaire author of *Unlimited Power, Awaken the Giant Within,* and other books and self-help programs has helped millions transform their lives with advice on overcoming fears, being a persuasive communicator, changing unhealthy habits, and achieving greatness by tapping into our God-given energy and potential.

Tony Robbins is the face of the hustlepreneur—one who has identified and exploited inherent and unique skills, dreamed skyscraper dreams, established a vision for his life, set goals, and executed a street-smart action plan. He's developed a unique recipe for success to beat obstacles and adversity head-on.

Now, keep in mind that being a hustlepreneur doesn't have to mean building your own business from the ground up. Though many hustlepreneurs find their calling as entrepreneurs or solopreneurs, you can use their street-smart tools to build any kind of life you want, whether that means striking out on your own like Domingo Diaz and Tony Robbins or finding a traditional job where you can use your unique strengths to get ahead and make a difference.

Street Smarts All Over

From 125th Street to Madison Avenue in New York City to 77th and Main Street in Los Angeles to Skyline and Meadowbrook Avenue in San Diego, street-smart people share and showcase qualities that explain why they find success in their vastly different worlds. They may not make the cover of *Forbes* or *Black Enterprise* magazines, but they're out there doing the impossible every day. They're serving tacos from food trucks or they're working the parking lot as merchandise vendors and selling the latest products from the back of their cars. They are the neighborhood handymen, the mom who runs a day-care operation out of her home, the folks who operate busy beauty and barbershops in the back room of someone's house, or the student who is the unofficial "tech-help" guru for his entire apartment building. They build businesses and make them work without the predictable resources that franchises or corporations enjoy. Or they work a job in someone else's business, always alert for ways to gain an edge and take the next step up the ladder of success. Either way, they know how to seize opportunities and keep their vision in motion—and you can do the same; all you gotta do is believe that you can.

Being street smart is not about breaking the law. Both book-smart and street-smart people indulge in illegal activity, too. No, being street smart is about recognizing boundaries and finding innovative ways to survive at their cutting edge. Street-smart characters become educated and skilled in nontraditional ways. Hard times teach them how to put food on the family table,

> Street smarters know what people are doing, saying, wearing, buying; they know what people are afraid of and what keeps them up at night.

stretch a dollar, keep the lights on, generate money without a 9-to-5 gig or a network of movers and shakers to open doors for them. Street-smart individuals create their own opportunities, in most cases out of nothing.

I'm talking about individuals who have the natural, nontraditional talents to make things happen in environments plagued with the ills of society. Any race, creed, or gender can be street smart. It doesn't matter if you're a Black person from "da 'hood," a White person from the trailer park, or a Latino from the barrio —people from all walks of life have put their street-smart skills to excellent use. They have masterfully put a grip on their signature strengths and personality traits. They've mixed these with their hard-won experience gained in the school of hard knocks. They've walked their own road in arenas that, on the surface, may not have seemed well suited for their talents.

Oprah Winfrey has shared her story from the heart of being raised in poverty by a single teenage mother in low-income Mississippi and Milwaukee neighborhoods. Mark Wahlberg was a gang member, street fighter, auto thief, drug dealer, and robber out of Boston, who wound up spending time in prison. George Foreman and Eminem were low-achieving students who dropped out of high school before finding their individual paths to boxing and rap stardom. Ellen DeGeneres and Jennifer Lopez dropped out after their first semester in college. Both worked odd jobs until they secured a footing in the entertainment business. Lopez stayed the course even though her parents believed that acting was a waste of her time.

All of these high-profile individuals, and so many others—Harvey, Snoop Dogg, Queen Latifah, P-Diddy, Jay-Z—in their own way merged their God-given talents with street-smart savvy, became great influencers of people, and found a way to fulfill their dreams.

Street-smart individuals are keen observers who know what motivates ordinary people. They rely on their ability to sense and seize the subtle opportunities in their worlds. Without focus groups, marketing surveys, or permission from authority figures who will green-light their identities, passions, or ideas, street smarters know what people are doing, saying, wearing, buying; they know what people are afraid of and what keeps them up at night.

Through hip-hop culture's extraordinary impact in global music, fashion, TV, and film, street-smart philosophy has become one of America's most iconic brands. Early pioneers in what is now a multibillion-dollar music industry started by sampling their tunes on bustling corners, throwing rap and DJ competitions at local clubs, selling their own mix tapes out of car trunks and at swap meets. Rappers, producers, and promoters created a distribution network that offered access to the new music outside of the mainstream record industry and turned tradition on its ear. Not long after the irreversible musical imprint was established, the planks of street-smart fashion and lifestyle were nailed into place, paving the way for so-called urban culture and the mainstreaming of the street-smart attitude.

All that said, it should be clear by now that you don't have to be from the mean streets to be street smart. There are street-savvy operators in every profession and every walk of life. A person who is truly street smart can function just as effectively in a corporate boardroom as in a nightclub back room. In fact, just because you were born in a low-income community or have had difficult circumstances in your life doesn't guarantee that you possess street smarts at all.

The good news, though, is that you can get them! You can learn, from the stories and insights I'll share as we go on, what makes a true hustlepreneur tick—what keeps him or her moving forward on the path to success. And you can cultivate these same qualities in yourself.

Your Best Self

Sometimes in the middle of a speech or workshop, it'll hit me: "Wow, Jeff, you're still the same homeboy, doing what you've been doing all your life. You were just doing it the wrong way." I was unconscious, unfocused, and using the lowest expression of my basic personality and natural talents for illegal gain. Like the youth in Professors McCarthy and Hagan's study, I was using my street smarts to succeed in all the wrong ways. Today, I am conscious, awake, and playing to the highest level of all the talents that I was born with. And I'm proving McCarthy and Hagan right by using those same street smarts to move me forward at high speed in the fast lane.

Not only am I working smarter today, I find that my journey—the life I've lived, the lessons I've learned from my days hustling on the streets of Los Angeles and San Diego, from surviving in prison to my early days finding my way in the corporate culinary world—has tons of value to others. If you've read the biographies or life stories of people like Oprah Winfrey, Bishop

T. D. Jakes, Tony Robbins, Jay-Z, Don King, or Mark Wahlberg, you see how these people who endured personal trauma or who navigated the mean streets, experienced hard times, or made big mistakes are expressing their gifts at the highest levels, and in doing so they have created extraordinary opportunities for themselves and others.

I want you to have your life-changing moments, too. And once you realize that the same character and skill sets that may have you running in place in a dangerous or dead-end space are the exact resources that will help you make your biggest picture-powered dreams come true, your life will be forever changed. Rest assured: the strategies that help you survive on the mean streets can be parlayed into Main Street success. And if you've never spent a day of your life on the mean streets, you can learn those same strategies, starting now, to help you in your lane. The key is to really understand street smarts and how to use them to keep you on the fast track to success.

As your mentor-coach, in the chapters ahead I will lay out in detail 12 straight-to-the-point and from-life-experience street-smart strategies. They are based on my life experiences and the stories of other people, famous and not, who've used these as the secret ingredients in their own recipes for success. And I'll help you discover how applying street smarts to the work you've already done will help move you from simply unconscious surviving to conscious living—the place where your dream can become reality.

part 2

The Street Smarts

In Part I of this book, you heard me break down how the hustle-preneur is a "master" of the street smarts you're about to discover. Truth is, the road to mastery is a lifelong journey of learning, one that I'm still taking along with you. So you don't need to be thinking that you'll read the 12 chapters ahead, put down the book, and bam—you're a master and don't need to work anymore. All that said, there are stages on the journey that you can use to mark your progress so you know you're moving forward—because you *are* moving forward! And I know something about those stages because I had to move through each one of them, though I didn't know that when I started out.

After running two prison kitchens as the top inmate cook and baker, I thought I was the you-know-what! I was convinced that my cooking game was tight and I was gonna take the culinary world by storm. My vision was pixel perfect, and my confidence was sky-high. I had graduated from Pen University with a GED, Toastmasters cred, and all kinds of praises for my prison accomplishments. Future Me was ready to claim a prize on the outside that I had envisioned for years inside prison walls.

Guess what? I was in for a rude awakening. I had been cooking government-issue buffet-style main and side dishes for a captive audience, literally. In the real culinary world, I quickly found out that I didn't know jack about how real kitchens worked. Prison chefs can't use real knives; the food is precut and steam-heated. Convicts have no access to sharp objects or fire! But professional chefs use knives and fire like an artist uses brushes and canvases —it really is an art and a gift. I also knew nothing about presentation or wowing customers who could damn well decide they were never coming back to the restaurant if the food, the service, or the ambiance of the place turned them off. The point I'm making is that I was light-years away from becoming the master I thought I was.

The 4 Stages of Mastery

While writing this book, I read an article about the "four stages of mastery" that perfectly described the phases we all go through as we attempt to transform our lives. Drawing on a model that's widely attributed to Noel Burch and the human-relations training organization Gordon Training International, the article defined the four stages as:

- unconscious incompetence
- conscious incompetence
- conscious competence
- unconscious competence

Reading it, I realized that when I was released in 1996, I was in the "unconscious incompetence" stage for sure. I didn't know what I thought I knew, and worse, I didn't know what I didn't know.

After I went to work for Chef Robert Gadsby, my first culinary mentor, in a real, upscale L.A. kitchen, reality slapped me in the face. I'd just been dropped headfirst into the second stage of mastery: "conscious incompetence." You can best believe I found out with quickness what I didn't know! This is the point when you've stopped pretending and accepted the fact that you're not the top dog you thought you were. Now you can either give up and move on to another skill in another lane, or you can decide to put in the work it's going to take to master this one.

Your best teacher is your last mistake.

— Ralph Nader

After you've dedicated years of study and practice—and messing up and recovering from mess-ups—to the skill you're trying to master, you've gotten pretty good at your game, and you're in the third stage of the mastery journey: "conscious competence." I got to this point after working at Gadsby's and moving on to other restaurants, putting in thousands of hours of practice and learning lessons, some the hard way. I had reached a respectable level in the hierarchy of established chefs; and managing 70 employees at the Bellagio, I was pretty well "conscious" of my "competence." But I wasn't a master yet.

That's because there's one more stage before mastery on this journey we're taking together: "unconscious competence." This is the intersection where you can do your thing with excellence and without any great effort—without having to give it much thought. I don't have to worry or think about my competence in the kitchen, whether I'm chopping an onion or searing a delicate piece of A-grade foie gras. I don't consider myself a master chef, but I'm secure in the knowledge that I can apply my skills in almost any culinary environment.

As you're learning and practicing the 12 Street Smarts, it's my hope that you'll pause from time to time to identify the stage you're at in this process—because even just doing that helps move you forward. If you realize you're unconsciously incompetent, well, you've just moved yourself out of the "unconscious" lane. And it only gets better from there. At every stage, you'll become more and more a master of the street-smart strategies that can take you from an ordinary place to an extraordinary space of power and possibility.

Your Recipe for Success

When I'm in the kitchen, prepping to create an unforgettable meal, I pull out all of the ingredients that I know are part of the basic recipe. Once those are in place, I unleash my imagination and raid my pantry and cabinets where the secret ingredients await. These are the ingredients that don't get written down—the personal touches that are part of my unique signature and sensibility as a chef.

In each of the 12 chapters ahead, I'm going to introduce you to the contents of my private pantry, stocked with the street-smart secret ingredients that you can use to create the meal of your dreams. Just like any of my culinary students, here in the kitchen of unlimited possibilities, you're going to choose the ingredients that pair best with your taste, your experience, and your vision for what you want to create. This is what will allow you to come up with a truly original and delicious dish—your personal recipe for success.

I'll hold each quality ingredient from the hustlepreneur's pantry up to the light so you can see what it looks like, taste it, smell it, and determine whether it's something you want to use. Maybe you have this ingredient already stocked in your kitchen; maybe it's brand new to your palate; maybe it's something you take for granted and need to appreciate in a new way; or maybe you've just run out of it and need to replenish your supply. Whatever the case, you'll decide if it's what you need to elevate your own success recipe. The special ingredients that you choose may be the ones that connect most naturally with the personality and signature strengths you've discovered in your work so far. Or they may be the ones that are obviously missing in your life right now. Either way, they're your secret ingredients!

To get that creative imagination in overdrive, I'll share stories of people who've used these secret street-smart ingredients in their own recipes to fast-pace their success, get ahead, and make a difference. Then, at the end of each chapter, I'll offer Street-Smart Challenges, which are designed to help you strengthen your newly discovered skills and start moving from seeing it to being it right away. It's time to get your hustle on up and get it cookin'!

The 12 Street Smarts

1. The Self-Controller: The strategy of self-discipline

Self-controllers don't make excuses, whine, or blame—they make decisions to do the things that advance their vision by staying on time and on task. They're disciplined doers, not talkers. When a task or a goal isn't serving them, they know when to let go, because endless perseverance isn't always an effective strategy for success—but when hard work is on the table, they've built the inner strength to buckle down and just do it.

2. The Sacrificer: The strategy of delayed gratification

Sacrificers aren't afraid to give up something they like to get something better, whether it's instant gratification or a relationship that's turned into a roadblock. In a culture of get-rich-quick schemes and instant results, sacrificers understand that you really do have to sow before you can reap. When it comes to surrendering right-now rewards to set themselves up for a bigger later-on payoff, they see the big picture and know how to do more with less.

3. The Knowledge-Jacker: The strategy of anytime, anywhere education

The knowledge-jacker seeks out vital information to create a winning advantage. Knowledge-jackers don't go after people's money or belongings—they go after everything they need to know to accomplish their own goals. They understand that imitation can be the one of the surest and most practical tools of personal growth, and they seek out mentors and role models who have mastered the profession, knowledge, or experience that they need to achieve—then take what they learn and apply it in a way that's all their own.

4. The ESP-er: The strategy of intuition

ESP-ers have a razor-sharp sixth sense that lets them sense their way to the heart of most any situation. Always on the alert with their antennae scanning for both threats and opportunities, they're highly aware of everything that's going on around them; they know how to listen to what people aren't saying. They can connect the dots in ways that others don't, and they hear and heed that "little voice" that speaks quieter than the ego but always tells the truth.

5. The Gambler: The strategy of calculated risks

The gambler knows when the time is right to roll the dice. Gamblers don't waste time sitting on the fence; they act in a big way to make the most of opportunities, and they know how to walk away when the risks have too big an edge on the potential rewards. They come to grips with their fear, they get back up when they fall, and they're comfortable walking the edge of uncertainty to get where they want to go.

6. The Gab-Master: The strategy of persuasion

Gab-masters can talk their way into almost anything. They truly have the "gift of gab": they know how to communicate with purpose, assess their audience, market themselves, and sell their brand—all the while moving potential clients to take action. They know that being artfully persuasive isn't about manipulation—it's about communicating honestly, listening, motivating, and truly connecting with others.

7. The Chameleon: The strategy of adaptation

Chameleons look the part, dress the part, and act the part—all in order to gain the access they weren't born with to the inner circles and upper echelons of success. They understand that they're going to be judged by their walk or their talk, their appearance or their ZIP code, so they change up their persona at will, whether they're applying for a job or a loan or trying not to stand out in a upscale neighborhood. Chameleons don't buy into the myth that "keeping it real" means not caring what anyone thinks, they are experts at "gettin' in and fittin' in."

8. The Crew-Master: The strategy of collaboration

Nobody gets where they're going in life by going at it alone, and there's no such thing as a one-man show. The crew-master knows you need top-notch people around you to provide the missing ingredients, filling in the gaps in your skills and strengths with high-level assets of their own. Crew-masters are experts at assembling the right team, creating effective and empowering partnerships, and managing people with diplomacy, grace, and tough love. They understand people power and know what a skilled team can accomplish when they come together for a powerful purpose.

9. The Winner: The strategy of competition

"Survival of the fittest" is the law of the street—and the blue- and white-collar workplace. Winners live on their toes, aware that there's someone making their move in the next lane, ready to snatch their opportunity away. They know that competition is a 24/7 proposition; they're experts at studying the opponent, zeroing in on real excellence, and keeping their competitive edge razor-sharp. They understand that there are no do-overs in life, but at the same time, as seasoned competitors they are ultimately comfortable with winning and losing when that's the way the cards fall.

10. The Last-in-Liner: The strategy of humility

The last-in-liner knows that "pride goeth before destruction" and a humble spirit is a strategy for success in any walk of life. They're confident without being arrogant, and they're clear that being humble doesn't mean that you're a sucker who's waiting to be exploited or humiliated. At the same time, they admit what they don't know, and they're open to listening and learning. Last-in-liners know that putting your ego in check to put the needs of others first may be just what you need to succeed.

11. The No-Strings Giver: The strategy of selfless service

The no-strings giver knows that it's never enough just to "get yours." No-strings givers pay it forward every step of the way: they give of themselves—whether it's money, time, energy, passion, or a ride to the grocery store—to those who have less or who aren't so far along on the journey to success. They understand that everyone has something to offer, and one of their gifts is inspiring others to find and use their gifts, too. They recognize that whatever you give in a truly selfless spirit, that's what truly changes the world.

12. The Shot-Caller: The strategy of visionary leadership

The shot-caller knows that when you're at the top of your game, you're ready to show others the way. Shot-callers are the visionaries who can see possibilities over the horizon and lead others to get there. Whether they're running a corporation or a community barbecue, they use the tools of trust, connection, and motivation with skill and grace. They know that leadership isn't about getting people to do your bidding—it's about firing them up to be and do the most they're capable of—and they understand that the very best thing you can do with power is pass it on.

The Self-Controller

The strategy of
self-discipline

Self-discipline is the engine that drives you whatever lane you're in.

— Chef Jeff

It took extraordinary self-discipline to wake up every morning in cramped cells and cubicles for nearly ten years and still dedicate time and practice to preparing for my life on the outside. At the beginning of my imprisonment, I mostly did what was easiest for me and passed the time (not that prison life was easy): I watched TV with the brothers—soap operas, sports, and BET—worked out on the weight pile, and waited for weekends when my dad or my girl would visit and buy me food from the visiting-room vending machines.

Then one sleepless night I started reading a book one of the other inmates had given me. I read until the battery in my nightlight died. Though I was never much of a reader, the Black self-help book began to make me think more about my life and setbacks; I started to see myself and then the world differently. And from then on I started doing more and more of the things that would move me in the right direction. I started helping organize programs for Kwanzaa and Black History Month. I joined the prison version of Toastmasters International to hone my speaking and presentation skills. And by reading whenever I got the chance in the law library and at night on my bunk after the 10 P.M. count, I earned my GED. I even volunteered to sit with inmates who were on suicide watch.

Later, when I was put on the pot-and-pan crew, I had to wake up not long after the 4 A.M. count to report to the kitchen at 6 A.M. As soon as I figured out that the kitchen was where I wanted to be, I washed those pots and pans religiously and worked as hard as I could to prove myself until a spot opened up on the cooking crew. At night, by the light of the small lamp in my cell, I committed recipes to memory and went over each step again and again. Without that discipline, I wouldn't have been close to ready to take on the world of professional cooking when I was released.

Self-discipline is the engine that drives you in whatever lane you're in. Without it, your vision, your goals, and your action plan won't be anything but words on paper and ideas in your head. With it, you can start moving ahead, focused and fast, toward success. In fact, it's across-the-board agreed among experts, coaches, and teachers that self-discipline is key to any kind of lasting success at all. It's not wishful thinking to say that it makes everything else possible. That's why you're reading about it before tackling any of the other street-smart strategies—so that you can apply this skill to all the rest of the work you're doing in this book.

The choice is yours—and make no mistake, it is a conscious choice you make. It's great to feel motivated and pumped up about the steps you're taking toward your vision, and you need that as a starting point; if you weren't motivated at all, you wouldn't be reading this book. But day by day, it shouldn't matter how motivated you *feel*. Philosopher Elbert Hubbard put this tough truth into crystal-clear words: "Self-discipline is the ability to do what you should do, when you should do it, whether you feel like it or not." It means you've made a decision to do the things that advance your goals, and you're going to do them no matter what.

Arming yourself with unwavering discipline, however, is more than just being tough and not whining. And discipline is a skill set that doesn't come naturally to a lot of us. The good news is that there are building blocks to a disciplined life, and we're going to discover them in this chapter.

Be All You Can Be

It's no accident that "Be all you can be" was the recruiting slogan of the U.S. Army for more than 20 years. The military—along with prison—is ironically one of the few places left in our society where discipline truly prevails. Now, I'm not asking you to enlist or do time! But I am saying to you, strong self-discipline is one of the most important keys to becoming the best *you* you're capable of being. Without it, I must say you'll always fall at least a little bit short of all you *could* be.

Discipline is the bridge
between goals and accomplishment.

— Jim Rohn

After 15 years, Arthur Boorman, a disabled Gulf War veteran, had basically given up. The knees of the former paratrooper had sustained too much damage from far too many jumps. Arthur, shockingly overweight at five feet eight inches and almost 300 pounds, couldn't walk without knee and back braces or support his weight without the use of two canes. Doctors assured him he'd never walk on his own again. And for a long time he believed them.

Any kind of exercise, Arthur believed, was out of the question. He thought yoga would help, but all the instructors he contacted turned him down. Even Diamond Dallas Page, the former pro wrestler turned fitness guru and yoga instructor, had doubts about his ability to help Arthur. But help him he did. With encouragement and consistent instruction, Page put Arthur on the specialized "DDP" workout to help him lose weight, gain balance, increase his flexibility, and regain his ability to walk.

As I watched a video of Arthur's story on YouTube, my heart went out to him as he struggled through the strength-building lessons, holding on to a chair for support. His fragile legs trembled; he flapped his arms to maintain balance only to tumble over on his side or fall flat on his face, time and time and time again. In one scene, Arthur attempts a headstand, but he crashes, feet over head, into a nearby cabinet. Kneeling on his yoga mat, long hair matted against his sweaty face, he talks to the camera:

"Just because I can't do it today . . . doesn't mean I'm not going to be able to do it someday."

Bravo, Arthur! Slowly, frame by frame, a slimmer, steadier, more confident Arthur appears in the video. He had a dream to walk again. With Diamond's help he developed a vision and an action plan to implement that vision. But it was Arthur's own determination and self-discipline that made it possible for him to struggle through those exercises each day, carrying him through the stumbles, flips, and falls and giving him the strength to get up and try, try again. He could see it, and his discipline paved the way for him to be it—all he knew he could be.

If you haven't heard or seen Arthur's story, I encourage you to look it up on YouTube (http://youtu.be/blXOo8D9Qsc). Take my word for it: you really need to see this. It's incredible to watch the time-lapse effect in photos of Arthur over a few months' time, each one slimmer and trimmer and standing straighter than the one before. It's thrilling to see him master that headstand at last and make it look easy. And it's unbelievably moving to see him, 10 months later and 140 pounds lighter, walking unassisted through a park—and not just walking. First he breaks into a jog, and then a full-out sprint—the man the doctors said would never walk normally again.

So what does Arthur's story have to do with you? Everything, because your vision depends on developing the kind of self-discipline that paved his path to success. It starts with realizing there's no room for excuses. Arthur could have made all kinds of excuses—that the exercises hurt, that he didn't have the time, that there wasn't room in his den for a yoga mat—but ultimately he understood that he had to step up if he ever wanted to stand up straight without those canes. And the same goes for you. It doesn't matter if you're starting a business, bouncing back from bankruptcy, trying to lose weight or conquer an addiction, or striving to achieve any other kind of life transformation; you absolutely must accept the fact that you and you alone are responsible for making it happen. It's as personal-development expert Brian Tracy says: "If it's to be, it's up to me!"

Start Where You Are

Many guys in prison have V-shaped torsos on top of I-shaped legs because they spend hours pumping iron on the weight pile to look tough. But the weights they're capable of lifting now are not where they started out. They had to build their strength gradually and deliberately, using weights that were within their capacity to lift but heavy enough to push their muscles to the limit. Too heavy and they wouldn't be able to get the bar off the rack. Too light and they'd never progress, even if they did endless reps all day long.

When you're beginning a workout program, you don't start by trying to bench-press your body weight. And you don't just pick up any old dumbbell you see and hope it's at the right weight. You have to figure out your level of strength at the start so that you can choose the proper weights to build it effectively. It's the same with any kind of self-disciplined endeavor. If Arthur Boorman had tried to do a headstand on day one, he might have become so discouraged he'd have given up, or he might even have hurt himself. Either way, it's safe to say he would not have mastered that headstand, even with great effort. He had to start with simpler moves to build the strength and flexibility his body was so sorely lacking before he could reasonably attempt to stand on his head.

So when you start to build your own self-discipline in the service of your vision, it's equally important to define your strengths at the start. Be honest with yourself, because it won't help you if you aren't. Let's say you've decided that you need to get up earlier so you have time to work on your action plan and review the day's tasks before you have to leave for work. If you normally get up at 8:00 A.M.—and find it hard enough at that hour—it probably doesn't make sense for you to suddenly set the alarm for 5:30 and expect to bounce out of bed. Try getting up at 7:30, or even 7:45, for a couple of weeks; that's a small enough shift that you can make it without much difficulty, and when you succeed at it, you'll not only feel encouraged, you'll be set up to move the time back to 7:15, then 7:00, until you get to where you want to be.

> *Discipline yourself, and others won't need to.*
>
> — John Wooden

Or if your goal is to find a job in an occupation you're gifted in, don't decide that you're going to send out a bunch of résumés a day right off the bat, because you'll likely be overwhelmed before you even get started. Instead, set aside half an hour a day to first read up on how to write a effective résumé, then draft and edit yours, then research companies and job openings, then write your cover letters and start sending them out. If half an hour feels like time you can spare, push yourself a little harder by making it an hour. In both these examples, what you're doing is using the discipline you already have to build your discipline muscle more and more. Over time, you can increase the challenge just the way you'd add more weight to your dumbbells.

Hard Work and Working Hard

Since coming to America, Gac Filipaj, a refugee from war-ravaged Yugoslavia, led a highly self-disciplined life. For years, working as a janitor at the prestigious Columbia University, he emptied trash baskets; cleaned restrooms; and mopped, buffed, and waxed floors. The job came with 14 free credit hours a year, so after his shift ended at 11:00 P.M., Filipaj headed to his Bronx apartment, cracked open his books, and worked late into the night—sometimes all night—finishing assignments or preparing for exams. The first few years, he studied English. After that, he enrolled in Columbia's classics program, studying Greek and Latin. Sleep or no sleep, he'd arrive at Columbia bright and early, attend his classes, then start his 2:30 P.M. janitor shift.

Filipaj had come to America in the early 1990s to escape the brutal civil war in the Yugoslav republic. Working at a relative's restaurant in New York as a busboy, he continued looking for a job where he could continue the studies he'd begun in Belgrade. He was intent on attending one of America's top schools, so he asked around. Since Columbia topped his list, he told an Associated Press reporter, he "went there to see if [he] could get a job."

In May 2012, at age 52, after a dozen years of study, Gac Filipaj received his bachelor's degree. Donning a cap and gown, he walked across the stage to receive his handshake and diploma with other students, some more than 30 years younger than the graduating janitor.

Filipaj honed in on his vision, set his goals, created an action plan, and was disciplined enough to stick to it for 12 years. He didn't let the curious glances and no doubt skeptical comments from those outside his circle of support dampen his fire.

What's so interesting to me about Filipaj's story is that he tapped into two equally important veins of self-discipline: he worked hard, and he did hard work. Those may sound like the same thing, but they're not. Working hard means just that: putting in a continuous, focused effort on any task. Emptying trash baskets wasn't hard work for Filipaj, but you can bet he worked hard at it—as he did at cleaning toilets and waxing floors. Cleaning up your desk may not be hard work for you, but you have to work hard to stay on top of it. Same goes for keeping your e-mail in-box clear of unread messages: not difficult, but it needs to get done consistently or it gets out of hand. Working hard is important because it trains you to complete your tasks efficiently and increase your productivity no matter what you're doing—so you can bring that industry and efficiency to more challenging tasks.

That's what hard work means: tasks that challenge you, like Filipaj's studies of Greek literature and philosophy at Columbia. The work I've been asking you to do in this book is hard: looking closely at yourself, drilling down on your dream, setting goals, and developing an action plan. Hell, *writing* this book has been hard work for me! Learning a new skill is hard work; so is exercising, or quitting smoking, or developing any new habit. What's hard for someone else may not be hard for you. But whatever it means for you, it's important to do this difficult work, because it's the work that's going to move you forward meaningfully on your path to success.

Be a Doer, Not a Talker

If words were dollars, there'd be a bunch of millionaires locked up in prison. I can't tell you the number of business schemes or life-changing products that inmates talked about in prison but never followed through on after their release. I know the game. Talkers talk because they want people to hear their value and worth. They hope their big schemes and big plans will validate them and make the felony jacket disappear. The motivation applies on the streets, too. People don't want to feel like losers for the rest of their lives. So they talk themselves into a fantasy life that allows them just to put one foot in front of the other each and every day.

I understand that desire, but I also know that society has little patience for talkers. After a while you start to sound like static, that annoying buzz between clearer-sounding radio stations. There are people who spend their entire lifetimes on the static channel and others who come to crystal clarity. The defining difference is that talkers run their mouths, while doers rely less on talk and more on the doing. Doers have the self-discipline that talkers, like some of those guys in prison, lack—the ability to buckle down and do what it takes to make their vision a reality.

> Are you going to be a talker or a doer? The choice is yours.

Talkers tend to see themselves as victims of circumstance. They consciously or subconsciously believe that others are better or just luckier than they are. They give up easily after a couple of setbacks (or just one!), and they don't really have a vision or goals or an action plan . . . they just have the talk. Doers, on the other hand, see themselves as equal with everybody—not luckless victims—and find a way when there seems to be no way.

If you create goals with timelines, then allow yourself just to blow them off for any reason, you're not a responsible doer. And if you call yourself a doer but you're still hanging out with talkers who sit around smoking weed all day, daydreaming and story-telling, well, you're not holding yourself accountable. Don't underestimate the importance of the company you keep, because self-discipline can be contagious, just like its opposite. It's like Larry Holmes, Muhammad Ali's onetime sparring partner, said of the great fighter: "Ali was a guy that had a lot of discipline. If you hung around him, you'd be able to get some of that discipline that he had. And I learned from that."

Are you going to be a talker or a doer? It's like I said before—the choice is yours.

Make Time Work for You

The story of Ivy Lee and business mogul Charles Schwab is well known in self-discovery, self-help, and business circles. It's a reminder that success comes through planned self-discipline. The famous tale goes like this:

Back in the late 1800s, Charles Schwab, president of Bethlehem Steel, sought the advice of Ivy Lee, a well-known business-management consultant. If Lee could show Schwab a fail-proof way to get more things accomplished in a day, Schwab promised a handsome reward.

As legend has it, Lee handed Schwab a piece of paper and asked that he write down all the things he had to do the next day. He had Schwab assign numbers to the items he listed in order of importance. Then he ordered the steel magnate to start working on number one first thing in the morning. He couldn't move on to number two until number one was completed. The same rule applied to everything on the list. There was to be no straying off course.

The secret, Lee told Schwab, was to do this every working day with no exceptions. This simple but effective system allowed Schwab to prioritize tasks, evaluate what had been done and the results it had brought, and set a plan of action that he could stick to. After Schwab was convinced that the system worked for him, Lee suggested he have his employees do the same thing.

Lee was so confident that Schwab would be satisfied with the results, he told the entrepreneur to send him a check for whatever amount he felt the idea was worth. A few weeks later, Lee received a check from Schwab in the amount of $25,000 (which is getting close to a million in today's dollars). In later interviews, Schwab said that Lee's exercise was the most profitable lesson he'd ever learned in his whole business career.

It's been more than 100 years, but Ivy Lee's lesson still serves as a key to self-disciplined goal setting and task and time management. You can use this approach yourself when you're doing what we discussed in Chapter 4: sitting in your war room, wherever that is for you, reviewing your action plan and making a list of things you need to do the next day. Try to keep the list manageable—four to six items. Put them in order of importance. Then, when you start in the morning, start with task number one, and don't move on to something else until it's completed. Don't be fooled into thinking that really self-disciplined people should be able to multitask effortlessly; the way to get things done is just to do them, simple as that, and then move on.

It's important to write your to-do list on an actual piece of paper. Sure, you can do all this on a computer, but that means you have to remember to print it out every night or turn the computer on in the morning. This, too, is risky and holds too many opportunities for distraction. A yellow pad right by your bedside, waiting for when you awake, is the best way to activate your day. At the end of the day, if some tasks are left undone, put them on the next day's list.

This basic exercise provides the structure you need to meet your goals and remain focused on the important tasks that are part of your action plan. It will also help you realize the value of your time. You will start to see money flying out the door with those wasted hours of playing computer solitaire, watching TV, playing video games, or just talking with friends and family on the phone all day about nothing.

The "self" in self-discipline means you make yourself submit and obey your inner coach. It is the motivator within who will urge you to turn off the TV or spend less time hanging out in nightclubs or with uninspired friends. Your inner enforcer will help you suck it up, stick to your plan, and do something every day to pull that vision of yours a little bit closer to the land of the real.

Know When to Let Go

Self-discipline means being persistent and consistent in your efforts, but it doesn't mean persisting when it's no longer productive or even reasonable to do so. We talked in Chapter 4 about how your goals—specifically, your short-term goals—are going to shift and evolve as you accomplish some and cross them off the list, getting ever closer to your vision. Here's something else that you need to understand: some of your goals aren't going to get accomplished at all. Now, this doesn't mean you have failed in any way! It just means that those goals, for whatever reason, have turned out not to be practical or still relevant for you. You need to be able to figure out what you *don't* need to accomplish—to know when to let go.

In a way, this takes the ultimate degree of self-discipline, because it can be so hard to put something aside before it's completed. If you're really dedicated to what you're doing, and you really want to be persistent, it can actually feel *wrong*. But sometimes, if you don't let go of one goal or task or project, it means you're preventing yourself from moving on to something new and more important.

*Self-discipline enables you
to think first and act afterward.*

— Napoleon Hill

There's a famous story about a company that was started in 1972 by a couple of computer whizzes named Bill Gates and Paul Allen. Called Traf-O-Data, it offered a microcomputer solution to tracking traffic patterns recorded by roadside counters, something that had previously been done painstakingly by hand. Have you ever heard of Traf-O-Data? Probably not, because it never got off the ground, though Gates and Allen ran it for several years. Eventually, they gave in and accepted that making Traf-O-Data successful was not a viable goal on their path to their vision of ultimate success in the computer industry. And I bet you've heard of the company they went on to found after Traf-O-Data folded—a small outfit called Microsoft.

You need to get this, because if something you're doing is just not working—if you're not making progress even though you're applying yourself to it with all the self-discipline in your power—you owe it to yourself to put that something aside and move on. If Arthur just couldn't get that headstand right, no matter how hard he tried and how consistently he worked at it—if he kept on falling over and crashing into the cabinet—he would have been wise to decide, *You know what? A headstand isn't in the cards for me,* and move on to other exercises that would challenge and stretch him just as effectively, but not frustrate him and keep him stuck. He would have crossed that particular goal off his list and put something else in its place as he worked toward his vision of being able to walk again.

The Lesson of Foie Gras

When I think about discipline and all that it means, I can't help but think that cooking in a professional kitchen is a perfect meta-phor. Few things are as disciplined as the preparation of a meal, especially when everything has to be timed to the minute—or even to the second. To make dishes come out right, you can't go about the preparation haphazardly. There's an order to things, from when you lay out your ingredients in the *mise en place* all the way to when the last dessert is plated for the last remaining customer at the table.

Now, chances are you're not heading for a career as a profes-sional chef, so I'll share a story that will show you just what I'm talking about.

It was the year 2001. Nearly every major hotel/casino had turned me down for a job on the Vegas strip. Finally, I decided to go after Caesar's Palace for a chef gig. I was hesitant because back in the day, I'd been a high roller there and I didn't want to bring back those memories of when I was a big-time baller. But it was my last and only opportunity of hope.

During the initial interview, JP, Jim Perrillo, a stocky Italian guy with slicked-back hair and an intimidating swagger, asked me two very direct questions: "Henderson, you ever kill anybody?" and "Can you cook?"

After my "No, sir," and "Yes, sir," Chef Jim offered me a shot to prove myself in the kitchen: "Come cook for me and my team. If you impress us with your food and your style, we'll consider an opportunity for you."

I thought maybe Jim and his crew believed I was a hash slinger. But they knew I had also cooked in some of L.A.'s top-notch hotels, so I decided that that probably motivated them to roll the dice and give me a shot. I had no intention of going in there and making meat loaf with some thick brown gravy and standard sautéed green beans that weren't shocked in ice cold water or seasoned properly. I was prepared to cook six courses in 60 minutes and I went in and put it down for them—Asian-pear-and-Gorgonzola salad, A-grade foie gras, pan-roasted Chilean sea bass, prime filet mignon—classic dishes with a California twist—and two old-school desserts on fancy bone-white French china.

Everything went off perfectly, with one exception. When the salad was on the table and I was ready to cook the foie gras, I freaked out on the inside, realizing that it had been sitting out at room temperature for too long. Now, foie gras is incredibly fragile, and if it gets too soft, you just can't cook it for any length of time—it'll turn into a shapeless mess. So I had to think fast and come up with a way to cook the foie faster than I imagined possible, over super-high heat for literally just a few seconds. It was nerve-wracking—but it worked, and the dish knocked them out. After my presentation, I was hired on the spot.

But before that happened, I had to exercise some serious self-discipline. First, I had to assess my starting point and plan a menu that would showcase my food and skills, but not overplay my hand far beyond my abilities. I had to do hard work—you can best believe that saving that foie gras was hard work!—and I had to work real hard to get six courses from kitchen to table inside of an hour. I had to manage my time and prioritize my tasks, otherwise the dessert would have come out before the filet and the fish would have been sure to overcook. I even had to know when to let go—to change up the way I'd planned to cook the liver and go for a different spin. The timing was key.

I share this story because I want you to understand what it takes to pursue any vision with real self-discipline—and I want you to know that you *have* what it takes! You can get this strategy down and use it to move you toward mastery no matter what lane you're in. Start by trying the Street-Smart Challenges on the next page to hone your no-excuse skills, then read on to get more street smarts under your belt.

Street-Smart Challenges for:

The Self-Controller

☆ **Take a small step.** For one week, set your alarm clock 15 minutes earlier every morning. Get up at that time whether you feel like it or not.

☆ **Form a habit.** Pick one thing you'd like to make part of your daily routine—like taking a walk after dinner or opening the mail without letting it pile up—and do it every day for two weeks. Then, if it's something you want to keep doing, you've got a habit in the making.

☆ **Get your priorities straight.** Starting now, put your daily task list in order of priority every day, and don't start a new task until you've completed the one before it.

☆ **Work hard.** Pick a task that's been hanging over your head—whether it's cleaning out your closet or answering old correspondence—and tackle it. Keep at it until you're done.

☆ **Do hard work.** Choose one thing that challenges you—that's difficult to do but important for your action plan—and make a commitment to do it (or start it, if it's a longer-term project) within the next week.

☆ **Move on.** Choose a goal that you've been working but not progressing toward, and consciously decide to let it go. If it's on a list, cross it off. If it's not, write it on a piece of paper and then throw the paper away.

The Sacrificer

The strategy of
delayed gratification

You've got to let go to grow.
— Chef Jeff

When I speak in front of an audience, I can feel the effect I'm having on them right away. I can see their faces, their eyes, the nonverbal expressions; I can see them smile and hear them applaud. Sometimes I can even see them get emotional if something I've said moves them deeply.

With writing, it's another story. You don't get feedback right away; you don't get that quick gratification of hearing your audience respond. In fact, sometimes there's a very long pause between putting words on paper and seeing their final impact on everyday people. I've written four books now, and I've learned that in publishing, that pause between first draft and books in the bookstore can be as long as a year or even more! Even though I have a treasured first reader right at home—my wife, Stacy, who looks over everything I write and often improves it or rejects it—I still have to put major work in before I'm satisfied with the words on the page or on my computer screen. As a wise writer once said, "I don't like writing, I like having written." The process of thinking through an idea, then writing, then revising and editing, is the ultimate test in delayed gratification, let me tell you. And there are no shortcuts, if you want what you're communicating to come across clearly and effectively.

Even if you're not a professional writer, always remember that all of us are communicators in every sense. Every time you write anything—a letter, an e-mail—you need to express your ideas to get people to understand your thoughts. Even a 140-character tweet has to be carefully crafted, because when you write some-thing these days, it lives forever. Going for instant gratification—skipping the steps of reflection and revision, or hitting Send too soon—can be a deal breaker. If you can't stay with the process and postpone the pleasure you'll get from hearing someone say, "That's great stuff," chances are you'll never have anything that's worth the time it takes to read it.

I'm telling you this not so that you can go off and become a published writer, unless of course that's your vision and you have a gift for writing. The kind of delayed gratification I'm talking about here is a secret to success in all sorts of enterprises. In this chapter, we'll look at why sacrifice is so important and check out some ways you can make it work for you.

Don't Eat the Marshmallow

Back in the late 1960s, Stanford psychologist Walter Mischel did a famous experiment you may have heard about on instant versus delayed gratification. The key ingredients were young children and a bag of marshmallows. A researcher offered each child a choice: the child could eat a marshmallow right away, or wait 15 minutes and get two marshmallows instead of one. Then the researcher left the child alone to decide.

Only about one-third of the kids held out for the second marsh-mallow—though videotape of the experiment shows how hard some of them tried to wait! They covered their eyes, turned their backs, even pulled their hair. That was fascinating, but the real payoff from the study came when the researchers followed up with the kids in the study to see how they were doing in school and in life. The kids who didn't take the marshmallow had aver-age SAT scores 210 points higher than the ones who ate it within 30 seconds. According to *The Wall Street Journal*, they were also less likely to drop out of college or go to jail, had fewer problems with drugs and alcohol, and made more money than their less self-restrained counterparts.

Today, we're all hustling in a world of instant gratification, no question about it. Just look at all the ads you see for get-rich-quick schemes or lose-weight-fast products, promising money-back guaranteed results with little or no effort. Information, movies, food and entertainment, and soul mates are all but a screen swipe away. Unlike earlier generations, folks today throw in the towel if the struggle is too hard or the situation doesn't change overnight. But what studies like Mischel's show us is that the ability to defer gratification can spell success

> **Life is not a game show. In real life, you have to earn your rewards.**

or failure in real life. Life is not a game show. You don't give the right answers or choose the right box and walk off the stage with the bomb rewards five minutes later. In real life, you have to work hard and earn those rewards.

This is the secret of what I call "strategic sacrifice": giving up what's in front of you right now in the interest of getting what you most want down the road in terms of your personal or professional growth. You're not giving it up for good, just for now. True hustlepreneurs know that sacrifice is not about losing something; it's an important choice that's all about gaining everything in the long run.

Strategic Sacrifice

To many people, the word *sacrifice* unearths painful images of self-denial, often with some serious suffering built in. But there's no need to invite all that drama. To be straight up, we need to change up the conversation on sacrifice. The way that I'm using the word, it doesn't mean you have to be a martyr. As self-help guru Bob Proctor, author of *You Were Born Rich* and *How Rich People Think,* says, "Sacrifice is giving up something of a lower nature to receive something of a higher nature."

So, in essence, when you sacrifice, you're simply opening yourself up for life's bigger rewards. In this light, we see that things like playing golf, going out with friends to the club, or even sitting on the couch and playing video games don't necessarily have to be permanently removed from your life. With strategic sacrificing, you simply move them down lower on your priority list, knowing that there will be plenty of time to enjoy that stuff after you've achieved your goals or activated your dream.

Adam and Jonathan Holland learned the importance of strategic sacrifice earlier than most. These two amazing brothers were 15 and 14 years old when they won the 2011 Black Enterprise Teenpreneur of the Year Award for the business they launched: AJ's Hawaiian Iceez, which sells flavored shaved ice treats at public and private events around Washington, D.C. For several years, the youngsters have given up their weekends—time when most kids are relaxing, playing, or hanging out with friends—to run the business, all in order to help their parents with the high cost of tuition to keep them and their younger sister in good schools. And they've achieved the goal they set out to meet: the business grossed some $30,000 in 2009, $40,000 in 2010, and around $50,000 the year of the award, $25,000 of it pure profit. "You have to make the sacrifice in order to reap the reward," Adam told *The Washington Post*. "The people out playing neighborhood ball aren't making the money or getting the experience I am getting."

Freedom Ain't Free

Let's be clear, my friend. No one forced you to make the decision to change your life or to aggressively pursue your dreams. This is on you. And this is powerful stuff that calls for big-time sacrifice without expecting any pats on the back or sympathy at all. As they say, "Freedom ain't free, baby." If you want the freedom to live an independent, meaningful life, you have to pay your dues by putting in the hard work and postponing the rewards as long as it takes. "Delayed gratification is a form of self-discipline that is necessary for emotional mastery," says personal-development expert Al Duncan, who counsels at-risk youth. "People often think it means 'no fun.' That's not true. It means sacrifice now to experience even more enjoyment and rewards later. You can still have some fun," Duncan explains. "You can still have a few nice things, but not too much too soon."

What happens if you don't heed this advice—if you let yourself fly high on the hog and go for "too much too soon," at the expense of the work you really need to be doing right now? It's important to be honest about cause and effect, but too often we aren't. When people work hard and get good results, you'll often hear them give credit to their hard work, and rightly so. But if those same people *don't* work hard and *don't* get good results, they'll often lay the blame at someone else's door—like a jacked-up boss or a sabotaging co-worker—or start whining about circumstances beyond their control, rather than admit that they cut corners or simply didn't handle their business in the first place.

I want you to keep it real right now. Think about a time when you delayed gratification and achieved something that made you really proud, and what you gave up to get those good results. Now think about something you let slip through your fingers, something you wish you had another shot at. Did you truly make a sacrifice of your time or your energy? I'm guessing you didn't. Did you blame someone or something else for the failure, or did you step up and take responsibility? Most important, what would you do differently if you could do it again?

Anything worth having is worth sacrificing for. But, as with everything else we've discussed in this book, our perspective on "giving up" starts with the discovery of who we really are and what we really want. If it's just about money, chances are you're going to get frustrated and give up if the cash doesn't flow quickly enough. But if your focus is on building a place where you can empower your vision, then sacrifice is seen as a crucial step on your journey.

---

*I think that the good and the great
are only separated by the willingness to sacrifice.*

— Kareem Abdul-Jabbar

And let's be clear: we're talking here about empowering *your* vision and working toward your goals, not someone else's. When you're sacrificing for others and trying to take care of everyone but yourself, sometimes it's a camouflage for the work you really need to do on yourself. Once you've done that work, then you can start thinking about giving to others, and we'll get to that later in the book. Right now it's about you—your personal transformation.

Prefer to Defer

Hang with me for a minute and let's bring this talk of sacrifice and transformation back down to what you can do right here and now. How can you train yourself to work toward your tomorrow at the expense of something that feels good today?

One of the best ways I know is to practice a simple, focused time-management technique. Instead of trying to make waves as a multitasker, focus on doing one thing with total attention. Decide that you're going to work on one task and one task only for a set period. I recommend 30 minutes, but the most important part of the exercise is to make it something a little different. One of my good buddies settled on doing one task for 33 minutes, and his productivity went off the charts. Customize the timing so that it will really work for you.

Once you start, spend that time working without any distractions at all. Resist the quick hit of enjoyment you get from clicking on your friend's Facebook post or your favorite celebrity's Twitter feed. Don't answer the phone or even check your e-mail. If you work around other people—colleagues in an office or your family at home—make sure they see your invisible *DO NOT DISTURB* sign. When your time is up, take a short break. Then you're free to handle the things that have come up while you were on task: the kinds of things that would have distracted or derailed you in the past.

Pay attention to how you feel as you're working with this kind of focus. You may feel restless at first; maybe you'll catch your hand reaching for your smartphone to send a text, or spot the mouse wandering over toward your e-mail as if it was moving on its own. But stay with it! You'll probably find that the more you get used to tuning out distractions, the more focused and clearheaded you'll feel. You may notice that you're getting more done more quickly, or even that the quality of what you're doing is better than it was when you were being pulled off course by all those instantly gratifying distractions.

Try to make a habit of this deferred-gratification practice. The great thing about it is that it works no matter what task you're on: thinking, reading, writing, cleaning, exercising, or working on your goals and action plan. Keep a log of the time you've spent and what you've accomplished so you can see your productivity stacking up. The good gut feeling you'll get from that is the kind of right-now gratification you *do* want!

Let Go to Grow

It's one thing to put off checking Facebook for half an hour (and don't get me wrong—that kind of short-term sacrificing is a very important skill to build). But what about the bigger things that may be standing between you and the success you desire and deserve? Figuring this out means you have to get your mind right and take a long hard look at what you do with your time and mental energy. If you're really serious about changing your life, you gotta get serious about how you spend the hours of your life.

According to a 2011 Nielsen report on TV usage (watching and gaming), average Americans used their televisions 5 hours and 11 minutes each day. The average usage for African Americans was 7 hours and 12 minutes. Now, a helluva lot of planning and self-work can be done in five or seven hours a day. If you spend five hours a day watching TV or hanging out with your crew, that's about 140 hours a month and more than 1,600 hours a year. Think of what you could accomplish in 1,600 hours!

To get an accurate read on how you spend *your* time, write down one week's worth of your waking hours. Do it every day for one week. At the end, you may be surprised at the amount of time you've wasted away. Go back and highlight the lost or idle hours. Then make a commitment to yourself that you're going to readjust your time.

If you want to be a rapper or a celebrated actor, you simply have to put aside anything that doesn't help you build your rapping and acting skills. If you want to be a big-name, well-paid chef, it won't happen if you spend the majority of your time on the golf course, at the nightclub, or in front of PlayStation.

So again, I urge you to take another look at *you*. Not only at what takes up your time, but at what influences your mind. If you're easily influenced by television or negative people, you have to limit your exposure to the tube or those energy-jackers. If you have trouble staying focused on specific tasks, you have to eliminate or reduce the distractions that take you off course. I can't do this for you. You have to examine what's getting in your way and commit to removing those obstacles even if, like excessive eating or drinking, you thoroughly enjoy those things.

Consider creating what I call a "got-to-go" list of people and things that are no longer aligned with your personal and professional growth. Really write it down on paper (or the computer). Maybe your list will include things like TV hours, excessive idle time, hours spent reading about sports or reading romance novels, or a co-worker who's always pulling you off your work to gossip or complain. If you're feeling beaten down by the idea that you have to give up anything at all—like it's not fair you have to work so hard to get yours—put that victim mentality right there on the list, too: negativity is one of the *ultimate* got-to-gos.

Here's what a got-to-go list might look like for someone like Sam Harris, who's trying to get his lifestyle lined up with his goal: to record a CD of original music in his time off from his job as a manager at a clothing store.

Sam's Got-to-Go List

- **Sleeping late on weekends:** that's time that could be spent in the studio, or taking care of household tasks to free up other time.

- **Going out on weeknights:** too much time hanging with the boys makes it hard to get up and get an early start the next morning.

- **Friends who bring me down:** people who don't get what I'm trying to do, or discourage me by saying how tough the music business is, need to stay on the sidelines while I'm working on this goal.

- **Regrets that it's "too late":** if I spend my time and energy bemoaning the fact that I didn't focus more on my music sooner, I'll never achieve anything in this field.

This exercise will help you nail down some of the sacrifices you have to make. But here again, it's not worth a wooden nickel if you won't commit to following your own list. This is where we start to separate the winners from the self-made losers. If you're part of the spoiled crowd who expect quick resolutions without long-haul commitment; if you think you can wave a wand and the distractions, obstacles, and negative people will magically disappear, you're in for a letdown.

Great achievement is usually born of great sacrifice, and is never the result of selfishness.

— Napoleon Hill

The fact is, replacing sports sections or skin magazines with self-improvement books and publications like *Fast Company* and *Inc.* isn't a sacrifice; it's a purposeful, strategic alignment of your reading material with the possibilities of the moment. Trust me: there'll be plenty of time for recreational reading or your favorite TV shows *after* you've signed the deed on your dream home or *after* you've created a lifestyle where vacations aren't luxuries but payoff for your hard work and determination.

Your got-to-go list will help propel you forward. Soon, you'll arrive at a place where the important things in life will take priority over the things that simply give you pleasure. Once you've reached a certain level of achievement, you'll be able to indulge yourself. But by then, you will have earned the right to play, and you will be so conditioned toward success that "play" will never again threaten your momentum or knock you out of the fast lane.

The bottom line is this: real-life transformation is never pain-less. It requires serious got-to-go commitment. Real street-smart hustlepreneurs embrace the challenge of sacrifice and surrender. And you can take it from me, because I know this stuff firsthand.

Reaping the Rewards

In the early days of my release from prison, when Stacy and I were first married, it seemed like everywhere I turned I was going to have to give something up so I could ultimately give my family all that I wanted them to have. I wanted a big family like Stacy did, but I wanted to provide for them right: bikes, nice clothes, tutoring, a pool, a basketball hoop. And by now it shouldn't sur-prise you to hear that in order to get closer to that vision of our life, I had to sacrifice a lot of things in the short term. Good times hanging out, the holidays, attending my kids' school programs— all went by the wayside to put us in a position to someday get our dream house on the hill with the white picket fence.

When I took a job at the Hotel Bel-Air, I had a 10- or 12-hour day plus an hour-and-a-half round-trip commute—less time with my family than ever. When I had the chance to become banquet chef—and the first Black chef in charge of a kitchen at the five-star Bel-Air—I jumped on it, even though it meant less money than I'd made in my previous job. I said to Stacy, "The money will have to wait." Hell, I learned that I would even have to de-fer the gratification of getting mad at people who deserved it: "You can't lose it at the expense of your family and your career," Stacy told me when a run-in with a front-of-the-house manager at L'Ermitage cost me my job there.

On the hunt for a new gig, I bought a plane ticket to Las Ve-gas even though our funds were short. I took the job at Caesar's Palace there even though it meant I'd be away from the family longer still; we couldn't afford to move everyone out until a few paychecks had come in. At one point we were getting only a few days a month to spend together. But they supported and believed in me, and I believed that everything we were giving up now was going to pay dividends later. And I was right.

Today, I've been out of professional kitchens for some six years.

I've reached a point where I can enjoy some of that gratification I delayed for so long. I've been able to spend more time with my family, raise my children, be home on the holidays, take my kids to school programs, and truly get to know my wife—the woman who gave me the foundation to evolve into the Chef Jeff people have come to know. I've actually reached a point where I get to sacrifice in the other direction—to pass up career opportunities if they don't make sense for my family and me.

When I was a young boy, when my dad visited my sister and me, he occasionally rode up to our house on his Harley-Davidson Sportster motorcycle. I would sit between him and the gas tank and we would ride for blocks. For those short moments, I felt removed from all worries. He eventually bought me my first pull-string mini dirt bike, and at that point I knew I was born to ride. Over the years I dreamed of owning my own Harley and riding with the kids, going out to explore new cuisines and taking family vacations. Today, it's no longer just a dream, and the highlights of my routine are Sundays in the park or at the beach, or watching my girls do their ballet classes, or going for rides on my own Harley. I'm living the American dream I saw 40-plus years ago, and the dream is finally legit.

He who would accomplish little must sacrifice little;
he who would achieve much must sacrifice much;
he who would attain highly must sacrifice greatly.

— James Allen

The willingness to sacrifice now is a sign that you're ready to "let go to grow." And if you are, you're in good company. Just look at Tyler Perry. Early in his career, before Madea hit the big screen, he poured his savings into producing his musical *I Know I've Been Changed*, and when it failed to take off (it ran just one weekend and had an audience of only 30), he supported himself by working odd jobs while he revised and regrouped. At one point, broke, he was living out of his car. "Can you imagine a six-foot-five man sleeping in a Geo Metro?" he told *Essence* magazine. But you know how this story ends: Perry's sacrifices ultimately paid off when he hit the big time. And if you take the long view, like Perry did, you don't even have to look at the choice to sacrifice as a hardship. As another actor, Jeremy Renner, put it in an interview, "You could call it making sacrifices, but those sacrifices have made me who I am, so I don't know if I'd consider them sacrifices or blessings."

Street-Smart Challenges for:

The Sacrificer

☆ **Hold that thought.** For one day, every time you write an e-mail or even a text, wait at least 15 minutes before you send it. Then review it to see if you notice anything you want to change.

☆ **Stay on task.** For one day, do all your work in focused 30-minute blocks. Don't allow any distractions in during that time; tend to other tasks when you take a break.

☆ **Track your time.** For one week, keep a record of how you spend your time every day. At the end of the week, look over your notes and see where you can make improvements.

☆ **Shift your focus.** If you regularly watch a certain TV show, decide for one week that you'll use that time slot to read up on your field or work on your action plan.

☆ **See what's "got to go."** Make the list we talked about, then go a step further and write down *how* you're going to put each of those things (or people) outside your lane.

☆ **Get perspective.** Talk to three people you know who have had to sacrifice to get where they are. Ask what they gave up, how they did it, what they gained, and what they learned.

The Knowledge-Jacker

The strategy of
anytime, anywhere
education

> *Don't hate the player, master his game.*
> — Chef Jeff

$\mathcal{R}$umor had it that chefs and cooks didn't last long at L'Ermitage (now Raffles L'Ermitage) in Beverly Hills during the mid-1990s, but I was confident that I could weather any storm. I was 35 years old and had been out of prison for almost three years. In that short time, I had worked in a few upscale hotel restaurants, earning the title of chef tournant (skilled in all cook stations), and had made history as the first African American banquet chef at the historic five-star Hotel Bel-Air in Bel Air, California. My goal was to become an executive chef someday, and I needed to expand my culinary résumé. So when L'Ermitage, the five-star, five-diamond hotel in Beverly Hills, offered me the position of sous-chef, I jumped at the opportunity.

It turned out to be one of the greatest challenges of my new-found career. At the time, a 28-year-old rising star in the high-end food world served as the executive chef and food and beverage director at L'Ermitage. A short time after I started, the young chef resigned under a cloud. The kitchen staff had the run of the place. It lacked discipline and consistency. The outgoing chef was way too cool with the line staff, so respect for the chain of command was weak. An obvious mutiny was in the mix to run the new guy (me) out of the place. Some ignored my directions and purposely worked slowly on the busiest of nights; the front-house staff systematically stacked orders that would, as we say in the restaurant biz, "crash the kitchen." And my counterparts, the other sous-chefs, refused to share the kitchen standard operating procedures with me.

In every restaurant, the executive chef manages the restaurant's recipes. He goes to the computer that everybody shares, develops dishes, calculates cost, figures out what should be changed and improved on the menu, and creates the specials of the day. It's his job to make sure the kitchen is stocked and the staff is trained to handle the high-end customers' special requests. Not so at L'Ermitage. Some of the cooks and chefs, envious and sometimes openly hating on me, kept the former executive chef's signature recipes on floppy discs that they shared only among themselves. It was their power play to keep me out of the loop and under their control, hoping I'd resign in frustration, like some other chefs before me.

But I kept cool and just observed them when they didn't think I was watching. One day, they slipped up and left the former chef's recipe discs on the desk we all shared. I started thinking like when I was on the streets. A big party on the hotel's rooftop was coming up that evening, and I knew the other assistant chefs would be busy for a few hours working the gig. I called Stacy and asked her to come to the hotel, bring her laptop, park in the underground garage, and wait for me—she had no clue to what I was up to. The timing had to be perfect. While the chef-haters were working the roof party, I was underground uploading the files onto my wife's computer.

My stay at L'Ermitage was brief—maybe four months. But I still savor that moment, looking at the faces of the renegade chefs when they couldn't understand how I was aware of exactly what was stored on those floppy discs. They had been outsmarted by a knowledge-jacker, someone who would do what was necessary to get access to the knowledge he needed to build his career and fulfill his vision of becoming top chef. Unlike those who steal money or someone's belongings, the knowledge-jacker is after information—he's like a heat-seeking missile that won't stop until it's reached the target. Don't misunderstand me: I'm not encouraging anyone to steal info—that's wrong, and my L'Ermitage experience was an extreme example of wanting to be successful, even though I didn't consider it stealing. The intellectual property belonged to the hotel, and in order for me to be an effective manager, I needed that information to do my job.

I had no choice but to become a knowledge-jacker!

What You Need to Know

Any self-help book worth its salt will tell you that researching, studying, and applying knowledge is key for growth—both in your personal life and in your working life. In the business world these days, you have to be adaptable and flexible, and you can't afford to be stuck in one lane; things move too fast and change too quickly. One day you can be a top-notch, highly paid computer programmer, and the next day that job has been outsourced to a third-world country. Being fully vested in a select range of skills and having the knowledge to back them up is your best defense against becoming irrelevant and unemployed.

Knowledge is like money:
to be of value it must circulate.

— Louis L'Amour

What those books won't turn you on to is the street-smart way to get your hands on the knowledge you need. Your life, your vision, and your happiness are no joke; they're a matter of do-or-die survival. Certified hustlepreneurs understand that if anyone or anything stands between them and the knowledge they need, they have to be hungry enough and resourceful enough to get around or eliminate the threatening roadblocks. But they always knowledge-jack with integrity—you don't have to hurt anybody or break the law to get ahead of the competition.

You don't need to be a rocket scientist. It's simple—it starts with knowing what you *don't* know. That wasn't hard for me when I started in the real culinary world after leaving prison. Like I told you earlier, I had been working in an environment where I couldn't use knives or fire, let alone develop the nuances of the art! It should be as obvious to you as it was to me that I had a lot more learning to do to make my vision a reality.

So I set out to learn from the best in the culinary game. I never attended culinary school or apprenticed in Europe; I didn't have the money or the necessary culinary book smarts to attend cooking school in the States. I did the next best thing: I studied the masters of the food world, the best of the best—Latino line cooks and Joël Robuchon, Sarah Bowman, Thomas Keller, Marcus Samuelsson, Robert Gadsby, Alfred Portale, and Patrick Clark—the most successful chefs on my admiration short list. I studied cooking techniques and learned kitchen Spanish from the Latinos who dominated kitchens in the L.A. area. I bought books written by renowned chefs to gain insights into their thinking and techniques. I sought employment with the best chefs to learn what they had paid top dollar for in the best culinary institutions around the world.

My goal was to knowledge-jack the pros to a point where I instinctively thought as they did. I memorized their philosophies on food and style in the kitchen the best I could. I paid close attention to the lingo they used and their style of communication and discipline. For example, in prison and in low-end dive kitchens, I'd say "veggies" when talking about produce. That's a no-no in the high-end food world. It's "vegetables." Gadsby laid down the food terminology law for me: "No nicknames for cuisine, no disrespecting the ingredients."

Jack Your Way Up

The aim of the knowledge-jacker is to get next to the holder of valuable information. And the best way to get next to any leader is to become a good soldier. In the streets or in the business world, you're labeled a good soldier after demonstrating your abilities and your loyalty to the point where the top dog takes notice—even when it means starting at the bottom.

In the high-end culinary world, many talented cooks and chefs start as dishwashers or "bitch workers." My first job at Gadsby's was sweeping and cleaning the restaurant, including the bathrooms, and washing pots and pans at minimum wage. Expertly trained by my grandfather, I was the best toilet-bowl cleaner Gadsby had ever seen. Honestly, I would have done the job for free. Gaining access to knowledge is like money in the bank. After janitor, I worked as a dishwasher, then a cooking assistant, and on and on until I was finally allowed to actually cook for customers at Gadsby's restaurant.

When I finally got to work in well-known kitchens, my talk game became key. I'd constantly use my "pump-up" strategy on chefs and line cooks, raining down praise on them: "Damn, Chef, that dish is wicked! Man, one day you will be selected to cook at the James Beard House in New York." Everyone wants to be recognized and acknowledged, and my bosses and colleagues were no exception. Before long, that complimented chef was offering me more and more insider information because I showed proper respect. A confident professional will share information with a promising prospect, if that good soldier has approached him or her respectfully and humbly.

At other restaurants, I had to work my way up the hierarchy, impressing the sous-chefs and the lead line cooks before I could get my shot to work the coveted sauté station, which was even closer to the executive chefs. When an opportunity popped up, I'd speak up: "Hey, Chef, I can work that station. I've been studying it, waiting and practicing. I would appreciate the opportunity to work that station, Chef!"

Once I got in, I doubled down on my work ethic, learning as many positions as I could and asking all the right questions. Sometimes—say, with a sous-chef—I'd volunteer to do the "bitch work" they didn't want to do. I'd peel potatoes, bust down lobster claws, pick fine herbs, anything. By doing that work with speed and attention to detail, I'd earn priceless advice and private cooking lessons from grateful supervisors who would say things, like: "Jeff, you have a lot of potential; you have come a long way. These are some areas you ought to focus more on—your sauté style, your meat temperatures, your knife skills."

After they became personally invested in me, I could ask more questions like: "Hey, Chef, can you show me how food and labor costs impact the bottom line?" or "How important are the 'five mother sauces'?" Before my shift or during slow times, I made sure the top chefs saw me writing notes. I called it "strategically shining." This isn't to be confused with butt kissing or brownnosing. Bosses see right through that B.S.

Now, don't get me wrong—knowledge-jacking wasn't something I just did when I was starting out, then put aside when I got comfortable in a commercial kitchen. Every step you take on your path, there's always something new you need to know. When I started doing TV, I had no clue how to parlay my personality onto the small screen. When the opportunity knocked, I zeroed in on the Food Network's Robert Irvine, Rachael Ray, Bobby Flay, and Ina Garten, the best of the best when it comes to cooking on camera. I had to knowledge-jack them to better my own TV skills. It was Robert Irvine for his ability to use his toughness in a nonthreatening way when taking over kitchens with new kitchen staff. I kept a keen eye on Rachael Ray's talk-and-cook-while-looking-at-the-camera style. Bobby Flay and the Barefoot Contessa, too, gave me the confidence I was lacking to talk through each dish as I cooked while looking up at the camera as much as possible—a key step in preparing for my own cooking shows. No excuses for failure, you must be a *beast in your field* if you really want to succeed.

Make It Your Own

I'm probably the only one who calls it "knowledge-jacking," because I'm trying to use language that will help ordinary people tap into their extraordinary potential. If I'm to be honest, though, I have to acknowledge that across the world of business there's a rich legacy of brilliant intellectual "jacking." America wasn't alone in pioneering the "network of networks" technology that today is known as the Internet. Apple didn't create the first desktop computer, portable media player, or smartphone. But under Steve Jobs's extraordinary leadership, the company built on the basics to develop cutting-edge products like the Mac, iPod, iPad, and iPhone. Today, it's increasingly common to seek out and borrow from the best to engineer your bulletproof success. As a hustlepreneur would say, "Don't hate the player, master his game."

Last year, as I was moving through airports flying across country, I spotted out of the corner of my eye a photo of a guy under the title "The Copy King" on the cover of *Inc.* magazine. I bought a copy and read the article closely during my flight.

This dude, Oliver Samwer, a German entrepreneur, is co-founder of Rocket Internet, an "incubator" that has invested hundreds of millions into companies that specialize in copying the formulas of other companies—like Alando, a Berlin-based company modeled on eBay's success, and Europe's City Deal, based on America's deal-of-the-day Website Groupon. And in every line I read, he

> None of us start from square one; we're always working off of those who have gone before.

validated my street-smart survival strategy. What he described was how I had survived and stayed employed over the past 17 years. "Most innovations come on top of other innovations, if you really look at it," Samwer told the *Inc.* reporter. Imitation, like they say, may be the sincerest form of flattery—but it's also the sharpest tool for knowledge-jacking.

Just look at how Black businesspeople operated in the era of segregation. With good-paying jobs in short supply, the entrepreneurs of the community looked at what needs weren't being met, then replicated basic services like beauty and barber shops, funeral homes, insurance brokerages, and restaurants in their own communities. They didn't invent beauty shops from scratch—they took a successful model and made it their own.

The truth is that none of us starts from square one; we're always working off of those who have gone before. People can be droppin' knowledge on you right and left, but until you own it for yourself, it won't take you far. Successful knowledge-jackers are imitators of intellectual property, but even more important, they are builders. They are strategic researchers and mind readers who take what they learn and apply it in a way that's uniquely their own. The exceptional ones, like Oliver Samwer, become so skilled at their game that they not only advance their own careers but help others excel and succeed. They've taken that crucial step from copying to creating.

Marcus Buckingham, the jump-starter of the strengths movement, fits the description of a master knowledge-jacker: he's someone who made his way on information he didn't invent, but applied and extended in new ways. Although the modern strengths movement is definitely Buckingham's brand, he's the first to admit that he didn't start it. The Cambridge University grad was fortunate enough to land a gig where accessing knowledge and information and the best practices of the best people was part of his job. He worked for the Gallup Organization, the company best known for gathering and publishing polling data and offering programs that corporate leaders can use to better understand their employee and customer bases.

Buckingham's duties included interviewing thousands of people —"from housekeepers to leaders"—who were excelling in their work. Along with two other Gallup team members, Dr. James K. Harter and Curt Coffman, he developed programs that centered on the best measures for employee engagement. That project served as motivation for Buckingham's first book (with Coffman), *First, Break All the Rules*—an immediate bestseller around the globe. Subsequent books—*Now, Discover Your Strengths; The One Thing You Need to Know; Put Your Strengths to Work; The Truth About You;* and *Find Your Strongest Life*—helped Buckingham become what *Newsweek* described as "arguably the business world's most in-demand management guru." All in all, Buckingham spent hundreds of hours interviewing thousands of people—known and unknown. With this information, he created his own niche, filled a void, and built an unbeatable brand—knowledge-jacking at its best.

I bring up these examples to stamp out any negative thoughts you may have about purposely studying people with the intent of borrowing and building on their ideas. As long as you act with integrity, acknowledge your sources, and give something back to others, you're on safe ground. That's what's so cool about

Mr. Buckingham: he gives others credit for starting the strengths movement, then sets out to share his unique brand extension for the benefit of millions.

Choosing Your Mentors

Doesn't matter if you're a scientist working with nuclear fusion or a cooking apprentice trying to master the art of chefdom—everybody starts with the work of someone else. They use the knowledge of others as their launchpad. In the same way, masters of any craft don't come out of a box. They're molded by *grand* masters. So a key part of your knowledge-jacking strategy is to find yourself the individuals you're going to learn from: one or more mentors of your own.

I was still locked up when I started putting together my mentor list—and Robert Gadsby, whom I'd read about in that *USA Today* article about the country's top Black chefs, was right at the top. Upon my release, I was determined to get myself hired at his restaurant. It took a month of knocking on his door, but he finally relented, and the opportunity was a game changer for me.

After I convinced him to hire me, I jacked Gadsby for every piece of knowledge he had in the realm of culinary arts, business, and how a polished Black man rolls. Almost whatever he did that was in line with my future, I did. I clean-shaved my face and head like his, bought the same style of casual clothes—Egyptian cotton chef jackets, clogs, and wireless-rim eyewear. I bought the books he read and duplicated his cooking style. Gadsby was my entrée to authentic chefdom. He shared cooking stories about his own mentor, the great Thomas Keller, while teaching me how to hold a knife and pick out salmon bones with fish tweezers and giving me my first glass of high-end sparkling water in a wine goblet. For more than two years, Gadsby served as my yardstick. Eventually, I developed my own techniques and style—but Gadsby was my stepping-stone to my true self and my true gifts. And that's a step the successful knowledge-jacker absolutely has to take. You don't want to spend your valuable time mastering someone else's gifts.

> *Leaders don't create followers,*
> *they create more leaders.*
>
> — Tom Peters

At the same time, you don't want to be jacking the wrong people for the knowledge that's going to hurt rather than help you. In *Cooked*, I wrote about my street mentor, T-Row (may he rest in peace). T-Row could operate in any environment and charm anyone—from the homeboys who worked for him to the women who did anything he asked of them. At first, I was T-Row's flunky, washing his cars and clothes, running his errands, doing little tasks to gain his trust. I got close to the man and adopted almost everything about him—the way I did with the Wall Street boys in the pen and then with Gadsby—I adopted the way T-Row dressed in creased 501 Levi's, crisp button-down shirts, and fresh K-Swiss sneakers. I copied the way he communicated with his prospects and homeboys, his thinking process, his whole swagger—I tried to walk and talk like him and incorporate his character and charisma. He was just that impressive to me. But the path he led me down didn't allow me to avoid the darkest period of my life—prison.

You may be walking a similar path, using your gifts to knowledge-jack someone on a crash course with destiny or wasting your time borrowing useless information from fools. There's nothing wrong with being a follower, but you must follow with a plan that fits your personality and strengths. You must selectively choose to duplicate the strategies of someone who's going to help you discover and manifest your vision. To do this, you may have to admit honestly what you know and don't know and recognize that it takes time to build your best self. Hustlepreneurs seek out the best of the best to fill the gaps in their knowledge, because nothing less will do.

Making the Mentor Connection

Remember that no matter how much you want to connect with someone who's a star in your eyes, just wanting isn't enough. Thoughtful preparation is every bit as important. I'm lucky enough to have come to a point in my life and my career where people now seek *me* out as a mentor, and I can tell you that the ones I really want to work with—the ones I'm excited to coach—are the ones who have done their homework first. I always ask them what they know about me—beyond the fact that they saw my face on TV or on the cover of a book. I ask them if they've thought through what they want to learn from me and how they plan to use what they learn. And I ask them what they're able and willing to give back to others as a result of my investment in them. How are they going to pay it forward?

What separates individuals who are serious about pursuing a dream or changing their life from the ones who just talk about wanting a better life and do nothing is that they're willing to put in the hard work to achieve results. A young man named Zo was cast on my Food Network docu-reality show *The Chef Jeff Project*. He was a standout among the rest of the crew. Zo wanted a way out of Pasadena's worst neighborhood, and he was willing to make the sacrifice for a better life. After the show ended, he and the other six earned a full-ride culinary scholarship to the Arts Institute. I took it upon myself to coach him through it. He chose to relocate to Las Vegas at my advice, because I saw his potential and believed he could finish school in peace. I don't take just anyone under my wing; by moving, enrolling in school, and taking a job while attending school full time, Zo committed to putting in the work before I committed my time.

So how do you find your own mentors? Start by asking yourself some questions to zero in on your role models.

Measuring Your Mentors

- Who is doing the kind of work I want to do—and being rewarded for it?

- Whose ideas are getting attention in the community, in the media, or on social media?

- Whose way of speaking, acting, or thinking do I want to emulate?

- Who is in a place where I want to be in three, five, or ten years?

Now, is it possible to get next to that person? It's great if you can establish personal relationships with high-profile individuals, but if you're like most of us, you might find it difficult to gain access, let alone get up close and personal with them. You may admire the hell out of Donald Trump, but your chances of getting on *The Apprentice* are slim to none. No worries—you don't need permission to be mentored by someone you admire. If you can't reach out and touch them physically, consider what you can gain by studying them through their writings, interviews, lectures, or lifestyles.

Another way is to find a Trump within your reach who is a master at what you want to master. So ask yourself a few more questions.

Finding a Master Mentor

- Who, in *my* community, has the information and knowledge I seek? What's the best way to get to him?

- Do I know someone who knows him, or knows someone else who could introduce me?

- Can I purchase his books, read articles online, or watch him on YouTube or Vimeo at the library or on my smartphone?

- Can I go to a lecture or event where he's speaking and introduce myself afterward?

- What can I offer in exchange for the help I'm requesting?

You can start working on this right now. Write down the names of five people you admire. Then start developing an action plan for becoming their virtual—or real-life—apprentice. Don't hesitate to add me to your list if you wish, because with this book, I'm invested in your transformation. And even though I can't mentor you face-to-face the way I'd like to, you can read my books and follow my journey through my Website and social media network.

In fact, social media, such as Twitter, Facebook, and LinkedIn, can be a real solid way to connect with your target mentors. Look for articles written by them or about them or their companies. In fewer than 100 words, comment on their success and tell them why you'd like to join their organizations. If you're an up-and-coming entrepreneur, see if your mentor is a member of SCORE, the nonprofit agency that works with the U.S. Small Business Administration to help entrepreneurs launch new business ventures.

And if you do make a connection, be prepared to get serious, get humble, work hard, and really take in what they have to teach you—because the rewards are huge. I'll never forget what Gadsby told me when he took me on: "If you follow directions and listen, stop that homeboy stuff, I will teach you everything I know, and when you leave me, no one will ever be able to take your job from you."

Information is the seed for an idea,
and only grows when it's watered.

— Heinz V. Bergen

Your Knowledge-Jacker Action Plan

I'm not gonna pretend that it's always easy. Knowledge-jackers often have to make hard sacrifices for the information they need. When I was offered the job at L'Ermitage, Stacy, who kept a keen eye on our family funds, pointed out that the $28,000-a-year salary was actually less than I was making as a banquet chef, including bonus, at my current job at the Hotel Bel-Air. But the experience as sous-chef and the knowledge I thought I'd get working directly under the L'Ermitage executive chef was more important to me than the salary at that time. Remember, extraordinary info is like money in the bank.

The truth is, you may have to take a pay cut, work an undesirable job, or even work for free if the information is that valuable to you and your career. That said, it's important to avoid being someone who seeks information forever and never puts it in practice. Throughout my career, I've always known when I have learned what I came to learn and when it's time to move on. To avoid stagnation, set a timer for yourself. Decide what information and experiences you need and who you're going to get it from, and then dedicate a timeline to access it, move on, and put it in motion.

Become strategic in your knowledge search. Write down what information you need and how much time you will dedicate to gathering it, and always leave a little space for the unknown. Finally, keep track of your progress by setting knowledge benchmarks, marking off what you've learned and how long it took, and, most importantly, how you have applied it. Don't worry if you go under or over the time you've allotted yourself. A disciplined and well-timed approach will keep your goals in sight and keep you right on pace to achieving them.

Whatever else you do, always jack with integrity, no matter what. Knowledge-jacking for manipulative, moneygrubbing, or destructive reasons is bad karma and can even be illegal. Seeking knowledge to hurt someone else's career or set them up for failure defeats all my street-smart strategies. I knew many of the flaws and bad habits of many of my superiors and could have used that information to make them look weak. But that route to success sets you up for future failure. You've earned a job or promotion illegitimately, based on deceit, not your skills.

If you act with integrity, there are no repercussions, even when your role model discovers that you purposely sought her out to tap into her data bank. She may not say it, but she knows it's part of paying her dues. You've flattered her and perhaps impressed her by the fact that you've done so much homework and gone through so much effort to model her knowledge and experience.

These knowledge goals can become a key part of your larger action plan—the one you're putting in place to make your vision a reality. I'm still knowledge-jacking even today; this time it's from the young generation, though. Their swagger, their lingo, and their one-liners are key to my ability to connect to youth in schools, in jails, and on college campuses where I speak. I know that as a father of six children, I had to be able to relate to my own children and my youth audiences. I found my voice by infusing my past youth experiences on the streets and by having a clear understanding of the thinking process of today's young people. I know that in order to stay relevant I must stay up on the voices of the people.

There's a great line from an unknown author that I always think sums up just what this particular street-smart strategy is all about: "Act as if you know nothing. Seek out the best of the best. Learn enough; borrow enough to turn a treasure chest of information into your own booty for life." Use the Street-Smart Challenges that follow to start filling your own treasure chest.

☆ **Know what you don't know.** Write down five areas where you need new knowledge to make your vision a reality.

☆ **Feed your mind.** Read articles in magazines, in newspapers, or online, or study videos that contain info you know you need.

☆ **Make a connection.** Write a one-page letter to someone you admire, describing what you think he could teach you. Send it if you can; if not, keep it to inspire you.

☆ **Recruit your mentor "dream team."** Make a list of five people you would like to be your virtual or personal mentors.

☆ **Get inside their heads.** Write down at least one way you can knowledge-jack each of the mentors you listed—whether it's by watching them on YouTube or asking them for an informational coaching session.

☆ **Return the favor.** Think of at least one thing you can give back to others in exchange for the teaching you receive.

Street Smart #4

The ESP-er

The strategy of
heightened awareness

> *Whatever it looks like,*
> *that's probably not what it is.*
>
> — Chef Jeff

I entered the entertainment world about five years ago as an absolute freshman. After we received the green light on my first TV show on the Food Network, I was naïve about production lingo and TV culture; I quickly started tuning in on production conversation around the set, as well as asking lots of questions. It was important for me to understand how production was going to tap into my gift of transforming troubled youth on the show through food more effectually.

Not knowing the flow of the business, I had to quickly learn the ropes of an industry swarming with some shady and slippery individuals. I prided myself on my ability to read the industry's street-smart players well; some of them were no different than how we rolled on the streets back in the day, just with a different product. But not the book-smart people with their polished appearances—executives in their power suits, sporting what I call "presidential hair." I was a bit intimidated by their rapid-fire, intellectual-talk game and their we're-gonna-make-you-a-star rhetoric.

I got schooled real quick, though. Especially after I got played once on a contract laced with tricky math and legal-heavy verbiage that I signed without my wife's or my attorney's blessing. I fell into this trap because I violated my own personal business code of conduct—I ignored my ESP, my extra-street perception. As a result, I lost my you-know-what. Lessons learned: watch out for too-good-to-be-true opportunities because they're just that; educate yourself about everything before you make any moves, and, last but definitely not least, trust your intuition, that inner awareness—that uncompromised little voice that doesn't shout like your ego. And once it gives you the 411 on a person or situation, pay attention. If it don't look like a rose and smell like a rose, it ain't a rose, my friend.

The Little Voice

When poverty and crime are off the charts in your environment and threats to your family, your security, and your livelihood are everyday realities, street smarters use heightened awareness as a crucial survival tool. They listen to their intuition, aka "the little voice." And this street skill is not only useful to spot external threats, what's going on outside; when your ESP is truly working, it means you're also conscious of, and up on, what's going on inside.

It means you're truly aware of the struggles and potential setbacks that can crush your dream, but you're equally aware of how your natural talents and unique gifts can shoot you right past the potential pitfalls. It means that you've looked hard at the situation that you find yourself in and mapped out your strategy for success.

Imagine a strange, generous someone gifts you with a million dollars. But there's a catch: the money is buried right smack in the middle of an overseas battlefield that's scattered with land mines and surrounded by snipers. What would you do? Give up and play it safe or find a way to get that money? The more fearless among us will develop a plan, get the training necessary, survey the land, find a way to avoid the snipers, detect and defuse the land mines, and do what's necessary to claim the money.

> Our senses are an incredible feedback loop **with tremendous power to make our lives better.**

I use this highly unlikely, dangerous scenario to stress the wide range and valuable nature of ESP. In that minefield, it's what allows you to know where your foot should hit the ground, when you should advance full speed, and when you shouldn't move an inch if you want to avoid the sniper's bullet. It's a highly developed sense that lets you see, hear, and tune in to things that others overlook or are blind to. If you're serious about claiming that million dollars (your vision), you have to become keenly aware of your skills, your surroundings, and the people in your environment —the dangers as well as the overlooked opportunities that will allow you to outwit the enemy and reap your just rewards.

That "overseas battlefield" I spoke of is really not that far away in many disadvantaged neighborhoods where crime and violence are common. Street-smart individuals learn at an early age that they must develop a strong sense of awareness of danger and forever stay alert to unwanted encounters—as well as those encounters that will bring them new opportunities and advantages.

The good news is that this heightened awareness is real, and anyone can use it. Today, even science is confirming what street smarters have known all along—that our senses are an incredible feedback loop with tremendous power to make our lives better, *if* we tune in to it. In this chapter we'll take a close look at the aspects of your ESP that can move you ahead at top speed.

More Than Meets the Eye

The downside of being blind to what's going on around you, or to the motives of the people you're dealing with, can be costly—as I learned the hard way so many times. So here's the street-smart lesson you must learn: whatever it looks like, that's probably not what it is. You have to look beneath the surface of people's words and actions. You have to ask, What's in it for them? When you learn to assess people's motives, you keep yourself from getting beaten. You're hip to people who may just be stroking your ego for the kill. You move beyond being flattered by what's on the surface—"They like me!"—to reading what's between the lines. If I had asked myself what was going on under the surface of the flattering praise my potential business partners were dumping on me, I might have taken a step back and had my lawyer look that contract over.

You may also find that when you tune in to what's going on under the surface of a situation, you can turn it to your advantage.

I was once promoted to an executive chef position that a non–African American had previously held. They offered me the job at $20,000 less per year than my predecessor. As my old "best me," I would have screamed foul play or discrimination. The new "best me" used my ESP to see a different angle: take the job and utilize the opportunity to get access to some of the world's most talented chefs, build my personal brand off their global brand, and put together an airtight resource list of relationships and suppliers. Street smarts are only as good as the outcomes. At the end of the day, taking $20,000 less positioned me to become a self-made businessman.

Since my rise to celebrity chefdom and a career as a sought-after public speaker today, many industry insiders who have book smarts and polished communication skills look at me as an uneducated Black male who got lucky and scored success by marketing my comeback-kid story. Hey, I just used my gift and opportunity to seize my dream, just like Mark Zuckerberg, Jay-Z, and Tony Robbins did. I once had a deal with a company worth $7 billion to do just that—to use my name and likeness and my comeback-kid story of transformation to market their socially damaged name to an inner-city audience in order to change the way the company was perceived in the 'hood. My street-smart ability to read people and communicate with them in a humble way gave them the confidence that I was the man for this delicate job of collaboration. They dispatched me in urban communities around the Midwest and South to empower and uplift at-risk youth and people who were stuck. I was no fool, though; I knew this company had a bad rep when it came to fair treatment and promoting minorities. They thought I would do the song and dance; well, I did, but to my own tune. I signed the deal to speak on their behalf, but my message was far from controlled. I spoke empowerment; I motivated my listeners to become smarter and to use their gifts to rise above their current circumstances. Instead of not taking the deal because of the company's shaky history with the minority community, I took the money and used the kill-two-birds-with-one-stone opportunity as a platform to uplift communities while building my public-speaking brand.

Practicing Perception

To hone your ESP, you have to become a street-smart detective, a laser-focused observer, taking in every detail. It's all about taking in the evidence of all your senses and then giving yourself the mental space to process that information. Often the dots are all there, but we don't connect them. When you connect the dots, you see the patterns, and you recognize those patterns when you see them again—so you can take the measure of people and situations with greater accuracy.

Some people are born with this awareness—like a sixth sense that lets you read people in the 'hood, trailer park, barrio, and even on the job to determine who's a friend or foe or who's about to bring help, opportunity, or trouble. If you didn't grow up in a tough environment where you needed this awareness to survive, it may not be your natural strength—but

> Try taking yourself to a neighborhood **where no one looks like you** and notice how **your senses get heightened.**

you can build this muscle just like any other muscle you work out. You can learn by watching your street-smart mentors, if you have them. But mostly you learn through experience. You can build your street-smart awareness by putting yourself in situations that are new, where you've *got* to have your eyes and ears open because you can't take your surroundings for granted.

You might do this, for example, by volunteering in various organizations—a homeless shelter or a youth detention center—whatever it takes to bring yourself in contact with people who run in very different circles from you. Or you might try taking yourself to a neighborhood where no one looks like you—and notice how your senses get heightened and your antennae perk up to what's around you, just like the Martian in the '60s TV show *My Favorite Martian*. You pay attention to what you're seeing, and that's not all. Maybe you hear music coming from a window, or people talking in a language you don't understand. Maybe you smell something cooking that you're pretty sure you've never smelled in your family kitchen before. You sense how the ground feels under your feet, and how *you* feel when you walk past people you know are watching you. It's real life, not virtual life. Take it all in and trust what it's telling you.

It's What They Don't Say

A couple of chapters from now, you'll read about being a gab-master and how the spoken word can speed you on the path to success. But successful hustlepreneurs know that what gets said out loud in a conversation is just the tip of the iceberg. There's another conversation going on under the surface, and your success may just depend on how well you learn to listen.

In other words, you've got to know how to read people—the way they walk, the way they stand, the way they move their hands when they're talking to you. You know how people say you can read someone like a book? That's exactly what you have to learn to do.

On the mean streets, this listening skill, which I call "ear hustling," can mean the difference between a situation that's cool for all concerned and one where your safety is seriously at risk. On Main Street or Wall Street, the gestures and postures may vary—the "cool swag" in the 'hood isn't the same as a corporate swag in a mainstream office—but the value is the same. When you can read between the lines and analyze people's hidden attitudes, agendas, and perceptions of you revealed in their non-verbal cues, suddenly you've got the upper hand in negotiations. Take a simple sign like a laugh. What's the quality of the laugh and the smile? If the person's laughing while also shifting uncomfortably in his or her chair, it's probably a nervous or shady laugh, and that tells you something worth knowing. Then you can start to ask yourself why this person is nervous and what that means for you.

There's no such thing as a poker face unless you're a professional poker player or you are in some kind of pain. Signals to watch for include shifting eyes, different kinds of smiles, a forehead that wrinkles up, movements of the arms and legs, hands touching the face or the hair, making or breaking eye contact. People avoid your gaze when they feel uncomfortable; you know the observation that someone "looks guilty." You can read a whole bunch of feelings this way: conflict, surprise, hateness, hostility, attraction, openness, interest, boredom . . . you name it.

Learning to read these signals is like learning a foreign language—and just like a language, as you get more fluent, you move around an unfamiliar world with more confidence and ease. So how do you study up? Like any language, you can read about nonverbal communication in books and on the Internet. But the best training is to people watch around you. Try watching them when you already know how they're feeling—that way you can develop a vocabulary of signs. Talk to your young nephew when you know he messed up at home by bringing home bad grades, and see what behaviors you can pinpoint that signal he's on the defensive. For example, people on the defensive may make eye contact with a hostile expression, and they often cross their arms or keep their jackets buttoned or zipped.

Consider this Chinese proverb: "Watch out for the man whose stomach doesn't move when he laughs." Ask yourself also whether the signals the person's sending are all saying the same thing. And pay attention to the nonverbal signals *you're* sending, too; you may be telling people a helluva lot more than you want them to know.

ESP in Crisis

When disaster strikes, we become aware of all the things we take for granted. In 2012, Hurricane Sandy swept ashore and brought the New York and New Jersey area to its knees. Millions immediately realized how, overnight, a lack of power, crippled subway systems, and extensive flooding can quickly drop you from a life of relative comfort to one of extreme circumstantial poverty.

In moments of crisis like this, heightened awareness can take on a whole new meaning—as a tool for survival, literally. That's what happened for Abby Wellington of Fort Lee, New Jersey, when she found herself going into labor, stuck in her high-rise apartment building with the power out. The birth of her first child had unfolded over many hours in a hospital, but Wellington's "little voice" was telling her loud and clear that something was different this time. With their ESP in overdrive, Wellington and her husband quickly gathered what support they could from their surroundings: a box of latex gloves from a neighbor, candles left over from a birthday party, and a pair of potato-chip-bag clips from the kitchen to clamp the umbilical cord. "My body knew what to do next," Wellington said in an interview, "and we just kept responding to it." And her intuition proved right on the money: her second child, a healthy girl, arrived in less than an hour.

It's also during these times of natural or man-made disaster that we assess what really matters. Some of us even think about the people who deal with rough environmental or social conditions every day. We wonder how they get by with no food, money, lights, gas, telephones, or Internet access.

What most of us don't think about is that the ability to cope with hardship and lack and to make do is a skill that savvy street smarters use for everyday survival. The Family Dollar or 99¢ Store isn't a lark, it's home. When you employ street-smart ESP in these situations, you're always on the lookout for free or low-cost alternatives.

My motto has always been that you can't say, "Oh, it won't happen to me." . . . Always be aware that things can happen.

— Venus Williams

Lights or gas turned off? They go to the library to stay warm and informed. If there are special sales, they plan trips to the grocery store with trustworthy neighbors or community support groups to stock up on food and supplies. They learn bus routes and subway schedules or the shortest path by foot to get where they need to go. They figure out how to feed their kids' bodies and their minds so they won't be another one of those sad statistics that get left behind.

What can you do to assess a threat with your ESP? Maybe the danger you're facing isn't as bad as a storm surge or an electricity turn-off notice. But you can surely understand what it feels like when the things you take for granted are taken away—and you know that that's when you need to listen most closely to that little voice. Maybe your job is about to be in jeopardy, or maybe your relationship is heading for the rocks. Pay attention to the signals your ESP is sending you, and figure out what you need to do to stay ahead of whatever is on your heels.

Alert to Opportunity

I said earlier that your ESP could open your eyes to advantages in your path as well as pitfalls. This is especially true if you're listening to the little voice tell you about the next big opportunity in your life or business, or even about a whole new lane you can move into.

What does "awareness" mean for you in terms of business? It means you look at what people eat, where they go for enjoyment or comfort, what they wear, and how they get from place to place. You seek to understand how businesses work, what jobs are involved, or what skills you can bring to the table that will make money for you, your family, and the Future You. You can assess your business awareness by asking a few questions such as: What skills do I have? What need will I fill? What skills do I need to develop? How can I change an everyday challenge into a future moneymaking opportunity? Who can I knowledge-jack right now or seek out as a mentor, to cut down on the time necessary to advance.

I'm reminded of a creative young man named Ink-Drop, an urban paint artist, graphic designer, and urban marketer. He once used the graffiti-artist skills he'd honed as a youth on the streets of Detroit to repaint rail cars, bridges, and abandoned buildings. After he relocated to Vegas with his family, business was slow, so he accepted a casino job in marketing and hotel branding, changed his street wear, and polished his lingo. First chance he got, he introduced to the casino creative ways to market itself to a younger and hipper crowd, using street-smart graphic designs.

He zeroed in on just what the downtown gaming business was missing; he knew exactly what was needed to bring the disappearing customer base back to the casino, and he knew how to fill that need.

Our world is full of opportunities like this, as well as serious social challenges that present opportunities of their own. Consider the prison industrial complex. The United States has the highest incarceration rate in the world, with more than 2.3 million people behind bars. Being in the personal and professional transformation business, I would like to see those numbers reduced, especially among juveniles who enter the system. But prisons require all kinds of services—laundry, food and merchandise delivery, educational services, and more. Can you offer a service or idea that will cut down the prison population or save cities, states, the federal government, and taxpayers money?

Some people visit their locked-up loved ones on a weekly basis. Is there a living to be made by arranging group shuttles to area prisons on the weekends? Is there a prerelease service that formerly incarcerated individuals can offer to prisons to make an ex-offender's transition back to society smoother? What about businesses that are built on the skills ex-offenders learned on the inside, like plumbing, electrical, culinary, brick laying, and barbering, to name just a few?

Let's look at our population numbers. The United States, with a population of over 291 million, is the world's third most populated country, after China and India. According to the Census Bureau, the population in the United States will grow by approximately 3.3 million per year. Yet the National Center for Children in Poverty reports that nearly 15 million children in the United States (21 percent) live below the federal poverty level ($22,350 a year for a family of four). Unless things change, a significant portion of the nation's children will be born and raised in poverty.

This painful social challenge creates a huge opportunity for those whose awareness radar is fully rotating. Children will need day care, food and shelter, early education, and after-school care and have a host of other unmet needs. If you grew up attending an inadequate public school, you have a jump-start on turning that negative experience into an innovative, positive outcome.

Listen to your intuition.
It will tell you everything you need to know.

— Anthony J. D'Angelo

Let's be clear, the goal here is *not* just to focus on prison or child poverty. It's to search for untapped needs. The challenges can be social or business-related. You may have a better, more cost-effective way to eliminate paper waste or save water when the office toilets flush. As long as it addresses an unmet need, you have a shot at being "that guy or gal" whose idea struck gold.

Whatever the idea, look for common practices and ask how you can make them better. Add good karma to your efforts by asking the *big* question: "Who will I help and how will my idea make things better for others and myself?"

What Not to Do

So how do we learn to maximize our awareness and hone our ESP? Like everything else, it's through practice and patience. We learn to trust that little voice a bit more every time we listen to it—and sometimes by watching what happens when we don't.

Laura Connelly was happy in her job as a copywriter for a marketing firm when her boss came to her with a proposal. He was being promoted, and he wanted to promote Laura into the job he was vacating, as manager of the department in charge of a dozen writers. It was flattering for Laura to be singled out this way, and she knew it was a great opportunity on paper, but she also knew that her old job used her skills better than the new one would. She didn't want to be in and out of meetings all day, supervising other people doing the work she really wanted to be doing.

She asked for time to think it over, and then a little more time. Finally, sitting in her boss's office, she knew she had to make the call. "My intuition was telling me to say no as clearly as if it had been written on the wall," she remembers. But her boss's faith in her, and her own feeling that this chance was "too good" to pass up, proved too strong. "I'll do it," she heard herself say.

Lying awake that night, Laura knew she had made a mistake—but it was too late. Or was it? In the days that followed, she did something that was even harder for her than the initial choice: she listened to the little voice she'd ignored the first time and decided to give up the position she'd agreed to take. Her boss's disappointment was tempered when Laura suggested another copywriter as a candidate—a woman who had been with the firm only a short time but had already made strong connections with her colleagues and people in other departments. That woman proved to be a natural manager who didn't miss the hands-on work of writing. Laura got to keep doing what she loved—and she got a lesson in ESP that she never forgot.

Tuned In to Success

It's important to realize that not every door that opens for you is the right way to go. Some of the time, your little voice is telling you what *not* to do, and you need to listen just as closely.

In 1963, Mary Kathlyn Wagner, a divorced mother with three children, had a stunning realization. As an employee with Stanley Home Products she realized the possibilities of promotion were limited because she was a woman. Finally, when she was again passed over for a promotion in favor of a man she had trained, Wagner chose to stop rolling in that particular lane. She retired, planning to write a book that would help other women struggling in a business world dictated by men. That book wound up serving as her business plan for a company she had reserved for her dreams. With the help of her sons and a $5,000 investment, Mary Kay Ash started Mary Kay Cosmetics, and history was made.

Mary Kay's story isn't just an inspiring tale of one woman's success. It's a story of finely tuned ESP. Mary Kay read the signs and hidden motivations around her in her corporate job, accurately read the demand in the marketplace for what she wanted to sell, and kept her vision in view until it became a reality. It's the ultimate story of making quality lemonade from life's lemons—and it's proof of how applying the street-smart strategy of awareness can change your mind-set and your life.

If you grow up with a tough life,
you have learned lessons
that cannot be taught in a book.

— Roy Juarez, Jr.

Life for me today is all about limitless opportunities that are aligned with my vision, goals, and action plan. All sorts of avenues are opening that allow me to fulfill my life's big dreams and passions.

This book is a direct result of my ESP: my own constant, clear understanding of what it took for me to discover who I was and how to parlay my dreams into reality. I realize that there are thousands, if not millions, of people who have been knocked off track in life, and I'm aware that we are all like lumps of coal with the potential to become diamonds. How many carats are you willing to rock for your family and the world?

The ESP-er

☆ **Study the language of looks.** Next time you're in public, watch the people around you to see if you can tap into what they're feeling or thinking. Who's looking forward to a date? Who's just tired and wanting to get home?

☆ **Build your nonverbal vocab.** Take a close look at someone close to you when you *know* how she's feeling. Notice how she expresses her pleasure, anger, apprehension, or trust. Have you seen these expressions and behaviors in others you know?

☆ **Listen deep beneath the words.** For one day, decide not to take anything at face value—but ask yourself what motivations and intentions are going unsaid in every conversation you have.

☆ **Take your ESP for a test drive.** Spend an hour or two in an environment that's foreign to you—whether it's a school board meeting or a farm in the country. Let your senses stay alert for new input.

☆ **Fine-tune your business awareness.** For the next week, keep your eyes open for unmet needs in your community or at your job. Don't make a plan to fill these needs right now—just see where there's a gap.

☆ **Tune in to the little voice.** For one day, every time you make a decision, pay close attention to the signals your ESP is sending you—could be a thought in your mind or even a feeling in your body. Notice how your little voice comes across when it's saying yes and when it's saying no.

The Gambler

The strategy of
calculated risk

> *Risk is a reality, fear is just a feeling.*
> — Chef Jeff

*O*n a busy Saturday morning at the Café Bellagio, the phone rang. "Chef Jeff, how can I assist you?" The caller was New York literary agent Michael Psaltis: "Do you have a second?" I said yes. "I read about your story online. Would you be interested in writing a book?" Of course I said yes. I knew that bringing my rise to chefdom to light would be risky, exposing the underbelly of the crack cocaine epidemic in the 1980s and the way that world functioned. To me, though, the benefits of telling the tale of the Black underground drug culture were greater than the risk. I thought about the fact that so many people could take away life-saving lessons and be inspired to go after their personal and professional dreams.

In 2007, my dream came true. Life for me was on fast-forward. After a surprising and, at times, seriously competitive bidding war, my memoir, *Cooked: From the Streets to the Stove, from Cocaine to Foie Gras,* had finally hit the streets.

Then shortly after the release of *Cooked,* I received "the call." Oprah Winfrey wanted me to be a guest on her show. The topic was "resilience" and I was one of three guests to be interviewed.

The invitation, to me, was the ultimate honor. It was also an extraordinary opportunity. I knew that authors who were guests on *The Oprah Winfrey Show* saw the sales of their books go through the roof. I knew what an appearance on her show could do for my career and the lives of others who had fallen down in life. But I had fears about the backlash, too. Oprah can be a tough interviewer when she chooses. What if she decided to grill me hard about my past role in drug trafficking and the impact drugs had in Black communities? What if she was going to beat me down in front of millions for the damage I had done to the lives of those who were addicted to the deadly product that I once sold? She and her staff were going to go over every inch of my life with a fine-toothed comb before I appeared on the show—what would they uncover that might do me more harm than good? I had rolled the dice when I put the book out, and when the time came to roll them again, it seemed like the stakes were even higher.

My fears, it turned out, were unfounded and completely put to rest during the interview. Oprah was an insightful, gracious host who zoned in on the true meaning of my story. It's hard to describe the emotions I felt sitting on the couch with Oprah. At times I felt like I was in the kitchen with a beloved aunt talking about my intense desire for full redemption and my determination to share the extraordinary blessings that I'd been given with others.

"You are a role model to little Black boys everywhere; so many of them don't have one, now they do," Oprah commented during the interview.

WOW! Those words, at that moment, struck me the way my granddaddy used to bust me upside the head when I being hard-headed. Those words intensified my call to action. Those words commanded me to keep on using my journey from drug dealer to prison cook to the first African American executive chef at the Bellagio Hotel as a catalyst to help transform the lives of people trapped in similar cycles of dysfunction, chaos, stagnation, ghetto life, and prison.

Rolling the Dice

Although my heart felt absolutely ready to put Oprah's compliment in motion, my mind was still a bit nervous about the risks. On one side of the coin, the time felt right to get out there and fully engage, inspire, and empower people with my life story. On the other side of the coin was the security that my wife, Stacy, and I had built for our family. We both had pretty decent gigs at the Bellagio. She worked the graveyard shift in the employee dining room, and I worked days as the executive chef of Café Bellagio. My vice president at the hotel had granted my request for a three-month leave of absence to go on a book tour, but the time to get back in the kitchen was quickly drawing near.

You can measure opportunity with the same yardstick that measures the risk involved. They go together.

— Earl Nightingale

I had a tough decision to make, and fast, about my employment future. I sought counsel with Stacy, my agents, and my attorney about what was best for my life. Many people stood to make lots of money off my success, but I knew that was how the business world works, no different from the drug game—everybody has to eat. Stacy and I saw it as our meal ticket, a way to secure our children's college education and our retirement, but also have the freedom to be in control of our own destiny. She is a gambler, too.

Ironically, it was the Oprah appearance that finally flipped the coin. The Oprah Effect is more than a myth. Days and weeks after the interview aired, my phone was blowing up with offers and new opportunities that were just unbelievable; it seemed like I went from ordinary to extraordinary overnight. Invitations for speaking engagements and book sales increased rapidly. In just a matter of weeks, *Cooked* hit the *New York Times* best-seller list. But the most mind-blowing opportunity came just two hours after the Oprah interview aired.

"Chef Jeff, this is Will Smith, I was watching you on Oprah..."

"Come on, who's playing on my phone!" I interrupted. "Who is this?"

"It's big Willie from Philly . . ." the caller responded.

It *really* was Will Smith—the superstar actor. He had seen the show, loved my story, and wanted to send a driver to pick me up to discuss film rights. I was still in a state of shock sitting in the back of the cream-colored Lincoln Navigator that Will sent to pick up my agent, Mike Psaltis, and me. I was headed to Brooklyn, where

Will was filming *I Am Legend*.

When I walked into his million-dollar, two-story trailer, I saw several copies of my book with colorful sticky notes inserted throughout. This was real! Will and his people were serious as hell about making a movie based on my life.

Within about ten minutes, Will entered the trailer.

"Chef Jeff, what's up?" he asked, with a big homeboy embrace.

We bonded instantly and started talking about our lives before our mutual successes. I don't know this for sure, but I feel Oprah— directly or indirectly—had something to do with our hooking up. What I do know is, within a few weeks, Will, Sony-Columbia Pictures, and I had struck a very impressive seven-figure deal. He had bought the rights and planned to develop a screenplay based on my rags-to-riches story.

I was down for the ride but I was thinking, *Man, this is crazy good stuff!*

By the time my three-month leave of absence had expired and I was summoned back to work, my mind was pretty much made up. I had to try to leverage all the high-power stuff I had on the table and seize the opportunity to go from an employed chef to a chef/owner in charge of his own brand, like other big-named chefs who had cut ties with the casino. I had a six-figure cook-book deal in the works with Scribner and a Food Network deal on the table to host my own TV show. *The Chef Jeff Project* was to be a docu-reality series where I'd recruit, mentor, and introduce a group of at-risk young people to the culinary arts game and my "tough-love life lessons."

Even with this amazing array of opportunities, I still felt a sense of loyalty to the Bellagio after Wolfgang Von Wieser, my boss, had given me a shot as executive chef of one of the most profit-able casual restaurants at one of the most prominent Las Vegas hotels. When I sat down with my chef, the VP of Food and Bever-ages, and then the former president and CEO of MGM Mirage, Terry Lanni, whom I have the utmost respect for, I offered sev-eral scenarios where I could still partner with the company while pursuing other opportunities of a lifetime. In my mind it was a win-win situation for both sides. I reasoned that the publicity I'd drum up through my books, TV, and film work would enhance the Bellagio's diversity and corporate responsibility mission. The top dogs didn't quite see it that way. I can only speculate, but maybe a redeemed ex-con wasn't something they wanted publicized on such a grand scale or attached to the Bellagio name.

Whatever their reasoning, Stacy and I walked away on faith and our gut instincts. We rolled the dice with everything we had, and we both resigned from the Bellagio. The choice between going full steam ahead with our dreams or clinging to our respectable combined six-figure income had been made.

Today, I travel the world speaking before Fortune 500 companies, financial institutions, government agencies, nonprofit and civic groups, hospitality and food service providers, universities, public schools, correctional facilities, and other diverse audiences. I mention this not to brag but to underscore that hustlepreneurs are the consummate gamblers. They know that there are no guarantees in life. Risk taking is as natural to business success as netting three-pointers was to Michael Jordan. If you're not a risk taker—well, as Ray Kroc, the founder of McDonald's, put it, "You should get the hell out of business."

I realize that most of you, at whatever crossroads you're facing in your life, don't have the extraordinary opportunities I had on the table when I chose to leave

> **Risk taking is a natural part of the survival game.**

a secure life in exchange for a promise of uncertainty. But more than likely, you share the fears and doubts that I once had. In fact, if you're like most people, you may find yourself occasionally sweating bullets in the face of *what can go right* and *what might go wrong.*

So how do you put out the fires of fear and cling to the faith that has to come with taking big, calculated risks? From the street-smart perspective, you'll begin to see that risk taking is a natural part of the survival game. But as with everything else in this book, the road to a sense of peace in the face of the calculated risk starts with you understanding you. With practice and good mentoring, you'll see big risks as little boxes to be checked off your list as you better understand how to take action to move your vision from the "I wish" kind of talk into the realm of cherished reality.

The Truth about Fear

The year my book was published, 2007, Robert Greene, famed author of *The 48 Laws of Power,* was hanging out with Curtis Jackson, better known by his hip-hop name, 50 Cent, discussing a possible collaboration on a book—which would turn out to be *The 50th Law.*

The most compelling aspect of Fifty, Greene observed, was the way his poor and chaotic upbringing had prepared him to be a success on the streets and in the entertainment industry. He grew up in the midst of the 1980s crack epidemic in a violent, low-income section of Southside Queens. Like so many urban youth today without believable options, he got involved in the illegal drug game, too. It was an environment, Greene wrote, where he could not avoid *feeling* fear. But he knew that *showing* fear was a sign of weakness and a badge of dishonor on the streets. So he worked to calm it. The appearance of fearlessness became his way of gaining respect from rival dealers.

Fifty also had to face his fears when he decided to drop out of the familiar and lucrative crack cocaine world and pursue a career in music. With pure determination, the rapper won himself a deal with Columbia Records. His days of risk, however, weren't quite over. Just before the release of his album in 2000, a street killer pumped nine bullets into Fifty's body. One bullet, Greene wrote, came within a millimeter of ending his life.

Columbia Records dropped the recuperating young rapper like he was poison. No matter. He had faced and overcome what for many of us is the greatest fear of all: death. With a new outlook on life, he relied on his hustlepreneur instincts and started pushing, selling, and even giving away his own brand of authentic hood life, hip-hop music. He became "street famous"; rapper Eminem took note and quickly signed the promising young star with Dr. Dre's record label. The rest, as they say, is history.

I share the rapper's success here because he's a prime example of a bold risk taker. He gambled it all at every stage: when he was an up-and-coming drug dealer, when he decided to exit the game, and again when he relaunched his career after being dropped by his record label.

Something else I like about Fifty's story is that it exposes one of the major barriers to risk taking: *fear*. No matter our personality or character traits, the fear of messing up, losing financial security, starting something new, being around people who are smarter than we are—and even, ironically, the fear of success—can sap the guts right out of a would-be risk taker. But roll with me for a minute, and I'll tell you something you need to know about those fears.

Lots of times, when people take big risks in their lives or do things that seem scary to us, we praise them for being fearless. The truth is that few people are really fearless, and you don't need to be. You just need to remember what street-smart individuals like Fifty know: fear and risk are not the same thing. If you're moving ahead in the fast lane toward your vision, risk— the gamble or chance you're taking—is more than likely a reality for you, but fear is just a feeling, and it's a natural thing.

Think about that for a second. *Risk is a reality, fear is just a feeling*. It's the feeling of anxiety and extreme stress that makes whatever risk you're contemplating seem so unachievable. If you let it, it can destroy your dreams and become the block that keeps you from the next big step you need to take in your life. Or you can face the feeling head-on like a pit bull, acknowledge it, then go ahead and take that step anyway. When I came to Vegas seeking a job, many said impossible, won't happen, can't happen, you're a felon. Those dream crushers became my motivators, and, as they say, the rest is history.

Facing Your Fear

When I was getting ready to launch my series on the Food Network, I was nervous as hell. I had to use self-talk and say to myself, *If I can cook in front of prisoners serving life and alongside killers, gangsters, and mystery men, I can cook in front of millions on TV.* Don't let fear stop your blessings.

The first step for me was identifying the fear. What was causing me internal grief and the dry mouth that happens when people going before an audience become so very nervous? Well, it's my personality and character; I'm competitive. Be it in the illegal drug world, the kitchen, or now in the world of TV, I'm hard-wired to try to be just as good as, or better than, those I identify as competition. It's just who I am. And the fear was that I would somehow fall short.

Strange as it may sound, coming to grips with that reality was all it took. Once I identified the barrier, I was able to work through it. My focus moved away from the gifts of others and how they might outshine my own and shifted to what I confidently brought to the table.

What are your fears? What's stopping you from starting that business you've been talking about for years? What is that one thing that gets you shaking in your boots when you look at your Future You picture-power dream board? Maybe it's a fear that you won't be able to sustain your success. Maybe it's a worry that people around you will feel threatened and turn against you. Or maybe it's a fear that on your way to getting what you want, you'll somehow lose what you already have.

> **What are your fears? Whatever they are, write them down. Now!**

Think about what you placed on your Past You board, too—the challenges and obstacles that have stopped you in the past. Where do fears fit into that picture? Can you gain confidence by remembering how you faced them and moved away from them?

What fears overshadow your stated vision or stop you from executing your goals and action plan? Whatever they are, write them down. Now! Pull out a piece of paper right now or type on your smartphone and lay out your top five fears in writing—those haters that threaten to sabotage your dreams. More than likely you'll find that just by naming the fears that weigh on you, you've already lightened the load up off you.

The Art of the Calculated Risk

Let's get something straight before we go any further. Taking street-smart risks doesn't mean just doing anything that sounds stupid, knocks your fear into overdrive, places your well-being in jeopardy, or puts you outside your comfort zone. Hustlepreneurs know that what's called for is *calculated* risk—which is simply a risk you consider worth taking because of the results it will bring if you succeed. It's about the timing. It means you've weighed the pros and cons—what you stand to gain versus what you have to lose—and your hand has tipped in favor of taking action, the way it did for me when I left the Bellagio.

A calculated risk is the kind of risk basketball star LeBron James took when he decided, first, to dive straight into the NBA without attending college first—a move that many in the sports world viewed as a *serious* gamble—and then to end his stint with the Cleveland Cavaliers early so he could become a free agent. He surely had to face the fear of what others would think and say—and in fact, press and fans alike came down on him hard when he left the Cavs. But today "King James" is #4 on *Forbes* magazine's list of the world's highest-paid athletes, he's emerged as a stronger on-court leader for the Miami Heat, and people are saying he'll ultimately be seen as the top b-ball player of all time. Those risks were significant, and they were worth it, and he'll be reaping the rewards for a long time to come.

So how are you going to weigh the risks and rewards of pursuing your own vision? You can start with a simple list. Take a piece of paper and divide it into two columns. Write your vision at the top to remind you of what it's all about. Then on one side, list the risks—the chances you'll be taking, the things that could go wrong; on the other side, list the rewards—all the amazing benefits that will come your way if you succeed.

For example, Martin Lewis, whom you met in Chapter 4, has a vision of being a successful freelance graphic designer with a profitable business that lets him live well now and save for retirement later. One of the first steps on a path like this, if you're already working a secure job, is to leave it and strike out on your own—something that's undeniably risky, especially in today's insecure world. So Martin, when he's debating this choice, might list risks like these:

Martin's Risks

- Losing company benefits
- Having trouble turning professional connections into freelance clients
- Running short of funds in the short term
- Feeling isolated working alone

On the flip side of the coin—or the page—might be rewards like these:

Martin's Rewards

- Having freedom in my schedule
- Being able to choose the work I want to do
- Not answering to a boss
- Feeling proud of running my own business

Once you've got your lists, you can compare them in a couple of ways. One is simple: is one longer than the other? If you've identified two risks and eight big rewards, it's a pretty good sign that you're good to move forward. But not all risks and rewards are created equal, so consider how serious each one is. Is there a risk on your list you truly can't afford to take right now? Now, do a "gut check." If your heart sort of sinks when you look at your safe "rewards" and starts to rise when you turn to your exciting "risks," those feelings are telling you something you can't afford to ignore. Listen to that little voice.

What's Your Plan B?

Now, let's keep it real. Not every story has a happy ending. Not everything you do is going to succeed, and not every risk you take is going to reap you a payoff. Even if you've calculated carefully, you have to be prepared to survive a calculated risk that fails—especially in these times, when survival is a high-stakes game for every player in every walk of life.

You need a hard-and-fast backup plan. You need a Plan B *and* a Plan C. And you can form that kind of plan only by understanding what can go wrong—this is no time to have a big head! So take another look at that list of risks you wrote out (and if you didn't make one, take some time to do it now). Take the first one, or the one that is the biggest and most gut-wrenching to you. Now write down the worst-case outcome of the risk. Under that, explain how you'd handle the imagined worst-case scenario. For example if you wrote, "Running short of money after leaving my job," write something like this:

My Plan B

Risk: Running short on money after leaving my job

Worst-Case Scenario: I go broke and have to start over by asking for my gig back

Backup Plan: Reduce my spending and find a job that may pay less until I save enough to try going out on my own again

Three things are happening with this exercise, and they go back to what we talked about earlier in this chapter. First, you've identified the risk. Then you've documented the worst thing that could happen should you decide to take that risk. You've got your mind focused now so when things line up, when opportunities come to the table, you're mentally prepared. And though that worst-case scenario probably has you tripping out, you've lessened the fear of the risk simply by acknowledging the fear.

If you're a real hustlepreneur, risk is going to rear its head every time you set a goal. As a hustlepreneur you don't have the safety net many others have—your safety net is your street smarts and the strategies we're talking about right here in these pages. And if hustlepreneurs fall, they get back up. They never give up no matter what. If you don't have resilience in your bloodstream, you've got no business taking risks in the first place—you'd better just stay in a safe space and not do anything stupid. If you want to be a hustlepreneur, you can't avoid risk, so you might as well strap your boots up and get ready to face the outcome.

> *Only a few act—the rest of us*
> *reap the benefits of their risk.*
>
> — Wynton Marsalis

When I left the Bellagio without any of my planned partnership proposals in place, I accepted the outcome because Plan B was already in mental motion. You may not have a book or movie contract in hand, but you could have another revenue stream in mind. You've told your higher self that you're ready for whatever comes your way should you decide to roll the dice and take the risks for your dream.

And you've called into play the part of you that you know is there—the part that rises to any occasion, recovers from any failure, and gets you through the worst of downfalls. Let's be real—if you were raised in poverty; had abusive, alcoholic, ignorant, or drug-addicted parents; lived in a neighborhood where violence was a way of life; or lost everything—life, for you, has often been nothing but risk, like walking down the streets in hopes you don't get messed with. Sometimes, with our ability to put our past behind us, we forget what it took to survive those crazy times and, occasionally, crazy people. We forget to remind ourselves how truly resilient we had to be to survive those times of personal and financial hardships. We forget that we were born with the gift to succeed in the face of extraordinary adversity. So I'm just saying to you: you have what it takes to stand up to misfortune and bounce back strong.

What's more, you have the ability to learn from your mistakes—and that allows you to take better risks. Because if you don't learn, even if you're taking what I've called calculated risks, you're just calculating the same failure over and over.

Acting on Faith

You are one helluva miracle!

Let's handle this right now. The fact that you are reading this book, that your mind is hopefully comprehending the words, that you're able to accept or reject the truth, go buy yourself a cup of Starbucks caramel macchiato and a slice of lemon loaf cake (my morning favorite, by the way), then go about your day accomplishing your business . . . all this is a part of the miracle that is you.

You're not here by accident. You're not designed just to exist. You have dreams for a reason, and you want your vision to become real for a reason, too. You have to have the inner faith and fight in you to transform your life, right now, today.

Faith is the shield you need to lessen the risks. It is the unshakable belief that you're in it to win it. Faith keeps passion alive and your vision clear. It provides the humbleness when your plan stalls, when discipline is weak, when your strength has been weakened, and when life feels as if it's falling apart. Faith is the rock when you're weary. It reminds you that your dream is not determined by others, it's determined by you—a walking, talking, thinking miracle. With faith, you know that whatever happens, no matter how hard the journey, you were born with the tools to survive, thrive, and live with purpose.

It was faith that led the Wright Brothers to defy the risk of falling out of the sky when they were learning how to fly. It was faith that made the risk of death and imprisonment bearable when Mahatma Gandhi, Martin Luther King, Jr., Rosa Parks, César Chávez, and others stood up for liberty, peace, and justice for all.

Applying the street-smart survival skill of risk taking means that—with heart, faith, careful thinking, and a crystal-clear understanding of your talents and strengths—you stand your ground and fight for your vision with your blood, sweat, and tears.

I started out this chapter by talking about the inspiration that Oprah Winfrey gave me when she told me I was an example to little Black boys everywhere—a model for them to take the risks needed to bring their own vision into being. In the spring of 2013, as I was writing this chapter, Oprah received an honorary degree from Harvard University. And what she talked about had everything to do with taking risks—even when they don't succeed. She spoke about the decision she had made a few years back to end *The Oprah Winfrey Show*—which had been #1 in its time slot for 21 years—and launch her own network, called just that, OWN, the Oprah Winfrey Network.

You might think that everything Oprah would touch would be golden, but in fact, OWN didn't take off the way it was expected to. After one year, to be candid, it was a flop, Oprah said— "Not just a flop but a big bold flop," obvious to everyone from media commentators to the people at home in front of their TVs. "Oprah, Not Quite Standing on Her OWN," read the headline in *USA Today*.

Failure is just life
trying to move us in another direction.

— Oprah Winfrey

But do you think Oprah gave up when that risk she'd taken didn't play out right away? You know she didn't. She thought about that old hymn—*trouble don't last always*—and she decided to learn from her missteps. She told herself, *I am going to turn this thing around, and I will be better for it.* And that is exactly what she did. Today, the network is alive and well, with new programming ahead, and the show *Oprah's Next Chapter* stands as proof that a failed experiment doesn't have to be the end of your story. As Oprah puts it, "Failure is just life trying to move us in another direction."

The Wright Brothers, Will Smith, Oprah, 50 Cent, you, and me—we all have something that no one else has, something that no one can take from us. Oprah gave me a platform to offer my story of transformation to others. I've built on "how to do for self" and have gained the confidence to face any risks there are. You can, too. Face your fears. Defuse them by writing them out, and write out a backup plan as well. Don't compromise or sell yourself short because the risks seem too high.

Remember, reaching success—personal, financial, or social—is all about taking risks. It's the only way to truly know and grow you. It is the only way to activate that miracle from within.

Street-Smart Challenges for:
The Gambler

☆ **Check the scales.** Make a list of risks and rewards that come with pursuing your vision. Which side is winning?

☆ **Face your fears.** Write down the fears that stand in your way.

☆ **Make a Plan B.** For every risk you're considering taking, think of the worst-case scenario if it fails, then make a backup plan. Write it down, too.

☆ **Take a chance.** Think of something that feels risky to you but isn't directly tied to your vision—like asking your boss for a raise or telling a friend the hard truth. Do it and make note of how it makes you feel. What happens if you succeed? What happens if you don't?

☆ **Consult an expert.** Think of someone you know who has taken great risks. Knowledge-jack to find out how he or she faces fear and decides to act.

☆ **Assess your risk.** Look at your goals and your action plan. Do you think you're trying to take too many risky steps at once—or do you need to roll the dice for even higher stakes?

The Gab-Master

The strategy of
persuasion

Persuade to upgrade!

— Chef Jeff

A few years back, I had the opportunity to speak at the UP Experience, named for Unique Perspectives from Unique People—a one-day conference that brings together innovators, creators, and thought leaders to inform and inspire. As usual when I speak to an audience, I walked back and forth across the stage, always in motion, feeling the audience members' energy and feeding it with my own. And I opened up by telling my own story. "Let me tell you something," I said to the audience of CEOs, business leaders, speakers, best-selling authors, and some of the most influential individuals in Houston, Texas. "As I take you on this journey, the journey through my childhood, the journey through prison, the journey through corporate America to the American dream, my mission is to get you to truly understand the power of potential." Just hold that thought while we go on. *My mission is to get you to understand.*

I continued pacing the stage, using my hands to drive home my points and make my case bulletproof for them, as if they could reach out and touch what I was saying. "We're called hustlers," I told them. "In the corporate world they're CEOs and businessmen." You can best believe the audience of businesspeople laughed at that! Then I held up a small plastic bag. "This—this is crack." (It was fake.) "How many of you have ever seen crack before?" I paused. "Raise your hand if you've seen crack. Now, you may not *want* to raise your hand . . ." More laughter.

But I didn't just want to make them laugh. I brought my voice down to a humble tone of seriousness to get across the emotion in what I was saying or to share something intimate and important with them. I tuned in to the way they were listening—and they *were* listening. Finally, I was ready to bring it home. "It was very important to me that I use my story to change lives," I said. "I thank all the people who have given me an opportunity. Not just me, but all people. Doesn't matter if you're a convicted felon. Doesn't matter if you don't have teeth in your mouth. Every one of us in this room is successful, every one of us is living the American dream because somebody reached back"—I reached behind my own back to show them—"and gave us access." Then I thanked them and bowed. That was all—and they gave me a standing ovation.

I spoke to that audience skillfully and from the heart, no question. But let's be clear—I had to *learn* to do that. I may have been born with the gift of gab passed down from my granddaddy, but to use it effectively, I had to study the street-smart art of persuasive communication. In this chapter I'm going to break that down and show you what it takes to get your gab skills on.

The Gab-Master in Training

I'd always been a talker since I was a kid, though I was punished for talking so much in class and at family gatherings. I heard a lot of fast talk growing up, from family members and from people on the streets. Whether I was talking myself out of trouble or up-selling gourmet candy to a potential customer in the 'burbs, I developed a credible talk game early on. Once in the drug world, I became a more polished salesman with an arsenal of sales pitches, sealing my deals 95 percent of the time.

In prison, your mouthpiece could mean life or death, literally. But it was there that my conversations and communication skills truly elevated, while talking with the kinds of people I'd never encountered before, discussing all sorts of subjects, taking the mic at inmate club meetings, and eventually speaking at the prison Toastmasters group that the Wall Street boys started. There were no rules as to who could join; most of the guys at some point before they became corporate crooks had been the best in sales, and to be the best in sales you must be a seasoned gab-master.

Taking the stage there, I felt like I was in control of the moment, yet a little unsure of how I would be received. When I got some applause, my confidence rose.

After my appearance on *The Oprah Winfrey Show* in 2007, life for me took off like a jackrabbit. All of a sudden, invitations to speak before frighteningly large crowds were nonstop, and I found myself thrust into the self-help arena as a motivational speaker. Yes, I had written a book, but it's one thing to tell your life story and quite another to teach from it.

There is only one rule for being a
good talker—learn to listen.

— Christopher Morley

The first big invitation to speak before more than a thousand people came from Gerald Fernandez, Sr. president and founder of Multicultural Foodservice & Hospitality Alliance (MFHA) in Boston. What could I possibly say that would captivate some of the top brass from Coca-Cola, McDonald's, the Bellagio Hotel, and other giants in the hospitality and food service industry?

To find out, I had to deep dive and dissect my story. I'm the former drug dealer who was sent to prison, who earned his high school diploma in the pen, discovered his passion for cooking, and, when he got out, made a name for himself in the culinary world. As I dug deep, a whole set of lessons and strategies emerged—all the ones I'm laying out for you in this book. I was amazed that the same street-smart skills that got me in trouble had also rescued me from a downward spiral life. Turns out, I had a whole lot to say. I became less and less nervous about what I would share at the MFHA event.

CEOs in the food service and hospitality industry employ people whose lives mirror mine all day long. My strategy, as the keynote speaker, was to show them how to go beyond the surface stories of their employees and co-workers and see their full potential. I wanted them to go back and see future Jeff Hendersons in their workforce. I imagined them telling their workers: "Look, if this guy can turn his life around and become such a huge success, you can, too."

Today, I speak to at-risk high school students, juvenile delinquents, teachers, counselors, employers, and employees of all kinds. I talk about resilience, never giving up no matter what, and setting goals, and I go hard to persuade the people in my audience that no matter where they came from or what they have done or not done, they can flip their scripts, too. They don't have to wear the jacket that society or circumstance has placed on them. I don't brag about my success; I use it, though, to show how I started at the bottom and now I'm here. I let them know that we are all born with gifts and talents; we just need to be schooled on the skills and on how to use them to succeed without becoming a crook or blamer.

It's been about six years since that first "big" motivational presentation, and I've continued to speak before larger and more diverse audiences with confidence and ease. I'm always in motion onstage because I love what I do. But I'll be the first to tell you that you don't have to be a professional speaker to benefit from mastering the power of persuasion.

The Ultimate Product—You

Hustlers who've lived lives on the razor's edge *have* to persuade people in order to get theirs. Their sales pitch must be short and convincing. They have to push emotional buttons and close the deal in an instant, all the while making their targets feel that what they've been sold is actually their idea or something that will bring them some great benefits or satisfaction. Persuading hardened homies on the block not to jam up their enterprises means they must have exceptional communication skills. Because at the same time that these gab-masters are defending their market share, they have to convince suspicious police that they were just walking home or hanging out and not doing anything shady.

By contrast, real hustlepreneurs aren't trying to "get over" on their customers. But they use their gab-master skills just like successful advertising, public relations, and political campaign people. They know that what they're doing really is just like selling a product. Except in their case, that product is *themselves*—their talents, their ideas, and their vision—just like my Wall Street buddy told me years ago on the South Yard.

These street smarters don't just come into their own onstage; their stage is every moment of everyday life, walking into a room or talking on the phone or writing an e-mail. You need the power of persuasion to be effective at your job or at a job interview, in a meeting with your child's teacher, in front of the frontline workers if you're the supervisor. You need it to head up a community project; raise funds for a good cause; deal with colleagues, friends, family members, and romantic partners—in short, to get the results you want in any personal or professional relationship or interaction you have, you just gotta know how to speak and speak right to accomplish anything.

You see, being truly persuasive is about much more than getting people to do your bidding. It's about marketing your "product" to get results, whether that's more dishes served at the food truck, more cars sold at the dealership, more fourth graders passing their statewide exams, or more and better job offers when you're searching. It's about marketing *you,* whatever lane you're rolling in. And in case you're thinking, *Hold up, Big Jeff, I'm a person, not a product*—I'm here to tell you that we are *all* our own best products, and if you get this mind-set, it can make the difference between failing to realize your vision and succeeding beyond your imagining.

The good news is that anyone can learn to become a gab-master and a masterful self-marketer. If you're introverted—quiet, reflective, or even shy in crowds—you may think you're an unlikely persuader. Extroverts—outgoing, talkative, energetic people who come alive at business mixers or gatherings—may think they're the godfather of persuasion. The truth is, both candidates can be weak if they haven't tapped into who they really are and if they don't know what values they bring to other people's lives. But both types of people can be compelling communicators if they use the right set of skills. It's all about becoming an effective persuader with excellent communication skills that allow you to ignite imaginations and generate trust and confidence, no matter who you're talking to.

> *To be persuasive we must be believable;*
> *to be believable we must be credible;*
> *to be credible we must be truthful.*
>
> — Edward R. Murrow

Marketers who successfully sell any product have the ability to motivate, inspire, and make people feel special and appreciated. This all requires charisma, the capacity to connect with others, the know-how to both listen *and* speak effectively, and the ability to articulate a big idea in simple terms. Persuasion is an art form that can help anyone, from any neighborhood, sharpen their game; motivate family, friends, and co-workers; win associates and alliances; and move from a life of barely getting by to that place where your dreams can touch the sky.

So let's get started learning the skills you need to market your own best product: *you.*

Cultivating Charisma

Charisma is one of those words—it may be hard to define, but you know it when you see it and sometimes when you hear it. It's a quality of personal presence, combined with an ability to charm, lead, persuade, inspire, or otherwise influence people. It's as useful on the street side as it is in the mainstream: I was fascinated at how my on-the-street mentor, T-Row, used his looks, charm, big smile, and wit to persuade rival gang members to broker peace for the love of makin' money. The word *charisma* comes from a root that means "God-given powers," which makes it sound like you either have it or you don't—but that's a myth. The truth is that anyone can develop a level of charisma.

There's even a book by that very name: *The Charisma Myth: How Anyone Can Master the Art and Science of Personal Magnetism.* According to its author, Olivia Fox Cabane, charisma comes in several forms. With "focus" charisma you're able to hone in on people's concerns and desires and get them to share just about anything they may not have thought to share. Leaders who get people to listen and obey have "authority" charisma. If you can inspire people and get them involved in the brainstorming or creative processes, you probably have "visionary" charisma. Finally, you may be like the Dalai Lama or Bishop Desmond Tutu, people who use "kindness" charisma that encourages others to open their hearts and souls to you and faithfully follow you through good and bad times.

Any one of these approaches—or a powerful combination— can give anyone an instant advantage the moment they walk into a room. Focus means giving your full attention to the person or people you're talking to. Authority comes from being genuine, as well as being on top of your game, and knowing it, so you project a sense of confidence and calm. You'll come across as visionary if what you say is driven by purpose and principles, delivered with real passion. And kindness can take the form of simply treating people the way they want to be treated, or the way you'd want to be. You can use charisma to make your product so appealing that the people you're dealing with will want it without even knowing why: the recruiter will want to hire you, the customer will want to buy from you, the friend or family member will want to fall in line with your ideas. Conversely, without it, you may find even an otherwise positive interaction falling flat.

Who do you know who's got these qualities? Is there someone in your world who's always described with "He's so charismatic"? Put your knowledge-jacking skills to use and study that person next chance you get. See if you can zero in on the specific moves and manners he or she uses that create that special aura. Charisma is very personal—no two people express it in quite the same way—so think about how you could do what this person's doing in your own unique way. How can you transfer some of these techniques to your street-smart bag of magic tricks?

The Emotional Connection

Listening to Joyce Meyer, the folksy, undeniably charismatic Christian evangelist, author, and speaker, is like visiting with a beloved aunt or wise neighbor from the block. She disarms with

221

a persona of authentic, motherly warmth backed by scriptural knowledge. But Meyer also has one heck of a story.

Born Pauline Joyce Hutchison, Meyer has revealed publicly that she was sexually abused starting at the age of five. She says she was raped some 200 times by her own father. Her story includes marriage to an unfaithful man who persuaded her to steal from her employer so they could go on vacations. After the marriage ended, the emotionally wounded Meyer frequented local bars trying to quiet the pain from her past.

"I was in a terrible mess in my childhood," she said during a 2010 interview on ABC's *Nightline*. "Just had so many devastating things happen to me: sexual abuse, verbal abuse, abandonment, just one mess after another. So let's just say by the time I was a young adult, I was really messed up."

Her life turned around after she met and married an engineering draftsman, Dave Meyer, in 1967. Meyer was "born again" in the mid-1970s and started attending Life Christian Center in Fenton, Missouri. She soon became the church's associate pastor, and as her popularity grew, she started her own ministry, Life in the Word, in 1985. Her ministry took off within the next ten years, fueled by the additional exposure of radio and television broadcasting, and she now has followers in the hundreds of thousands.

Meyer used to regret the tragedies in her young life, but she learned to embrace the experiences because they provided the pathway to God, she says. That story, told honestly, touches people deeply. Meyer readily admits it's her story and the way she delivers it that draws people in and cements their loyalty: "I think it's my transparency," she said during the *Nightline* interview. "It's just the way I am."

If you tell the truth,
you don't have to remember anything.

— Mark Twain

Meyer makes it sound pretty simple, but the ability to make this kind of authentic emotional connection with a listener is a key aspect of the gab-master's art. It's said that people make decisions based on their emotions 80 percent of the time, even when they don't realize it, so don't discount the power of the other person's feelings when it comes to marketing yourself.

As Meyer notes, an emotional connection calls for real honesty. Always speak the truth, and when you're wrong, don't hesitate to own up. This doesn't mean you have to let it all hang out, or reveal more about you than is comfortable or suitable for the situation. It just means that what does come out of your mouth has to be rock-solid honest. That's how people know they can trust you, and trust opens a channel for real connection. My audiences know they can trust what I'm telling them because, like Meyer, I'm completely straight up with my story; I don't spin it to make myself sound better or different than I am. When I spoke to the Disney Dreamers Academy, an audience of at-risk teenagers from across the country, I told them, "When I see you, I see myself"—words of shared connection that I meant from the heart.

Always keep in mind that an emotional connection is a two-way street. If you want people to really get where you're coming from, and care about that place, you've got to give them the same caring and understanding. This is what empathy means: to put yourself in someone else's place and see how things might look from their point of view. When you do this, not only do you create the goodwill that comes from their feeling understood, you can also tailor your message in the way that's likely to make the most sense to them and get them on your side.

There's a way to create the sense of empathy that's so crazy simple, you're almost surely doing it already without even knowing it. It's your body language: the way you hold yourself, stand, move, or gesture while speaking with another person. When people are on the same page, there's a subconscious effect called "mirroring" that takes place; their movements and stances match each other. So one person might lean forward when the other person does, or cross her legs, or tilt her head a certain way. And though it's often subconscious, as I said, the skilled gab-master can use this effect consciously to *create* a sense of accord. Watch what the person you're trying to persuade is doing, and do the same thing yourself. As long as it's pretty subtle, he won't notice that you're mimicking him, he'll just get a feeling that you're in agreement and on his side.

Stop, Listen, and Roll

Dig deep and you'll find that most successful, persuasive people follow the wise advice of our elders: "Listen when someone else is talking," "Speak the truth or don't speak at all," "Shut up, and you might learn something."

These down-home and back-in-the-day directives might sound familiar but perhaps surprising if you're thinking that marketing yourself means constantly broadcasting what you want people to hear about you, your work, or your ideas. But intelligent listening is a key element of powerful communication, too. In order to touch people, you have to really know people. In order to inspire and motivate them, you have to know what buttons to push and what desires need to be satisfied. This information comes only when you sincerely listen and look for ways to get inside people's heads, so listening is a key driver of empathy as well. It's about understanding what the other people mean, not just what they say. If you can approach them from the perspective of their needs and wishes, not yours, honest criticism and feedback is accepted more easily. If you can disarm them with charisma, your brand of authority is tolerated and appreciated. If you can show kindness and empathy, people will feel it's safe to speak from the heart and share their deepest dreams and desires with you. If they trust you, they will be willing to share ideas that can increase their bottom line and yours.

The good way to get there is to act as if you were a talk-show host like Oprah, Tavis Smiley, or Barbara Walters. Ask questions that get people to open up. Ask about their children, their hobbies, their passions, and their greatest wishes. Try to avoid the topics of religion, politics, ex-spouses, or anything that might bite you in the you-know-what later.

---

*I like to listen. I have learned a great deal
from listening carefully. Most people never listen.*

— Ernest Hemingway

You have to become an expert listener, and that means listening to yourself during conversations, too. Are you a "hogger"? Do you just take over the conversation by talking about yourself or your accomplishments? Do you find yourself preparing an answer while someone else is talking instead of working to get at the "big idea" he's trying to communicate—really just waiting for him to stop talking so you can talk some more? If you stop thinking about what you're going to say next and really focus on what he's saying right now, you'll pick up on cues, like his expression and tone of voice, that you might otherwise miss. And if you practice this one well-timed line: "That's enough about me; tell me more about you," you'll increase your ability to persuade by leaps and bounds.

Listening to yourself can also keep your speech from running away with you. There's a great piece of advice from Ann Landers, who knew a thing or two about advice (*and* about listening): "The trouble with talking too fast is you may say something you haven't thought of yet." Whether you're interviewing for a job or making a sale, you can't afford to say something you'll wish you could take back. Take time to pause, breathe, and reflect so that what you say gets carefully considered and what the other person says gets heard.

The Means to an End

Remember what I said in my talk at the UP Experience? "My mission is to get you to understand." Doesn't matter *what* you want people to understand, whether it's the value of a product you're selling, the importance of a request you're making, or, like me, the truth of a big idea you're presenting; when you get right down to it, your message is *you*, and your mission as a street-smart gab-master is to get that message across in the most compelling and convincing way possible.

It starts with knowing exactly what it is you want to accomplish. Don't just start in talking; start by thinking of the results you want (a promotion, a sale, a change in someone's behavior) and work backward from there. Have your facts at hand, if facts are necessary, and know the main points you want to make to get where you're going. That way, everything you say will be on point and you won't get sidetracked by the other person's responses, or by other ideas or feelings that come up.

Next thing is knowing who you're talking to. To some extent this comes naturally; you just don't speak the same way to your boss as you do to the neighbor's kid on the block, and you don't talk to the kid the same way you do to someone in your own family. But like many of the skills we're talking about, it becomes more powerful when you think about it consciously and apply it deliberately. I do this whenever I address an audience, and sometimes the differences are extreme! At that Disney Dreamers Academy I mentioned, I was interviewed by a student reporter, a little boy in a suit with a big microphone. I talked to him in a way he would understand, without talking down to him, even though he was about three feet shorter than me.

Before you start a conversation, think for a minute about the other person (or people): What are they likely to be feeling about the subject at hand? How do you think they're feeling in general right now—tired or energetic, edgy or relaxed, combative or receptive? Is their background similar to yours, so you can share a kind of cultural shorthand and know they'll get your insider references, or very different, so you can't take their comprehension for granted? And what do *they* want to get out of the conversation? Give yourself a little time to plan and prepare how you're going to carry yourself and how you're going to approach them. But don't get tied up in knots trying to predict how the whole conversation is going to go—just get your mind right and then relax and let things unfold.

> *The most important thing in communication*
> *is hearing what isn't said.*
>
> — Peter Drucker

Last but not least, stay clear and positive. What do I mean by positive? Not necessarily keeping everything light and happy, but framing what you're saying in positive terms. Ever notice how politicians and political movements don't describe themselves as "anti" anything—they're always "pro" something? It's subtle but true; using words that have a positive emotional punch can help shift people into agreement with you. So if you're trying to change someone's behavior, talk about what you do want to see happen, not what you don't. "It's no good saying to my daughter, 'Don't mess up your room,' when I mean, 'Tidy your room,'" says author and persuasion expert Nicholas Boothman. If you want your spouse to do more around the house, don't say, "You need to stop being so lazy"; try "I'd like it if I could have your help with some of these chores." By the same token, Boothman says, it's important to be clear and specific: "If you say to a customer, 'Don't hesitate to contact me,' they don't know what you mean. What you really mean is, 'Phone me Friday,' or, 'Call me if you need some help.'"

All these rules of persuasion hold true in face-to-face talk—but also when you're chatting on the phone or communicating via e-mail, text, or instant message. If anything, the verbal cues are *more* important when the other person's not in front of you, because you can't rely on your "mirroring" technique to create empathy or on your physical presence and facial expression to generate a sense of trustworthiness. When it comes to electronic communication, you don't even have tone of voice to fall back on. So when you write an e-mail, ask yourself the same questions: What do I want to accomplish? What are my key points I want to get across? Who am I talking to? Am I being positive and clear? Use correct grammar and spelling—no LOLs or IMHOs, no

Internet abbreviations or slang. Be careful about cracking jokes, because the humor can get lost in cyberspace, and be aware of the tone you're setting: Is it so businesslike that it seems cold, or so friendly that it's a little less than professional? If you do this, you'll avoid many of the misunderstandings that arise because someone misread the tone of an e-mail and got offended or failed to pick up on an important instruction.

One final word on the subject: if you're uncertain about speaking to people, and want to get some on-the-ground experience, consider joining a Toastmasters club, like I did when I was locked up. Toastmasters International has been around for almost 100 years, with clubs in over 100 countries; it's very inexpensive; and anyone can join. There's no teacher at their meetings, just members who listen to one another's presentations on a wide variety of topics and offer constructive on-the-spot feedback. These no-pressure, learn-by-doing workshops are a great way to get more comfortable talking to anyone about anything, and the more comfortable you are, the more you can bring your gab-master techniques out front.

The Big Idea

We've talked about how to communicate persuasively in your everyday encounters—a conversation, a meeting, an e-mail exchange. Now I want to circle back to where we started and talk a little more about the bigger picture—how you persuade people of *who you are* and move them to take action through the sheer power of you.

Les Brown, one of the top motivational speakers on today's stage, didn't start out with the gift of gab. Adopted along with his twin brother by a caring, hardworking domestic worker, the young Les was a restless daydreamer who couldn't concentrate on his schoolwork. In the fifth grade, a teacher labeled him "educable mentally retarded," and Les was sent back to the fourth grade. Although his mother told her boy that he had the potential to accomplish whatever he desired, Les's self-esteem was shot. In high school, a speech and drama instructor noticed his way with words. When the youth confessed to the teacher that he was "retarded," the teacher checked him: "Do not ever say that again! Someone's opinion of you does not have to become your reality!"

With the teacher's encouragement, Brown learned the power of eloquent speech and persuasive, rhythmic, stirring words that lift and inspire. Working as a sanitation worker after high school but longing to be a radio disc jockey, he nagged the owner of a local radio station until the man finally relented and hired Brown to perform odd jobs. He was in the right place at the right time when a disc jockey was so drunk on the air, the owner had no choice but replace him with the only other person at the station— Les Brown.

The rest, as the saying goes, is history. Brown killed it in his on-air debut and was eventually offered a full-time DJ spot. As his audience grew, he went from becoming a political commentator to a community activist to a three-term Ohio state legislator.

In the early 1980s Brown met master motivational speaker Zig Ziglar. Realizing that he, too, had the power of persuasion, Brown decided to become a motivational speaker himself. He devoured books, tapes, and anything else he could find. He lived and slept in his office until his career took off. He went from speaking at elementary schools and high schools to small groups in hotels to stadiums packed with audiences in the thousands.

> Being able to **tell your story in a way that motivates people** is huge.

Today, Brown is a world-renowned speaker, author, and television personality. His strongest gift is his ability to persuade with a great life story. And being able to tell your story in a way that motivates people to change their lives is huge. Many rappers do this—they use their street-smart gab-master skills to make albums that tell lifelong stories of pain and poverty and the hope of one day finding yourself a way out of rough times. Snoop Dogg, Tupac, Eminem, all came from the bottom by transferring their quick talk to wax to carve out their own version of the American dream.

Like Les Brown, I can move people with my stories of life in and out of the kitchen. My story gives me the credibility to walk into any hungry audience of workers and entrepreneurs and fire them up. I can get them to begin to see themselves in the big picture of life. Like Brown, I'm selling them my best product—myself and my personal transformation. And I get them to see how they can become their own best product, and market that product persuasively and successfully, just like I'm telling you to do in this chapter.

Marketing Your Brand

What's the one thing that your story is supposed to get across to your audience? The big idea from my story, and from Les Brown's, is transformation: convincing people that they have within them what it takes to change their lives.

But let's say you're not a motivational speaker with a come-back-kid story to tell. You still have a story—a story of who you are and what you have to offer. This is how you define yourself in whatever space you're in—entrepreneurial, corporate, social, or personal. In effect, it's your brand. I know you're not Nike or Chevrolet, but yes, every hustlepreneur has a brand, whether you're a small-business owner promoting your services or an employee looking to advance in your occupation. You already have one yourself, whether you know it or not. The only question is whether you're defining your brand or letting others do it for you. You need to get this, because if your brand isn't crystal clear, your marketing efforts will never move your product the way you want.

So what is your brand? To focus in on it, try to describe yourself and the way you want people to see you in one defining sentence. For me, it might be "Chef Jeff, the guy who went to prison, turned his life around, wrote a book, and became a celebrity chef, TV personality, and motivational speaker." Now, I've done and I do so much more than the sentence describes, but so what? If that's how people immediately identify and connect with my brand, I'm okay with it.

Chesley "Sully" Sullenberger will forever be remembered as that "heroic pilot who landed a plane in the Hudson River and saved everyone on board." Like it or not, it's Sullenberger's brand—

and a damn good one, I must say. President Barack Obama will always be known as "the first Black president." Now, that's one helluva defining sentence. And I'm sure Keme Henderson won't be mad if people define her as that "cookie lady who makes to-die-for, original, homemade cookies and cheesecakes."

So what's your defining sentence? What's the identity you've established that will compete for attention even if you're not in the room? If you're running an auto repair shop and willing to make house calls, it might be something like "Leroy, the dependable, professional mechanic on wheels who comes to the customer." Once you've got it down, start playing with condensed versions. Try something like this: "Leroy, the Mechanic on Wheels. We come to you, no matter where you are!" If you're looking for a job, your brand should zero in on the expertise and professional qualities you offer. Perhaps you're a "certified medical assistant with ten years' experience and a gift for working with patients." Or an "IT professional who can solve any tech problem in ten minutes or less."

Okay, that's probably promising too much—but you know what I'm saying. Write your defining sentence down, use it as often as possible, and promote it as many different ways as you can. This is where social media can really help you out. If you can, create a Website that showcases your business or your professional accomplishments (you can do this even if you don't have your own business—lots of job seekers do). If you do have a business, create a Facebook and Twitter page to promote it; link this to your personal page, if you're confident there's nothing there that makes you look unprofessional or unreliable. If you're in a corporate space, create a LinkedIn profile; use a short version of your defining sentence as a headline right below your name, and use the tools that site provides for showcasing your skills and experience and connecting with others in your lane.

If you're job hunting, don't forget that your résumé is a marketing tool, too. You can use some of the same skills we've talked about in this chapter to make it the sharpest tool possible: make it clear and positive (what results have you achieved in past jobs?), targeted to its audience (what qualifications do you have that perfectly match up with the job description?), and carefully considered (have an eagle-eyed friend, or two or three, proofread it before you send it anywhere).

Gregory Evans, once known as the *Hi-Tech Hustler* back in the day, has a different profile today: he's become a nationally known technology expert. After serving federal time for his tech crimes against some of the world's biggest corporations, today Greg is reformed and has marketed his extraordinary tech skills into a highly profitable cyber-consulting firm that works with companies to help them avoided getting hacked. He branded his unique story in the media as a regular on CNN, FOX, the *Tom Joyner Morning Show,* and the *Steve Harvey Morning Show.* Like me, Greg was born with gifts but used them for illegal gain; but today his street-smart skills have given him a second chance at life, and he's honed his brand to a fine point just like I described above.

What you're doing in all these steps is the heart of the gab-master's art: persuading people of the value of *you.* In the new world we're living in today, it's simple: this is what you have to do to get yours. To put it another way, you have to *persuade to upgrade!* If you don't market your product, no one's going to buy it, and you won't be one step closer to where you want to be in your life. If you *do* market yourself skillfully and tirelessly, your product's going to fly off the shelves, so to speak—and you're going to reach top speed in the fast lane to achieving your goals and making your vision real.

Street-Smart Challenges for:

The Gab-Master

☆ **Join the club.** Find a Toastmasters group near you (www.toastmasters.org) and visit a meeting—visits are free. If you like what you see and hear, join up.

☆ **Stop and listen.** The next conversation you have, make it a point to pause every time the other person stops speaking. See if they have more to say—or if the extra space allows you to form a better response.

☆ **Keep it positive.** For one day, frame everything you say in positive terms. Try not to let the words "don't" or "not" pass your lips.

☆ **Refine your brand.** Write out your "defining sentence," then show it to three people who know you well. See how accurately your sentence represents the way other people see you.

☆ **Write your résumé.** If you don't already have one, draft it now—you can find good samples online. If you do have one, bring it out for an overhaul. Challenge yourself to find new, compelling ways to frame your skills and accomplishments.

☆ **Get the word out.** Set up a LinkedIn profile for yourself or a Facebook page for your business, then invite as many friends and colleagues as you can to connect with you to build your network.

Street Smart #7

The Chameleon

The strategy of
adaptation

> *Adaptation is not about selling out, it's about gaining access to what you want in life.*
>
> — Chef Jeff

On the streets of L.A. and Southeast San Diego, my life and livelihood depended on my ability to navigate in neighborhoods dictated by gang and ZIP codes. I was never a violent guy, so I had to rely on my ability to blend into the neighborhood culture in order to do business and survive. I had to dress and act out the role strategically, depending on whom I was dealing with. When I was in the "red neighborhood" I made sure I had red on me somewhere; when I was in the "blue neighborhood" I made sure at the very least I had on a pair of Levi's 501 blue jeans. I was in full hustler mode around my old and potentially new customers. The thick gold rope chain around my neck, pinky ring laced with pavé diamond chips, my rag-top white 500 SEC—all the bells and whistles—legitimized the illusion that I was a real big baller. It impressed and motivated those who worked for me and with me and intimidated some who viewed me as a threat to their piece of the pie.

Yet I had to tone down all of these trappings of 'hood wealth in public settings as much as possible to avoid getting on the radar of the drug task force. When I made runs to L.A. to cop with a quarter of a million in the trunk, I drove a family-oriented rental car or my four-door Chevy Celebrity complete with a car seat and the original hubcaps. The diamond-crusted black-face Rolex watch and solid gold 14k benzo medallion stayed at home. I tried to look the part of a legitimate businessman wearing Polo khaki pants with a tucked-in Le Tigre golf shirt; I tried my best to really downplay my street persona. Because my illegal street hustle was wrong and there were too many uncontrollable forces against me, like jealous rivals, crack addict informers, and undercover narcs whose job it was to watch and bring down drug dealers, my little shenanigans were destined for failure. Still, the street-smart abilities that backstopped my million-dollar status were authentic, and they served me well in my prison and professional lives.

Being adaptable—a chameleon—was a matter of life or death on the streets and even more so in the joint. I learned when to play hard, when to be respectful, and when to be a quiet and detached observer. I was able to fit in with the Christian brothers, the Muslim sects, and the pan-African and socialist factions. When I was dealing with the mob bosses, I was reserved and courteous, calling them "Mr.," as in "Mr. Gambino." Respect is not only critical in the Mafia world, it's also a big part of the whole prison environment. In prison, my goal was to survive and get out unharmed and reformed. And when you're truly street smart, you play the role necessary to achieve the goal.

The Switch-Up

Unlike many inner-city youth, Dana Elaine Owens grew up in a two-parent, working-class home in Newark, New Jersey, and was surrounded by examples of stability, hard work, and independence. Her father was a policeman and her mother was a teacher. She learned about entrepreneurism from her grandfather, who owned a hardware store in Newark.

Intelligence is the ability to adapt to change.

— Stephen Hawking

At an early age, Dana was taught that if she wanted money, she had to go out and earn it. She did, taking a job at a local Burger King while still in high school. She learned that "success isn't guaranteed"—a lesson she holds on to today. And griping about things she didn't have, she also learned, was a waste of time.

"My thing is, I try not to complain about anything. I always go back to what my grandmother said about things. . . . 'Don't complain. No one wants to hear it anyways.'"

No one may have wanted to hear her complain, but millions today want to hear and see Dana E. Owens—aka Queen Latifah—sing, rap, act, and proudly celebrate her beauty in cosmetic commercials or on the covers of fashion, beauty, and entertainment magazines.

After she conquered the male-dominated hip-hop world, Queen Latifah's ability to strategically switch up her image allowed her to fit in in Hollywood, too, and to make her mark with diverse comedic, dramatic, and musical roles in such films as *Jungle Fever,* *House Party 2, The Bone Collector, The Secret Life of Bees* and *Set It Off.* Queen has won a Golden Globe Award, two Screen Actors Guild Awards, two Image Awards, and an Academy Award nomination for her role in the musical film *Chicago.* She wears multiple hats as an entertainer; entrepreneur; artist manager; co-CEO of her own record label, Flavor Unit Entertainment; author of *Put on Your Crown;* and the woman behind the Queen Collection, her Cover Girl cosmetics line.

The Queen is the ultimate chameleon, without a doubt.

Those little lizards that you see (or often don't see) between rocks and leaves are known for their ability to change their colors to match their surroundings—a life-saving defense mechanism that lets them evade predators so they can survive and thrive. For the street-smart human chameleon, it's very much the same. Certain tough neighborhoods demand that people adjust quickly to their surroundings. Some individuals can change characters on the drop of a dime, from square to wannabe gangster, depending on their perceptions of opportunity or immediate danger. These strategic chameleons understand they're prejudged by their ZIP codes and body language. They instinctively change the way they walk, talk, or dress when applying for a job or a loan or when they pass by gangbangers on the streets or the police in high-crime neighborhoods. Some tone down the bass in their voices to appear less threatening. Others adopt an aggressive persona so they won't come across as weak or soft.

In truth, there's nothing weak about being a chameleon. The word itself means the very opposite—it comes from Greek words that mean "ground" and "lion," so it translates, essentially, into "the lion on the ground." And this lion's skill has never been more necessary. Technology today has led to a world of easy global access. We no longer compete just on the block, in the neighborhood, or within a city. We now have to fit in with cultures and people around the world. Business opportunities and challenges come from China, India, Africa, and everywhere in between. My success, your success, everybody's success in today's game of life depends on our ability to adapt to and capitalize on ever-expanding and exciting change.

In this chapter, we look at what street-smart chameleons have to do to blend in for success in the places where their vision can take root and grow.

Adapting for Access

My chameleon ability to change quickly came in mighty handy when I got out of prison. Oh, I still have a bit of street swagger on occasion, but I had to master the ability to turn it up and down at the right times, like the flames on a gas stove. If you catch me having conversations on the block or with a group of juveniles or felons who are locked up, on parole, or on probation, you might see me with my arms crossed, or with my hands in my pockets, laid back and using broken English. But catch me in the corporate world or in the first-class section of a plane and you'll see and hear a totally different Jeff: arms at my sides, head up, walking straight up, smiling, and maintaining eye contact. Those profiles require a polished self-presentation. Believe it or not, even the most polished person has a totally different persona on display when he's not onstage, addressing superiors at an important meeting, or in front of a camera.

It's not about being phony. I'm an authentic person with chameleon skills, strategically surviving and thriving in a world of multiple audiences. The chameleon is the master of defining, respecting, and delivering what his audience needs. He adapts to the world around him because he understands that it doesn't work the other way around.

The rule of street-smart adaptation can pose a challenge for those who've always lived by the street credo that credibility comes from not caring what anyone thinks—that authenticity means you are who you are and that's that. The truth is that when you step into the mainstream, you need to understand that it isn't all about you anymore. You need an attitude of "we're all in this together," not "I'm the only player in this game."

Before you start thinking that the odds are stacked against you, let me say this: adaptation is a two-way street, my friend. I've met big-time hip-hop artists in person who are not in the least like their onstage persona. Most were never raised on the mean streets, or should I say the 'hood. They've just knowledge-jacked gangster life stories and incorporated them to promote a thug-life brand, playing roles to hype their music and get paid. Offstage their mental game and conversation is as suited for business as a mainstream CEO's. And we all do some version of this, most of the time. We don't dress the same way to go to church as we do to go to a basketball game or to shop at the mall. We don't put our feet up on the table at a restaurant. Adapting is just a matter of knowing which "you" to put on display.

> **Adapting is just a matter of knowing which "you" to put on display.**

Even if you were raised in a trailer park, you can give an impression of being a Main Street veteran if you switch up some things about you. It's possible to incorporate the look, the talk, the walk—the shoes, eyewear, hairdo, watch, and lingo to reflect where you want to go instead of where you've been. You can jack it all day long and make it your brand. However, you must make these changes consciously and consistently. If you overapply them and come off as way out of your league, you'll have the value and credibility of a three-dollar bill.

Do a written inventory of yourself, vow to change what's not consistent with how you want people to perceive you, and then make sure you track your progress. Keep in mind, if you get a job based on the personal brand and the skills you sold the employer, you *must* deliver. And never oversell your abilities. A chameleon can always get a job, but it's the smart chameleon who can keep it.

Dress—and Walk and Talk—for Success

Let's say your gift of gab has landed you an extraordinary opportunity and you have the attention of your boss's boss. You've finally landed that interview for a dream job or a chance to advance your career. It's time for your switch-up.

Many of the people who conduct job interviews come from the 'burbs or outside inner-city areas. They watch the news and see mug shots of people arrested for robbery, murder, drug sales, or cheating the welfare system. Don't walk into their offices looking and sounding like the images they've seen on the evening news or on *The Jerry Springer Show*. They may not say anything, but believe me, red flags are going up like crazy. In the back of their minds they're thinking, "OMG, he (or she) is one of them!"

A legit change-up defuses negative projections of you and creates some space for reasonable doubt. That's when you can use prejudice to your advantage. When you bust the stereotype, the person who wrote you off is confronted with the fact that she's prejudged you. Your appearance and performance may have caused her to doubt her motives, and that could spark a change of heart to make her mistake right.

Americans love a great "comeback story." Most people are moved to help somebody who appears to be helping himself. If you've made mistakes in life, make sure you have a legit comeback story, not a victim's blame game or begging plea—few people have time for weak feel-sorry-for-me stories today.

With all that said, there are lots of people from low-income communities with huge amounts of low self-esteem. Many use clothing, jewelry, or cars to subliminally say "I am somebody, too, look at me." Some like colorful clothing, loud four-piece suits with bright hankies, godfather derby hats, knock-off Coach purses, and multiple rings on their fingers and gold chains around their necks. Others go around rocking low-rider jeans and Major League baseball caps.

Sporting ghetto fabulous wear like Timberlands, Jordans, or Chuck Taylors to interviews is like going swimming in body armor: you know it's just a matter of time until you sink. The non-White job candidate most upscale employers want wears Johnston & Murphy wingtip shoes with tassels and socks that play to the belt and shirt. Women often have to ditch the booty-fitting jeans, the high-heel knockoff red-soled pumps, the too-long overdecorated French nails, and the fake designer handbags. These played-out fashion trends are rooted in the narrow-minded attitude of "I live my life the way I want, this is how I roll, love me or hate me." But the chameleon understands that one-color, conservative business and dress suits are what catch the corporate eye, the one that's constantly observing who is fit to move up the ladder because he reps the company culture and who will be kicked off it faster than Donald Trump can say, "You're fired!"

I had to drop my gold chain, goatee, and street gear when I entered the high-end corporate culinary world. That look just didn't fit in. As I transitioned in life, I became what fellas back in the neighborhood called "hip square" or "a buster." I studied the way the up-and-coming Generation X CEOs and dapper William Morris Endeavor agents dressed, the way they wined and dined and carried themselves with their colleagues and clients. Their hip-square swag translated into a golden ticket into the upper middle class. That's how I wanted to roll. I covered my earring hole with my wife's foundation and made sure I was well groomed—no hairs hanging from my nose or ears, clean-shaven, and nonthreatening.

I even focused on the way I sat. I stopped the slumping in chairs with my legs spread apart gangster-style. I started eating differently, trying sushi, Thai food, and various Italian dishes I'd never eaten before. When dining with corporate executives or top chefs, I'd take little bites as opposed to throwing down on my food the way I did in prison and as a kid. I started sipping high-end imported bottled water and ordering salads with ingredients like herbed goat cheese, cranberries, and candied pecans and dressed with wood-barrel-aged balsamic vinaigrette.

A true champion can adapt to anything.

— Floyd Mayweather, Jr.

You see, as a street-smart chameleon, I'm always aware that some of these people may know my background and be looking for the signs of my past life. I don't give them the expected; I carry myself with an aura of class, intelligence, and humility—the unmistakable signs of my personal growth.

I tailor the way I speak to my audience, too—just the way I do when I'm speaking in front of a group of schoolteachers or a group of felons. Chameleons know when it's time to be done with the street talk, substitute for the curse words, and say "How are you today?" instead of "Waddup?" They know when standard English rather than street slang is the preferred line of communication in their lane—and when it's okay to let things get a little more colorful, you know what I'm saying.

They also know when to keep their mouths shut altogether. When I managed kitchens at the Marriott and the Bellagio, I did not discuss race, religion, or politics unless an authority figure asked my opinion. Even then, I'd give short natural answers that didn't relay my loyalties or betray any alliances. Opinions can be a problem in some conservative or liberal environments, so I don't go there, whether I'm Republican or Democrat, Christian or Muslim. The chameleon doesn't disclose personal stuff, at least not right away; it's an invitation to stand out in the *wrong* way.

How to Be the Chameleon

So far in these chapters we've talked about ways to increase your knowledge base and your ability to take risks, sacrifice, heighten your awareness, and discipline yourself from within. Now we have to work on your outside—the parts of you that people see and react to first. The way for you to build up your strategic chameleon strength is to consciously change your outside game.

You do this by always asking key questions about your audience and your environment: "Where am I and who am I talking to?" You have to closely scrutinize the field in which you want to play and honestly ask, "Do I fit in, with no second-guessing?" If the answer is no, then you have to ask: "What must I do to get in, where I fit in?"

You start the process by clearly noting and breaking down the top visual impressions and impact created by the people you admire who have already achieved what you're aiming for in life. Let's say your list includes some of my mental mentors who I knowledge-jack all the time—Jay-Z, Marcus Buckingham, Chef Thomas Keller, Bishop T. D. Jakes, Tony Robbins. Take a look at how they roll. What can you pick up and use in your own playbook to blend into the environment where you want to be? Maybe they wear dark suits, matching ties, and modern jewelry; maybe they wear white Egyptian cotton chef coats, dark chef slacks, and black-rimmed glasses; maybe they're clean-shaven, with hella white teeth and manicured hands. Let them inspire you to find ways to strategically change up *your* swagger.

Chameleons are never-ending change agents. They are the first-class role players, and they have to be to fill the openings available for a good, marketable employee who blends in with the company's brand and culture. This is why, before I applied for top-notch jobs, I'd conduct reconnaissance missions. Just as a burglar cases a joint before breaking in, I'd check out places where I might get hired before officially applying for the job. I'd go to the restaurant and have a meal so I could chat with the waiters and hostesses. I'd hang out in alleys behind the restaurant where the employees took cigarette breaks. With a carefully worded compliment or pump-up, I'd start a friendly conversation: "Hey man, how are you? Who's the head chef here? Do you know if they're hiring? What's it like working here?"

As if studying for a part, the change agent has to get as much information as possible to land the role. Go online and find information about the company where you wish to be employed, the bank where you'll be applying for a small-business loan, or the neighborhood where you're thinking of moving. Try to find out about the department head's likes and dislikes, the company brand, the workplace atmosphere, and how people conduct themselves. Get to know the company's mission statement, its goals and objectives. Learn something about its unique niche in the marketplace. Use this information when you get to the interview to blow away any negative perceptions the interviewer might have had.

Man in the Mirror

Long before there was a Queen Latifah, there was Ronald Reagan—a master chameleon who went from acting in films to playing the ultimate role of President of the United States. He was versatile enough to switch roles and make people believe that he wasn't just an actor; he was a charismatic statesman and a leader capable of governing the state of California and, later, the nation.

Like Latifah, Reagan was also a salesman. In the 1950s, he served as the host of General Electric Theater on television and went around the country speaking at GE plants. He was transitioning from an onscreen actor to an everyman who understood the circumstances of everyday people. As writer Lou Cannon noted in a commentary after Reagan's death in 2004, the actor had a way of "using folksy anecdotes that ordinary people could understand."

> Getting your foot in the door is just the first step; you need to keep earning your access.

On June 12, 1987, Reagan stood before the Berlin Wall—a real and symbolic divide between Eastern and Western Europe—and issued the now famous directive to Mikhail Gorbachev, leader of the Soviet Union: "Mr. Gorbachev, tear down this wall!"

It was part diplomacy and part showmanship. Those words didn't make Gorbachev quake in his boots, run out, and start chipping away at the wall. They did, however, help seal Reagan's legacy as the leader of the free world.

Hollywood or politics may not be your destination, but you still have to draft an image that mirrors who what you want to be and what you want to accomplish. Chameleons know the bottom line of adaptation: when you're deliberate about creating a certain impression, you're doing it to create a specific and desired result. You're working to fit in not just for fun, but so you can get the thing you really want—so you can execute your action plan and achieve your goals.

It's time for the kind of straight talk that's beyond political correctness. There's no use denying that light skin/dark skin, nappy hair/straight hair, and urban style/suburban style discrimination still exists. Your look depends on the job or career you're trying to get.

You have to stay real with this. Black men, especially dark-skinned Black men with full beards, have to accept the fact that some in our society fear them because of negative stereotyping in the media. So you can't play to the stereotype. A cowboy hat and a full beard may be a good look if you're seeking a gig with the rodeo or in a country-western bar, but it won't work in the Ritz-Carlton or Bellagio VIP services. A Latina woman who wants to work the front desk at the Four Seasons or Hotel Bel-Air won't be taken seriously if she shows up for an interview popping gum, with black pencil-drawn eyebrows and pierced body parts. That image doesn't reflect or enhance the hotel's high-end brand. Forget about it.

Now, this is not to say you have to chop off your beloved locks, slick back your spiky hair, plug your earring holes, or drop the urban culture you grew up on. There are some industries—fashion, hip-hop, entertainment, social media—where hip and urban is cool and profitable. Jimmy Iovine, the iconic music producer and chairman of Interscope Geffen A&M, still sports his trademark baseball cap and hoodie at age 60, because it's part of his brand. As I mentioned earlier, Dr. Dre, Iovine's partner in the designer headphone business Beats, is just as effective in the streets as he is in the business world, adapting his attire to the people, the places, and the business he needs to accomplish.

If your intended career path caters primarily to African Americans or Latinos, then maybe the locks or braids or that particular Latino or Afrocentric swagger is just what the employers are looking for to gain deeper penetration into the lucrative urban market. However, if you want to get your foot in the nonurban door, I recommend shaking the urban look. Once you get past the probationary period, once you're classified as a permanent and a valuable member of the crew, then you can let your hair down, literally and figuratively, for real; I mean, then you can take your costume off. But when you do, make sure your game stays tight and your contributions to the company are beyond criticism. Getting your foot in the door is just the first step; you need to keep earning your access.

Now, don't be thinking it's only those of us from the mean streets who have to watch the signals we're sending with our look. Mark Zuckerberg, the young CEO of Facebook, made the news from *The New York Times* to *Forbes* to style blogs when he showed up for meetings with potential investors in the social-media giant's first public offering, wearing—you got it—his habitual hoodie. The critics didn't know what to make of it: Was it a slap in the face to the business establishment that a new generation was staking its claim in the elite billionaire club? A signal of disrespect for his would-be investors? A sign that Zuckerberg was just too busy changing the face of social media to worry about things like his clothes? Perhaps you're thinking that when you're a 20-something billionaire, you don't need to adapt to your surroundings in quite the same way as an ordinary striver. But even Mark Zuckerberg can change his colors when it's called for: he wore a suit to meet with President Park Geun-hye of South Korea in 2013 before putting the hoodie back on for a visit to Samsung.

Even Zuckerberg knows how powerful visual impressions are, what a strong signal of belonging. And this was tragically apparent in another set of headlines in 2012, when teenage Trayvon Martin was shot and killed in a gated Florida community by a neighborhood watch volunteer. Trayvon had looked "real suspicious," the shooter told police. What he was wearing at the time? A hoodie, and he was a Black male.

Leave Your Comfort Zone Behind

We're all comforted by people who look, behave, and think the way we do. The rise in cable news over the past 20 years can be attributed to the fact that people can pick and choose news programs—be it FOX, CNN or MSNBC—that complement or validate their points of view. This may be convenient and soul-soothing, but it does little to open your world to new ideas and perspectives.

Living in your comfort zone slows your potential to grow

> **Truly successful people force themselves out of their comfort zones.**

mentally, psychologically, and socially. Likewise, if you only hang around people who mimic your lifestyle and values, you're never challenged to analyze, recognize, or change your deficiencies.

Truly successful people force themselves out of their comfort zones and build their chameleon muscle every day. They go places and hang around people who are totally unlike them to sharpen their social and communication skills. If you're Black, spend more time with non-Blacks, and vice versa. Asians, Latinos, and other ethnicities should mingle with Blacks and Whites, just to understand what social or political values and experiences they share.

If you're a Democrat, attend a Republican function—seek to respectfully learn their passions and platforms. Be bold! Get out there and mingle in unknown arenas. Join book clubs and groups, go to museum exhibit openings, political rallies, mosques, and synagogues. Learn how people outside your norm socialize, think, talk, dress, and congregate.

The point is to force yourself outside yourself. If we were to walk out to my car right now and open the trunk, you'd find a set of golf clubs. Honestly, my golf game is weak. But I force myself to play outside my comfort zone because influential people I know or want to know *love* golf. It doesn't matter how good I am at the end of the day; what matters is that I've strategically placed myself in the company of men and women who are currently in the lane I want to roll in. This welcome discovery has led to great rounds of golf and even greater rounds of opportunity-making conversations with influential people.

That said, here's a piece of good advice I picked up in my earlier life: know your role. We're all actors in this production called life, but playing a role not suited for you can quickly blow your cover. Know your stuff and stay in your lane. I'm a pretty good chameleon at times, but I can't pretend to be an engineer or an architect. I'm a chef, speaker, and deal-maker, and I'm pretty good at what I do, too.

Beware: there will be individuals inside and outside your circle who really will accuse you of "selling out" or compromising for "the man." Block out the haters. Like I said before, it's not about selling out; it's about gaining access to information so you see beyond your current views, change your circumstances, and adapt successfully to your new reality. You can either be a player or a pawn in the game of life—there's no in between.

The Chameleon

☆ **Spot the standout.** The next time you're in a public place, look for someone who isn't fitting in. What sets him or her apart?

☆ **Follow your model.** Choose someone you see frequently; for one week (subtly!) snatch his or her look or behavior traits. It doesn't have to be someone you want to emulate in the long run—it's just for practice!

☆ **Talk the talk.** For one day, make it a point to speak in a way that's different from your normal vocabulary and tone. Choose a mode of speech from a world you'd like to enter.

☆ **Walk the walk.** For one day, carry yourself the way one of your role models does—whether it's someone in your life or someone in the public eye.

☆ **Play the role.** Take yourself into an environment you're not familiar with—a neighborhood, a restaurant—and do your best to fit in in the way you dress, speak, and act. Bring a friend with you for some objective feedback on how well you blend.

☆ **Learn from an expert.** Interview someone you know who has adapted to a new workplace, home, or school environment. How did he do it? What can you learn?

The Crew-Master

The strategy of
collaboration

> One is never enough—
> you need your crew to get yours.
>
> — Chef Jeff

A few years back, I had the opportunity to work on a very special cookbook. The *America I AM Pass It Down Cookbook* showcased Black Americans' collective food history in 130 soul-inspired recipes, plus stories and essays and cooking tips, gathered from real home cooks across the country who came together to share their knowledge and love, food and family.

In the preface to the book, I recounted my interview with Maya Angelou—the great poet, civil rights activist, and American icon who also happens to be a celebrated cook—about what food means and has meant in the lives of Black people from slavery times to today. Let me tell you, I was a little nervous; I knew what food meant to my family, but I would have never imagined I would someday discuss the power of food with a cultural icon.

Maya put me right at ease, though, when she started talking about how her grandmother always kept a pot of rice on the stove and how much she loved and admired her—the person who had helped form her deep connection with food. Her intimate conversation with me about her grandmother in the kitchen and the older woman's food philosophy felt magical. And it transported me back in time in my own life, back to the late 1960s and early '70s, when my sister and I would visit our grandparents' home on 77th Street in Los Angeles nearly every weekend and on every holiday. When we were over for dinner, they'd set out large platters of crispy fried chicken, slow-cooked collard greens, smothered pork chops, stuffed bell peppers, and hot link sandwiches, plus traditional side dishes like candied yams, red beans and rice, and string beans with neck bones—food that connected them to their New Orleans and Alabama roots and, more importantly, connected us all to one another.

As I traveled across the country for *Pass It Down,* gathering recipes and talking about the importance of sharing our legacy in food, I met many extraordinary people who shared their own stories of food and life. And when it came to putting the book together, so many people had a hand in it—talented cooks, writers, food and wine experts, food historians, and editors. Through it all, even though I had already stacked up some serious culinary cred at Hotel Bel-Air and the Bellagio, and as a best-selling author of *Cooked,* I started to get a whole new take on what it means to be "top chef." In a word, whether you're at the stove in your home kitchen or in front of the cameras on the Food Network, cooking is all about the crew.

Larger Than Ourselves

In many ways, food—the cooking, eating, and sharing of it—is the ultimate collaboration. We build our first so-called crew right in our family, and our first shared efforts are all about food, from the time we start setting the table as small children to the time we're heads of households in charge of getting the whole family fed. That's the principle behind my new TV show in national syndication, *Family Style with Chef Jeff,* which is a collaboration like no other. Invited guests come to my kitchen, where together we cook America's comfort food made healthier—which also means partnering with local farmers, growers, and food producers to get the best and the freshest, whether it's just-picked greens or fresh fish line-caught in the local lake.

One time in Atlanta, while shopping in a local grocery store for ingredients I needed to do a cooking demonstration at the National Black Arts Festival, I got into a conversation with an elderly White woman. She was navigating her way with her electric scooter, heading toward the baking section. As I assisted her, our casual conversation rapidly turned to Southern cooking. We talked about canning peaches and the best way to cook collard greens using scrap meat. She even told me quite passionately that fried chicken is best if cooked in pork fat. Our cook-to-cook exchange reminded me that Southern White folks' cooking was not radically different from Southern Black folks' cooking, because we'd helped to define the region's food.

For centuries, this was the kind of sharing that kept our people going. On a daily basis, family and friends came together for the main meal of the day and for conversation. Growing up in poverty, dinner was the one daily event that put a smile on our faces. We've lost a lot of traditions, but holding my family close during Sunday dinner, that's one special moment that I try to hold on to, to this day. There are other family values that still connect me to my family as well: just like my grandparents, I always keep a private stock of my granddaddy's inspired seafood gumbo in the freezer.

> Food, for most of us, gives us **our first lesson in working together.**

Passing down food customs and recipes from one generation to the next like this is another form of collaboration—not just on a meal, but on a cultural legacy. Everyone has his or her own approach to a dish, and every home cook collaborates with family members or friends to give a new twist to a family favorite and pass the new flavor on down the line. And when this legacy is all you have to leave for those who come after you—the way it has been and still is for many people—it's all the more precious. Any way you slice it, food, for most of us, gives us our first lesson in working together in the service of something larger than ourselves.

One Is Never Enough

One person can prepare a simple meal, but that same person can't assemble a family feast singlehandedly, or everything would be cold by the time the last dish made it to the table! Let's face it: not much that's bigger than just us can be done successfully by just one person all on his or her own. Unless you are a master of all things—and I've met none—it's not humanly possible to be a one-man show. To put it another way, one is never enough—you need your crew to get yours.

On the streets, your crew can determine life or death when you're living in the fast lane of illegal gain. My Meadowbrook crew back in the day in San Diego was an all-star team of gifted street smarters that consisted of hustlers, shot-callers, salesmen, gab-masters, and fighters, all with major street and prison credibility. We all had our own collaborations in different neighborhoods with individuals who played a role in our organization's wealth development. Relationships, sales, and marketing were my unique gifts, which allowed me to chart the course of the crew and forecast yearly revenue. Though I was never voted boss of the crew, I was respected and looked to for direction—but when you got right down to it, we relied on one another for our livelihood as well as our survival.

On Main Street it's much the same, though the stakes aren't always life and death. Thinking back to the world of food, where we started this conversation, an event like a neighborhood picnic or bake sale takes coordinated collective action: someone is assigned the task of making flyers and getting the word out. Another dependable person makes sure the meat is cooked right or the baking is done. And of course, there's probably a trusted person in charge of collecting, counting, and turning in the money. One person can't do it alone—and if the people doing the work don't work together, that picnic isn't going to go down right.

Collaboration is also a must for a successful business of any kind. Thankfully, collaboration has always been in my DNA. It's a street-smart survival skill I adopted early on in life. Delegating responsibilities to those who do them best works for me. It's part of what I did best on the streets and what I do still today: smart leaders don't work hard, they work smarter than the competition.

Smart leaders of all kinds of crews—whether they're corporate executives, street CEOs, or bake-sale ladies—know that effective collaborations include delegating, networking, and the art of alliance building. You're not doing anyone any favors by trying to do all things yourself. Not only are you spinning in circles and slowing your journey to mastery, you're denying someone else the chance to combine his or her unique strengths with yours so that both of you can reap the rewards of a strong, strategic partnership.

About five years ago, as I mentioned, I had the opportunity to meet Gerry Fernandez, president and founder of Multicultural Foodservice & Hospitality Alliance (MFHA). This nonprofit organization is dedicated to advocating and educating about workplace diversity. It helps corporate leaders effectively tap into, engage with, and build strong and efficient multicultural businesses and communities. Back in 2008, Gerry asked me to join his lineup of presenters who could inspire audiences from hospitality companies and the culinary industry that had interests in helping inner-city kids succeed.

Both of us stood to benefit. Gerry was in need of someone to shake up the culinary industry with a little street swagger, someone from the rank and file who came up in the business and could relate with young people from low-income communities. As for me, I still work off and on with Gerry today because speaking at his events has opened many other professional doors for me and has led to other chances to share my story and lessons of life transformation with diverse audiences. It's because of this collaboration with Gerry that I've met and shared the stage with *New York Times* best-selling authors like Malcolm Gladwell and Stephen Dubner, co-author of the acclaimed book *Freakonomics*.

Working with Gerry was a win-win situation all around—collaboration the way it's supposed to go down—in part because we didn't just recognize how it could help us; we put in the effort to make it happen. As Henry Ford put it, "Coming together is a beginning; keeping together is progress; working together is success."

Your Missing Ingredients

In my collaboration with Gerry Fernandez, each of us had something the other needed—and understanding just what that something is, that's the first step toward a successful partnership. When I have a challenge with a recipe for my TV show, I have three or four chefs I call who help me in certain cooking areas where I'm weaker. It really is just like a company has a board of directors, or the President has the cabinet members. The President may not be an expert in defense, intelligence, or land management, but he has people with the necessary know-how holding down those cabinet posts.

Now, don't be thinking there's any shame in admitting someone else might have something you need. We've already seen that no one can do it all alone—not even the President! Even players at the top of their game need to lean on others for skills, strengths, or connections they don't possess.

Jimmy Iovine began his career as a recording engineer in the mid-1970s. Today, the iconic music producer and chairman of Interscope Geffen A&M is one of the hippest cats in the music biz. He has been credited with putting Eminem and Dr. Dre together —enough said—and he co-produced *Get Rich or Die Tryin'*, which featured 50 Cent in his debut acting role.

Five guys on the court working together can achieve more than five talented individuals who come and go as individuals.

— Kareem Abdul-Jabbar

Iovine was savvy enough to know that he needed someone with raw street credibility to market gangster rap successfully. In young 50 Cent, he found someone with a direct connection to the audience Interscope wanted to reach, and the two teamed up, first to release 50's debut album and then to start the rapper's own label within Interscope, G-Unit Records. Iovine has since collaborated with Dr. Dre (who's equally effective in street and mainstream business) to produce and market Beats by Dre, a high-performance line of headphones designed for today's "hard-beat" music lovers. The headphones were designed to tap primarily into the urban and suburban youth markets, but Iovine and Dre were savvy enough to design an executive set for street-smart executives as well.

To reach the new heights that both 50 Cent and Iovine dreamed of, they needed to combine their greatest strengths. That's what collaboration is all about: bringing your very best to the table along with somebody else who's bringing his very best, so that together you can elevate your game. But let's be clear: serious collaboration isn't for egotists or idlers. It's for savvy visionaries who know how to "see it," and at the same time are street-smart and committed enough that they can "be it," too, and not just talk about it.

Your reasons for creating effective partnerships through collaboration may be like mine: to gain experience and exposure to other opportunities. Or they could be like Iovine's and Dre's: to create something that's going to help you live large and fulfill your dreams. Whatever the reason, building your crew starts with asking yourself a few simple questions.

The Five Questions

The first step in masterminding collaborations is to get clear on what you're trying to accomplish. What is your vision, what are your goals, and what's the action plan that's going to get you there? Once you got that, you're ready to move forward with five straight-up questions—the **what, who, why, how,** and **when** of building your crew.

What are my missing ingredients? The only way you're going to find the people tailor-made to help you make your vision a reality is by first identifying exactly what you need. You may have brilliant ideas but suck at explaining them in a way that people get it. Maybe you got major gift of gab but you're weak at pricing, accounting, and paperwork. Whatever you lack, write it down. Get it on paper so you can continue to focus in on exactly what you're missing and build an A-team of savvy collaborators.

In your "know thyself" inventories, you had an opportunity to get up close and personal with some areas that are not your most natural strengths, so this shouldn't be difficult for you now. Being able to call those weaknesses out is a great asset because it gives you a map for figuring out some of the skills that you need to make sure are reflected in your crew.

If you're not detail-oriented, it's important to have a crew member who sweats all of the small stuff. If you're not a helluva gabmaster, then make sure you recruit someone who possesses those skills and will enjoy using them on your crew. If you're generous to some degree, then you better have someone who doesn't wear his heart on his sleeve to manage your inventory and keep an eye on the books, or your business may go broke from offering too many freebies for friends. Your team should be like the five fingers on your hand: they are always more powerful when they operate together than when they operate separately.

Now that you've written your shortcomings, it's time for the next question: **Who can supply what I need?** Set out to find those in your neighborhood or town who have the skills to complement yours. In the best-case scenario, who do you need to partner up with?

> Your team should be like the five fingers on your hand: always more powerful working together than separately.

Just the way you made a list of potential mentors in the chapter on the knowledge-jacker, write up a list of the people you want on your team. Then go get 'em! It may seem like I'm making it sound easier than it really is, but that's the spirit of the American dream. You have a vision. It's achievable and real and will benefit others. The key is to take the time necessary to find someone with the skills you need who's willing to work with you.

Which leads to the next question: **Why should these people work with me?** What are the benefits of partnering with you? How does an alliance with you help someone else accomplish his own goals? What's the best-case and worst-case outcome of the collaboration you're putting on the table? What's the win-win for all players? Are you offering a moneymaking enterprise, community service, or collective growth—or are you pursuing a deep personal ambition, such as something you want to accomplish for your family? How are you going to convince the people on your list that it's in their interest to support your vision and buy into the outcomes? Write your answers down and use them as part of your selling points after you've pinpointed your potential partner.

Now you've got the what, the who, and the why, we've arrived at the how. The same way you did with that list of mentors, ask yourself, *How can I can get next to each of the people on my crew list.* Do you know them personally? Does someone you know have a connection? Next to each of the names on your list, make a note of how you're going to make contact.

There's just one question left: *When is the right time to put this partnership together?* Think about when you'll realistically be ready to take the next step in, say, your business venture. There's no point in putting your crew together too early in the game—it could even backfire—but if you wait too long, you may let opportunities pass you by. Set a timeline for yourself with the steps you'll take to go after the people on your list. Write the timeline down, too.

Assembling Your Smarter-Than-You Crew

You don't want just anybody on your crew; your selections must be business- and outcome-driven. This is your vision, your livelihood we're talking about, ladies and gentlemen! Trust, integrity, and character are mandatory for building lifetime, productive collaborations. In some ways, it's just like a personal relationship. The most bulletproof relationships are those where the partners enhance one another's strong points and lessen one another's weaknesses.

Book smarters and street smarters, for example, may operate in different lanes, but they can complement each other's strengths. True, they come from different worlds, and that can make relationship building awkward or threatening. Reducing suspicion and fear takes time. Think of collaborations as the investment necessary to build a successful relationship. Let's be real—jumping into bed with a late-night call can be very hazardous in many ways. Likewise, with collaborations, you need to take your time. Strategically speaking, dates hold hands, find common ground, and discover each other's dreams and desires. Look for people who have what you really need, take time to give real tests along the way, and make absolutely sure that your potential collaborators can pass the tests. To gain a spot on your crew, each person you invite to the table needs to share your vision, expand the skill sets of your enterprise, and deliver with timeliness and integrity. And they all need to bring something you don't already possess; that's why I call them your "smarter-than-you" team.

I've told you how I basically stalked Chef Robert Gadsby because I knew that landing a spot on his culinary crew would sharpen my cooking game and give me the in-kitchen exposure and knowledge of chefdom that I needed to reach my full potential. And you can best believe he made me pass some tests before I gained a spot on his crew! I had to prove myself by showing I could work well with others from the very bottom up—remember, I started as a janitor/dishwasher—and proving I was someone he could trust.

And that's exactly what you need to be doing, too. Doesn't matter if you're building a crew of 2, 4, or 400. Just the way you need to bring your A game every single time in the pursuit of your vision, you need to bring your A team, too. Don't settle for anything, or anyone, less.

The Street-Smart Manager

The unfortunate truth is that most business partnerships, whether they're made on the streets or on the golf course, will crash and burn because not enough work has gone into creating a well-functioning collaboration—the parties involved haven't thought through the questions you now know to ask, or given themselves a chance to get to know each other. Partnerships must have solid foundations like concrete, with powerful purpose, and there must be trust in order to please all players. Oftentimes, we place our own selfish, ego-driven interests ahead of the people we've recruited to our teams. We forget that they have dreams and desires, too, and we fail to fully engage their talents. But it can never be just about you. We shortchange ourselves and create animosity when we don't ask their advice or give them the authority to act. Crew members wind up feeling dissed and shut out of the process, so they eventually bail and go right to the competition. I set out to avoid this as soon as I started supervising employees in major hotels: I didn't run a "me" kitchen, I ran a "we" kitchen. After all, the crew-master is only as good as his or her crew.

The crew is the basic unit that needs to function as one in order to achieve any goal—think of a work crew fixing potholes on the highway—and street-smart crew-masters are the managers, dispatching people and resources to get results. They're team leaders who know exactly how each member of the team functions best. They're not afraid to take charge; they understand that someone has to be the head cook, or else the meal turns into chaos. And they know that what keeps a team bonded is a strong sense of shared purpose and shared experience, just like the experience I had with the team that put together the *Pass It Down Cookbook*.

> I didn't run a "me" kitchen, I ran a "we" kitchen.

I don't care if you're the owner of a neighborhood dive or the head of Apple, the manager of a small office or the person who steps up to coordinate a family member's health care: effective team leaders move with charisma, conviction, integrity, and respect for those they lead. They understand the power of the team and how important it is that all members feel appreciated and involved in the process, like some of the power to achieve a purpose is in their hands. If they don't—for example, if you don't delegate—envy and doubt set in and leadership comes into question. Your team starts to feel that you regard them as incompetent or untrustworthy. They can't see how their dreams are going to materialize if you insist on being the only star of the show. But great team leaders, once they've locked in their key players, become like coaches never allowing their players' talents to go to waste on the sidelines. They make them feel appreciated, valued, and involved all the way to the bank.

What if you're not a manager—yet? What if you're an entry-level employee reporting to a boss? Well, I hope you're gaining a new appreciation for the street-smart skills your boss has to bring to the table. But I also hope you're appreciating what *you* bring, too. Collaboration is a two-way street, and every single member of a team is a key part of its success. You can use the same strategies we've discussed in this chapter to figure out how the different parts of your team fit together—who's strong in one area, who's rock-solid in another, and how all of you stand to benefit from your collaboration—then use that knowledge every day to do your own job smarter and better.

Out of the Spotlight

When you take the spotlight off yourself, it shines on the needs and desires of your team. The team members become stakeholders in your dream when their honest pushback, feedback, and contributions are respected and acted upon. And if the personal and professional benefits are clear to them, they have an incentive to work productively so they, too, can reap the rewards of the crew.

It takes humility and checked egos to maintain good collaborations. Make sure you check yourself constantly as you go through the process. I've got an old saying, "little mouth/big ears," that applies perfectly here. Practice keeping your opinion to yourself at times and truly listening to your partners as much as possible. Don't let ego discount the contributions of others, even if you don't always agree with them. Force yourself to use the skill of compromise. There may be a time when that little internal voice tells you to stay on a certain course, even when you're advised to change lanes. If you have to follow your gut (which I recommend), do it in a way that acknowledges the input of others. Here's an example:

"Kasha and Alfonso, you've helped me see the big picture clearer. I've made a few minor modifications, but your work has definitely moved us forward. Big thanks to you two. If we do this right, we'll all be able to cash a nice bonus check this coming holiday season!"

With statements like these, you've acknowledged the contributions of others, alerted them that you're going a different direction, but also let them know that they are included in the possible rewards.

My ex-boss Wolfgang Von Wieser at the Bellagio was a master of this. He always showed his underchefs love and praise as he made his rounds, with pump-ups such as "Good morning, Chef, what can I do to assist you?" or "Great job this month." It went a long way for us chefs on the line." Result? I would have taken a bullet for Wolfgang any day. He understood the power of collaboration, and it made the job easier for himself and everyone else on the crew.

Collaborating for the Greater Good

Collaboration, at its most basic, is people coming together to work for something larger than themselves—whether it's a one-time project, a small business, or a movement for social change. In low-income and working-class neighborhoods where people have dealt with generations of economic disadvantage, there is a proud history of coming together across societal lines to fight for grand causes. Farmworker, labor leader, and civil rights activist César Chávez was an expert at collaborating with migrant farmworkers, labor union members and leaders, and sympathetic politicians in his fight for fair wages, worker's rights, and safer working conditions. Without the collaborations of Blacks, Jews, Christians, the rich, and the poor, civil rights gains would have been next to impossible.

At the level of the larger community, the street-smart rule of collaboration is based on the very real need to build alliances for survival. It's when opposing groups, businesses, or individuals join forces to become stronger against bigger entities or challenges. A group of concerned neighborhood residents will work together to end gang violence; owners of small, struggling businesses will collaborate to corner larger percentages of the market against huge corporate companies moving in on their turf. These collaborations have real purpose, based on the needs of the moment; as Congressman William Clay says of politics, "There are no permanent enemies and no permanent friends, only permanent interests."

Sometimes these interests intersect in surprising—and life-changing—ways. In St. Louis, Juvenile Court judge Jimmy Edwards,

whose job was to see justice done in the cases of young offenders
—which sometimes meant time in a correctional facility—set out
to reduce the number of children he had to sentence. In order to
access what was at the heart of a child's disruptive behavior, Edwards assigned court-appointed deputy juvenile officers to every
case. Whatever problems they saw, it was their job to get that
child and his or her family the resources needed to reverse negative behaviors.

Judge Edwards is a collaborator who initiated youth-related
programs through partnerships with agencies and individuals
such as MERS Goodwill, universities in the region, the mayor's
office, the city police department and several other area non-
profits and private enterprises. In 2009, through a partnership
with MERS Goodwill and the St. Louis Public School District, Judge
Edwards opened a school that specifically addresses the needs
of at-risk youth who have been expelled from regular schools,
offering compassionate, tough, and dignified instruction with a
focus on providing the students everything they need to be successful in life.

The full-time judge couldn't possibly handle his duties from the
bench and operate a school at the same time. So he reached
out to partners who shared his passion for intervening in the lives
of troubled youth. Their work has had national influence—and
they have inspired me to jump in: I've visited the St. Louis Juvenile Center on a couple of occasions to hold one-on-one cooking presentations or group discussions with the kids. This work
benefits me because I'm exposed to youth with whom I can share
my street-smart recipes for life transformation. I guess you could
say I'm part of Judge Edwards's extended crew.

If the crew ain't happy, ain't nobody happy.

So what's the end result?
What's the secret ingredient for keeping a crew together and
working for maximum results? The big dogs at Google, those
top-notch data doctors, got a reality check when they analyzed
performance reviews and feedback surveys to hone in on the

qualities that made a good manager. Turned out it wasn't the iron fist or running a tight ship, and it wasn't a technical skill set, either, like being a genius at writing code. It was all about being there for your people: listening to their concerns, getting them involved in setting the team's goals, giving them the right mix of freedom and support, helping them develop their careers, caring about their lives.

But I could've told them that from day one. What I've learned on the streets, and taken with me to every street I've navigated, is that if the crew ain't happy, ain't nobody happy!

☆ **Sign up.** Identify two places where you can volunteer, like a soup kitchen, where you'll be working as part of a team. See what happens.

☆ **Step up.** Put yourself forward to lead a team working together toward a goal, like a project at work or an event in your neighborhood.

☆ **Give props.** For one week, practice this crew-building technique with the people around you: as Alex Haley said, "Find the good and praise it." Acknowledge people's contributions and see what happens.

☆ **Check yourself.** Contact someone who supervised you at a job in the past and ask how well you functioned as part of his or her crew. Think about whether those strengths and weaknesses have changed since then.

☆ **Find a model.** Identify someone you admire who has built a successful team and ask about how they did it. If you can't connect with such a person one-on-one, read an interview with him or her online or in a magazine.

☆ **Meet up.** Make coffee dates with three people you would like to collaborate with. Make sure you've done your homework by answering the questions in this chapter, and treat these meetings as if they were job interviews.

The Winner

The strategy of
competition

You got to win it while you're in it.

— Chef Jeff

As a young boy, I rarely played sports at school or at the local park, so I never fully realized the value of competition on the playground or the abandoned fields in the neighborhood. Don't get me wrong, sports were cool, but I just knew I wasn't gifted at sports and play. I needed to make money—no way to help my mother bouncing a ball around the school yard. I was naturally competitive; whether I was selling school candy or my city's newspaper, I wanted to be the top guy and sell the most and make the most money. But it was truly while working with my grandfather, Charles Henderson, Sr., in his janitorial business that I really started to pick up on the strategy of street-smart competition.

You see, Granddaddy carved new paths in L.A., winning contracts with White-owned ice-cream shops, laundromats, bakeries, and delicatessens up in the Wilshire district in West Los Angeles. And Charles Henderson, Sr., always delivered on his skills. He didn't play when it came to his money or his family's livelihood. In the early 1960s, there were few opportunities for Black people to make decent wages, especially in the South. My grandparents didn't pack up and bring their family all the way from New Orleans to Los Angeles to be unemployed and outhustled by competitors.

My granddaddy was real cool and a street-smart hustlepreneur who accepted the fact that he not only had to compete for customers and business, he had to compete for survival! When you learn at an early age that your parents are struggling, too (especially if you're being raised in a single-parent home), and that there's no safety net in place to break your fall, you start to understand that you've got to outthink and outmaneuver your competitors on every level if you want to win. No matter what game board you play on, gaining and maintaining a competitive edge increases your odds of getting a good education or a decent job or achieving success in a start-up business.

Some people are simply competitive by nature, like those who are E-gram Type Threes—the Achievers—they can be competitive to a high degree! But even predators in the wild aren't necessarily born with that killer instinct—they have to be taught to hunt—and the good news is that street-smart competition can be learned over time and your competitive strategy carefully mapped out to fit your vision, your goals, and your action plan. As Zig Ziglar said, "You were born to win, but to be a winner, you must plan to win, prepare to win, and expect to win." There are *rules* to the win, and we're going to go through them now.

Okay, so you've had a setback or two or three in life—who hasn't? We're going to deep dive into how upping your competitive game can make the difference between barely living and living large. I'll show you how your dark past can either be like chains around your neck or the life jacket that will keep you afloat while riding the waves to your dream destination.

Shoot for Excellence

You often hear people talking about "the competitive spirit"—but what is that really? In part, it's making a commitment to becoming the best you—to playing at the top of your game and always striving to be the best, no matter what game you're playing or what field you're on.

Excellence means no excuses, no whining, and no complaining. Real winners are always accountable for their success *or* their failure. If you're always coming up with one reason or another why you didn't close a deal, or meet a deadline, or win a raise, then you're not a winner, you're an excuser. It's up to you to decide if you're ready to put aside that kind of woulda-coulda-shoulda reasoning, step up and start increasing your competitive spirit to take your seat in the winner's circle.

Excellence also means loving what you're doing, embracing that competitive pressure, and enjoying every minute of the game, even when your back is up against the wall. Winners go about their work with real zest—which you'll remember is one of my signature strengths! Their reactions are lightning-quick and their efforts every day are nothing but the best they can give. Their goal is unmistakable—they want to be the top dog. Nobody has to push them, because they're already pushing themselves because they have clearly defined goals and a bulletproof action plan.

> *Excellence is doing ordinary things*
> *extraordinarily well.*
>
> — John W. Gardner

Now, you've also got to know what excellence looks like in whatever lane you've decided to roll in. You wouldn't expect to win a game if you didn't know the rules, would you? It's the same in any kind of competition: you need to know what it takes to be the best at whatever you're doing. Winners get schooled in excellence as they go, whether it's by watching others in their field, or reading a how-to book, or being blessed with having a personal mentor. You become a competent competitor by being aware of your surroundings and tuning in to the spoken and unspoken rules of the game. Keme Henderson knew what made a great cheesecake, *and* by learning the rules of the baking game, she became an excellent saleswoman; that's how she got her win.

Here's another reason why you've got to zero in on real excellence in your field: because not everyone who looks like a winner really is one. These days, the standards in our society have been lowered so far that lots of people have lost sight of what excellence *is*; they think the winners are the ones who shine the brightest in the media spotlight and on street corners. But that doesn't make you a winner, it just means you're playing the PR game. "Fake" winners like this are all over the place, from politics to entertainment to sports to the illegal street hustles. And there are always going to be haters looking to undermine the people on top; what you need to know is that sometimes their criticism is pointing to something you need to pay attention to. For years cyclist Lance Armstrong looked as if he was on top of his game, successfully riding out the accusations that he used performance-enhancing drugs, only to fall far and fast when it finally came to light that he'd been systematically doping for years.

If I'm to be honest about it, that's what I was when I was on the streets, a fake winner, with the house on the hill and fancy cars. Now, I know what it takes to win for real in the areas where I'm committed to excellence—from cooking to writing to speaking. Don't be the kind of "winner" who's getting the win the wrong way and just hasn't been found out yet—and don't be fooled by these people, either. It's important to know there is a standard for performance in any field, and to be discerning enough to see if people live up to their hype.

Fight Fear with Confidence

Real winners come into the game with a capacity for sky-high confidence. Like Zig Ziglar said, they *plan* to win. They fully expect to win, and they "rehearse" winning in their minds so convincingly that they attract success to themselves like magnets. However, this doesn't mean that winners never feel doubt or fear. It's just that they've learned how to confront it in their own way. Courage doesn't mean never being afraid of anything—authentic courage comes from facing and overcoming our deepest fears.

When I was first released from prison, I was a bit frozen with the fear that I would be sent back for some stupid stuff. My imagination created different scenarios—a hater ex-homeboy would set me up, or I'd be talking with one of my old boys who happened to be carrying and, me being on probation, I'd catch another fresh case. My fear was so intense and real, at times I was afraid to socialize with anyone from the 'hood, and I had headaches and many sleepless nights. Inside my head the fearmonger was competing for my attention and energy. If I hadn't confronted the monster and quieted its voice, I would have never built up the nerve to go hunt Gadsby down and repeatedly ask him for a job.

What's your fear monster telling you? That you're not good enough or smart enough or middle-class enough? Believe it or not, just identifying the fear is a huge step in the right direction. Now it's not some scary unknown thing that can be bigger than it really is. You know what it is, so now you can start chipping away at it. It took me a couple days of serious self-talk before I worked up the nerve to go across town to visit Gadsby's. But I knew the fear. So every day I avoided bad influences or unwanted encounters with negative people, my fear of being sent back to the joint lessened.

Don't let the fear monster beat you down. Face it down with the courage and good vibes you know you've got inside you. It's a critical tool if you want to win in life.

Know Your Opponent

If you want to be a winner, you have to know who's in the game with you. If you don't, how are you gonna beat them? In athletics, coaches have their players watch films of other teams before they ever meet on the field; they study the opponent's moves, their strengths, and the places where they're weak. They pay attention to what other teams or players have done to come out on top against this particular competitor. And then they plan their strategy to take maximum advantage of those chinks in the enemy's armor.

On the streets of L.A., as Granddaddy built up his business, it wasn't long before other janitorial crews tried to muscle in on it. But Granddaddy knew how to watch and listen, and he knew that some of his competitors had been burned in the past with bad customers. So he used his gift of gab to strategically "down talk" his job. He'd tell the competition when they rolled up on us how hard it was to work in the rich people's part of L.A. The police would harass us, he told them, because he had keys to the shops we cleaned at night. Hell, a Black man with keys to White-owned businesses in that part of town was unheard of at the time. Granddaddy talked about how the store owners underpaid him, knowing the effect that would have.

He'd play the other side with the same street-smart savvy. If he knew that one of his clients had bad experiences with poor service in the past, he might say, "Such and such a client had two other janitor companies before me, and the work was weak and sometimes the guys were a no-show. He says our service is the best at a can't-be-beat price." For him, being a winner also meant being a self-promoter, because if he didn't sing his own praises to the client, there wasn't anyone else who was going to do it for him.

If you push me toward something
that you think is a weakness, then I will
turn that perceived weakness into a strength.

— Michael Jordan

No question about it, my granddaddy gave me my first introduction to the "survival-of-the-fittest" rule. The drug world exposed me to that rule at a whole different level and showed me the dangerous and ruthless side of competition. Everyone in the game tried to outsmart, outstrategize, and outmuscle their way to kingpin status. I fell back on the lessons of my streetwise granddaddy by focusing on my competition and studying the strengths, weaknesses, and strategies of all the players in the game on my side of town. I carefully watched how they rolled, how they recruited and jacked new customers from rivals, how they treated their regulars and marketed their stuff. With this information, I created a blueprint for my own illegal business approach and structure.

Practice Survival of the Fittest

In the Brian De Palma film *Scarface,* Tony Montana (played by Al Pacino), a Cuban refugee turned small-time nickel-and-dime drug dealer, comes to realize that his boss, Frank Lopez (actor Robert Loggia), is weak and soft. Sure, Lopez has Colombian connections, but on the streets he's dwarfed by Montana's cutthroat cruelty and fearlessness. After studying his boss's illicit business practices and making his own connections, Montana uses Lopez's weaknesses against him to take over his empire.

My story follows a similar track—without the cutthroat practices and the murder, of course! Before I was finally sent to prison, I moved up rapidly in the game. I adopted the practices of my L.A. mentors and noted their drug connections. I studied their strengths and weaknesses and came up with strategies to capitalize on both. When one of my mentors went to prison, I was positioned to break out on my own and make a name for myself as a "credible player" in San Diego's Black underworld. As smart and savvy as I thought I was, though, I wasn't smart enough to pay closer attention to law enforcement who were watching me just like I was keeping an eye on my competitors.

When I left prison, I was introduced to yet another new level of competition in the culinary world, where rivalry can really heat up when employees compete either to keep their jobs or to get that rare promotion management dangles in front of them like a fresh carrot. Making extraordinary food with flavor and managing the workforce go hand in hand, and determine who will become the top chef in the kitchen. If you can't hack the sometimes military-style grind, you're out. The possibility of your entrée into the middle-class world is gone as quickly as the job.

Competition is good for business, and it's good for individuals who desire continued personal growth, development, and mastery. Being competitive keeps you from becoming too comfortable, bored, and complacent. From a street-smart perspective, being competitive is a 24/7 state of being. It means you're always on the lookout, always aware that there is someone waiting in the next lane to snatch your opportunity or dead-end your best efforts.

If we're to keep it real, we must admit that the same kill-or-be-killed strategies that work on the mean streets apply in some of the most respected corporate and political arenas around the world. When it became front-page news that accelerator pedal problems on some Toyota models had been linked to 19 car-crash deaths, the company's public image, sales, and stock plummeted. To specifically take advantage of the dent in Toyota's gold-plated reputation, competitors like Ford, Hyundai, GM, and Honda—like gangsters—increased their own advertising to hype the safety of their models. Without mentioning Toyota, they were able to capitalize off the damaged brand all the way to the bank.

Taking out the weak is standard practice in politics as well. Remember back in 2008 when then-candidate Barack Obama's presidential campaign was on the rocks as a result of the controversial comments made by his former pastor, Rev. Jeremiah Wright? Obama's chief opponent, Hillary Clinton, quickly used the scandal to slap Obama down in the polls and boost her chances of becoming the nominee. Two politicians were competing for a highly valuable spot. It wasn't personal, as evidenced by the fact that Obama later chose Clinton as his secretary of state.

I'm not glamorizing my past. Let's be clear, though; I used my God-given talents in a dishonorable and destructive way. However, I never resorted to violence or any activity that brought physical harm to my competitors or users. You see, when you adopt a winning attitude, when you work on your own brand and make sure your game is tight, you don't have to set out specifically to eliminate the competition; your sloppy, overconfident competitors will eliminate themselves in due time.

Who's your biggest competitor right now? Maybe it's a co-worker who's angling for a promotion you want, or it might be another business that's selling a product that's similar to yours. Identify at least three areas where they're weak and you're strong. Make a plan to capitalize on that so that in the "survival of the fittest," you come out on top.

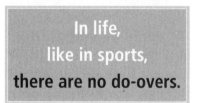

In life, like in sports, there are no do-overs.

Win It While You're In It

Even though I never was an athlete, I've developed a great appreciation for what it takes to be one—and I've noted how closely competition on the streets lines up with competition on the court. I'm not a B-baller, but I am what you might call a "street-baller"; I've learned my lessons on the court of life.

One of them is this: in life, like in sports, there are no do-overs.

You can only win today's game right now, today. You don't get to play this exact same game over again—you got to win it while you're in it. That said, every smart winner discovers early in life how to learn from losses. You learn to find the time to hit the Pause button and figure out exactly what went wrong. This is the true competitive edge, and what allows the "best" to get their win another day.

In the 1970s, Bernie Marcus and Arthur Blank were executives with a big home improvement retailer, Handy Dan Improvement Centers. There was every reason to think their careers were on track to keep them winning big in the exec lane. But then, in 1978, they both got fired. It had to be a serious blow, but Marcus and Blank didn't stay down. They got back up and started their own home improvement company, opening their first two stores in 1979.

Have you ever heard of Handy Dan Improvement Centers? Probably not, because the company went bust more than 20 years ago. But today, Marcus and Blank are both billionaires. The name of the company they bounced back from defeat to launch? Home Depot.

Bernie Marcus and Arthur Blank didn't get a second chance to succeed at Handy Dan. No do-overs. That game was lost. But they went on to compete successfully and win big in an even bigger arena. Today, their story, told in their book *Built from Scratch,* is looked to as one of the great entrepreneurial success stories of all time.

Even Will Smith didn't set out winning steadily from square one. He hit a dead end with his first big venture as part of the hip-hop team DJ Jazzy Jeff & the Fresh Prince. Not long after they won a Grammy for best rap duo, Smith was on the hook with the IRS for nearly $3 million. He climbed out of near-bankruptcy to star in *The Fresh Prince of Bel-Air,* and you know the rest. Today, he's making more money in the movies than he ever did as a rap star.

Winners are people who learn from their losses, like all these guys did. If you don't learn, you'll just keep on doing the same thing that *doesn't* succeed over and over. Which would you rather be, a winner or a serial loser?

Know the Value of You

Whether you operate in a profit, nonprofit, or entrepreneurial space, to be truly competitive, you must know exactly what you're bringing to the table. This means that you have to break down the product (you) honestly and really understand how you're better than the rest or how you can at least become equally as good.

There are a lot of celebrity chefs out there, but many don't have my experience or back story and I don't have theirs. Ina Garten, author and host of the Food Network's *Barefoot Contessa,* is a former White House nuclear policy analyst whose cooking and home-entertaining tips have been recognized by the likes of Martha Stewart, Oprah Winfrey, and Patricia Wells. Garten has a unique brand that's hard for just anybody to snatch or duplicate.

Armed with genuine integrity and professionalism, we can disarm our competition without engaging in negative, emotional, or confrontational behavior. Remember how my granddaddy used classic sales tactics to intimidate his competition. He made his job seem harder than it really was while upping the quality of service to his clients and keeping his prices reasonable. Granddaddy was a mental martial artist with a Teflon brand.

It's people with an iron-clad brand that you've added to your list of real and virtual mentors. They've built their success from the inside out, and now their light is bright enough for the whole world to see. And as you build up more and more wins in the service of your vision, you're getting ready to build a brand of your own. Make no mistake—it takes a lot of wins! Oprah couldn't become Oprah until she had competed successfully in the world of broadcasting. By winning in *your* lane, whatever that is—and showing that you can hit your mark consistently—you build your track record, and people start to pay attention.

Through it all, you need to stay focused on the straight-up value of *you.* Top tennis trainer Pat Dougherty tells this story from an interview he did with star Maria Sharapova when she was only nine years old. He asked her what players she used as role models, and she named a few—players she looked up to and studied to help her improve her own game. "However, when I asked her if she wanted to become the next Graf or Seles," Dougherty says, "her answer was a resolute 'No . . . I intend to be the first Maria Sharapova.'"

Work Out for the Win

I'd like to bust a myth for you right now. Rich people, successful people, celebrity people . . . whatever, they're just people. They cry, they laugh, they bleed, they're insecure, and they make mistakes just like everybody else—no matter their background or economic advantage. The major difference is that those who've become winners have stopped fear in its tracks, found resources, and built relationships to get a second, third, or fourth chance. This is why you hear about CEOs who bankrupt one company and get a chance to run another. Opportunities increase if you're born into a family with means; if you attend college, join fraternities or sororities, and wind up with a frat brother or sorority sister with connections who can open corporate doors for you. If you're at the shallow end of the opportunity pool, if you were born as one of the "have-nots"—well, as rapper Eminem phrased it: "*You only get one shot, do not miss your chance to blow. . . .*"

A winner is someone who recognizes his God-given talents, works his tail off to develop them into skills, and uses these skills to accomplish his goals.

— Larry Bird

You may have fewer opportunities in life, but that doesn't mean you should accept defeat. It just means you have to work harder, dream bigger, get smarter, and stay alert and ready when that rare bird "opportunity" does fly into your life. In other words, your patience has to equal your strength.

Your circumstances do not define the real you. Opportunity is surely coming your way because you have a dream, a vision, specific goals, and a bulletproof action plan and people around you who want you to succeed. And you can start building your competitive muscle right now—think of it as the workout you need to get *your* win.

The Winner

☆ **Skip the excuses.** Practice not being an excuser, whiner, or complainer—it's the only way you become a winner. For one week, decide you're not going to make any excuses for why you didn't do this or that, or why something you tried didn't succeed the way you wanted it to.

☆ **Define your best—then do it.** Write down the very best you're capable of, then for one week, ask yourself at the end of every day whether you gave your very best that day. Did you push yourself, or did someone else have to get behind you and shove?

☆ **Name the winners.** What can you borrow from the playbooks of the top three winners in your field to sharpen up *your* game and support your action plan?

☆ **Shake out the fakes.** Pinpoint at least one person in your field who has a great image but may not have the real stuff to back it up.

☆ **Ditch the do-over.** Think of a time in the last six months when you didn't do as well as you could have. Decide right now to let that loss go and fix your sights on the next game you'll play.

☆ **Know the value of you!** Write down three qualities or practical skills you bring to what you're doing that are going to help you compete successfully in your lane. Go back to your VIA and E-gram results if you need a refresher on what makes you *you*.

The Last-in-Liner

The strategy of
humility

> *When ego takes the wheel—watch out.*
>
> — Chef Jeff

I was the shit!

It had been 18 months since my release from federal prison; I'd had one year of white-tablecloth-dining experience under the watchful eye of Chef Robert Gadsby, and then I landed the chance to work in my first hotel, the LAX Marriott.

MC Hammer raps it best: "You can't touch this!" Or so I thought.

Marriott's executive sous-chef, Sterling Burpee, could have been my brother from another mother, we looked that much alike. I rolled up on him with a half-street and half-corporate approach when I met him in the hotel lobby: "Hey, Chef, how are you doing, sir? I'm Jeff Henderson, a cook. I want to apply for a job here, but I need a way in."

Burpee was a professional, too, but with a bit of been-there-done-that swagger. He asked if I had filled out an application. "Yes, sir," I responded, whipping out my résumé.

He was down-to-earth, so I decided to tell him I had been to prison right on the spot. Burpee appeared unfazed: "What were you in for?" he asked. After I told him, he asked if I had ever been involved with robbery, violent crimes, or fraud. I told him, "No, sir"—I was never into that kind of hustle.

A few days later, I received a call from LAX Marriott HR. After a drug test and an interview with an HR intake specialist, I was hired. Burpee put me to work in the pastry department. There had never been a Black person in that department before, I was told, so he must have wanted to mix it up a bit. After about a month, I was upgraded to working the banquet department as a lead cook.

At the time, Marriott didn't have any high-end restaurants. The dishes I had learned from Gadsby were many steps beyond what they offered in their casual restaurants and buffets. I also represented on a professional sous-chef level. Like Burpee, I was always clean-shaven, except for the handlebar mustache I sported at the time, and wore crisp white chef attire.

My low-level management skills impressed the higher-ups. I took ownership in the kitchen, taking orders from my direct supervisors like any good soldier would do. I was always courteous (except when someone tried to play me), timely, efficient, and commanding. The crew took me seriously—because I gave and demanded respect, but most of all, because I saw the big picture when preparing food for events. The bosses liked that I wasn't some robot who just took orders.

Soon my chefs were shop talking about this new Black cook they had in the house who could make all these elevated dishes, who from time to time shared a new trick or two with the co-workers. They were so impressed that after three months on the job, Curtis Dean, Burpee's boss and LAX Marriott's food and beverage director, asked me to join a special task force. Marriott had taken on a new property in San Diego, a former four-star Le Meridian Hotel on Coronado Island. The food and beverage department gathered the hotel's best employees to oversee the opening and operations of the casual, upscale three-meal restaurant.

Working with a team of culinary superstars, I grew kinda bigheaded and overconfident. The head of the culinary team was Chef Sarah Bowman, a middle-aged White woman. She was a Johnson & Wales grad with a long blond ponytail and short tolerance for bullshit and male egomaniacs.

Bowman put me in charge of L'Escale Restaurant as the kitchen supervisor. It was the first restaurant I had ever run on my own. I was in charge of three meals—breakfast, lunch, and dinner—plus bar food and pool food. Again, management was thoroughly impressed with my skills. Then came the day Bowman asked me to submit a few new menu items. I did, giving her all the fancy stuff I had learned from Gadsby with my own creative twists.

"What is this?" she asked straight up before ripping my ideas apart like shredded leeks. "This isn't in season, and neither is this," she said, pointing to my dishes. "Based on flavor profiles, this doesn't go with this . . ." On and on she went.

I had mad respect for Chef Sarah. She was, and still is, one of the most talented chefs in the business. Although she was a pit bull in the kitchen who had no problems busting my chops, she was loyal to those under her charge. With her help and mentorship, I created the right menu items that reflected the seaside enclave, and my star continued to rise at the Coronado Island Marriot Resort.

With confidence restored, I went back to Sarah a few months later and told her I wasn't satisfied running the breakfast, lunch, and dinner restaurant anymore; I wanted to try my hand at cooking at the fine dining restaurant, Marius.

"Jeff, you can't work over there right now. You're not quite ready yet."

Bullshit, my ego screamed in my head. To convince her, I rattled off all my work experience with Gadsby and accomplishments at L'Escale.

Sarah's cool but brutal response unsettled me: "Chef, you can't even cook a cheeseburger right."

She ordered me to prepare three burgers—a perfect rare, a perfect medium rare, and a perfect well done without being burned. I made the burgers, presented them to her, and, once again, she ripped me apart, informing me that the temperatures were all off.

That was another blow to my ego, and I easily could have gone there with her. But then I remembered something Robert Gadsby had told me: "Jeff, no matter how good you become at this cooking game, you will always be a student for life." It took a lot, but I stepped back and got my ego in check. I realized that Sarah wasn't giving me a beat down; this was a chance to learn something.

Through it all, Sarah and I bonded and formed an extraordinary teacher/student relationship. I still feel somewhat guilty about leaving her tutelage to pursue a once-in-a-lifetime opportunity at the Ritz-Carlton. She was pissed and for good reason. Sarah had put in a whole year, taking me under her wing, investing so much of her personal time, and sharing extra lessons with me. I regret leaving Sarah so soon, but I will always treasure what she taught me.

---

*Humility is not thinking less of yourself,
it's thinking of yourself less.*

— C. S. Lewis

"Be Humble or Stumble"

What Sarah Bowman taught me, to put it bluntly, was that I was *not* the shit, not even close. I had skills, yes, and talent and passion. But I wasn't a master at my game yet; I had a whole lot left to learn. And in that, I was like every single other person. It was, in short, a lesson in humility.

Humility isn't something you hear a lot about in our society. We might say how great it is that someone famous is so humble, like Maya Angelou—but when you get right down to it, most of us don't want to be humble. We want to avoid being humiliated or brought low in any way. We follow leaders who are bold and aggressive; we cater to big executives as if they were celebrities. We always want to be first in line. We push our children to achieve and be proud of themselves. And that's fine, if it helps them grow into secure, productive adults. It's just not the whole story.

Real humility doesn't have anything to do with being humiliated. It's simply a calm awareness and acceptance that we aren't perfect and don't need to be. It means we don't set ourselves up above other people, but see and celebrate their gifts. It means we're grateful for what we have without feeling like it's our due. And it helps us to fulfill our true destiny, because it allows us to inspire and support others without thought of reward.

It's also a strategy for success in just about any walk of life. The humble truly understand "There but for the grace of God go I," and you can bet that they profit from that knowledge. It's important for CEOs, heads of companies, teachers, police, and everyone else to put themselves on the same level as the people they serve or interact with on a daily basis. With humility, a teacher or a counselor can discover untapped talent. A cop who tries to figure out *why* a youth is on the streets in the morning is less inclined to jam up or punish that teen.

In the TV show *Undercover Boss,* top execs went out into the office or the field incognito to experience firsthand what their employees dealt with every day. So many companies go under because the workforce is disgruntled or feels disconnected from the company's success—but a strategically humble CEO understands that the frontline workers can make or break any organization and makes it a point to put himself or herself in their shoes. Without being in tune with everyday people—their wants, needs, and challenges—President Barack Obama wouldn't be where he is today. Leadership steers the car, but the workers are the wheels; if the wheels don't roll, the vehicle won't move.

Humility is the opposite of arrogance. It allows you to be human, to accept the fact that you're not weak, and to actually choose to say no when you feel you're not ready. Even if you're the type who enjoys living on the edge, by cultivating humility as a starting point, your appetite for adventure and achievement will be balanced by your awareness of self and appreciation of others.

You can't fake humility; in fact, you can usually spot false humility a mile away. It's just a way of fishing for other people to praise you and tell you that you really *are* all that and then some. But you can develop genuine humility, and in this chapter we'll take a look at some ways to do just that.

Know What You Don't Know

When I was on the streets, I always gravitated to people who were smarter than me and had what I wanted in life. When I was in prison, I rolled with the smart guys who taught the business, marketing, and history classes. I was humble enough to know what I didn't know—and you need to get this if you ever want to expand beyond your limitations right now. Individuals who think they know it all have no room to take any new information in. Knowing that you *don't* actually know it all makes space for new ideas, new approaches, and new growth. It gives you the chance to knowledge-jack the best in your lane and use what you learn to elevate your own game.

Gadsby knew this when he told me, "No matter how good you become, you'll always be a student." And he proved it when took me along with him on his weekly dining reconnaissance missions. Robert was a pro. Whenever some hot new chef was getting a lot of media attention, he would go to the restaurant on a spy mission and see what all the hype was about—and he wasn't the only top chef to do this, all business-smart people roll like that. He checked out the operation, the menu, and the waitstaff and tried to figure out what helped the chef get all the buzz or what made his or her dishes the talk of the town. He understood that they might know something he didn't, and he was willing to learn.

People who don't get this are simply trapped in their own illusions of thinking they are the shit! They have big mouths and little ears, always focused on their desires and wishes, not those of others. To these individuals, other people's successes aren't a positive thing, they're a threat. Life to them is like a gladiator sport where someone has to be defeated or eliminated—and it isn't going to be them.

Power is dangerous unless you have humility.

— Richard J. Daley

Humble people, by nature, are open to challenge and change, to listening and learning. They welcome diversity and are appreciative, not intimidated, when someone in their orbit shows potential. And this doesn't just apply to people who are low on the totem pole; it's just as important for leaders as it is for line workers. Leaders who are humble enough to learn and grow this way help their workers grow, too, by setting the right example.

Learn from the Downturns

Learning in a humble spirit is key to stretching your own limits—and the lessons can be especially effective when they come in the form of setbacks you can't avoid and mistakes you don't want to make over again. So it's important to welcome those trials as opportunities. People who think they can do no wrong seem to make the same mistakes over and over and blame others when things fall apart. But if I'd taken an arrogant and defensive attitude in the face of Chef Sarah Bowman's gut-crunching critique of my skills, I might have responded angrily when she burger-checked me. Then I would have missed out on a huge opportunity for professional development. Instead, I humbled myself, took a clear-eyed look at my mistakes, and learned how not to repeat them.

One way to get this in your head is to change the way you think about criticism. Instead of thinking, *Chef showed me up* or *Chef criticized me,* I could think, *Chef gave me a correction.* Right away it sounds better: I'm being "given" something, and it's something I want, because who doesn't want to be more correct? And once you get this, you can go even further and not only accept corrections but actively seek them out. Ask your boss or your co-workers to give you their honest opinions of your performance. Don't flinch from what you hear. The path to success isn't paved with your co-workers' approval; it's lined with opportunities to do better tomorrow than you did today.

The same is true for those downturns and disappointments that life serves all of us from time to time. That lost job, business decline, or divorce—even if it's not directly due to some clear mistake you made—becomes an opportunity to start over and learn something about yourself in the process. When you can see your current humble circumstances as a temporary stay and not a lifetime sentence, it's because you are beginning to get the power of humility in your head.

This may sound like an unachievable aim when we're talking about serious setbacks in your life. Here's a trick I learned: if you can look at these hard times, as well as the good times, with a grateful attitude, you'll have an easier time with the "fresh start" part. Tough times show you that you can't take success—or health or relationships or anything else—for granted. You aren't entitled to these blessings—now that's a pretty humbling thought! So always being thankful for everything and everyone good in your life is guaranteed to help keep you humble, and that's going to set you up for more success down the road.

As for me, I learned the lesson of gratitude back in the day. Although poverty and crime were familiar elements in my childhood, there were also extraordinary people in the 'hood. They didn't have much money but were very grateful for what little they had. They were always willing to offer a meal, a place to sleep, or a kind word to anybody, even if the individual seemed to be unworthy. An old-timer in my past once quoted Scripture: "God opposes the proud but gives grace to the humble." Today, I'm endlessly grateful for the grace I've been given, and it's my hope that I can help you get some of that grace into your life, too.

Be Last in Line

Many who have escaped violent or dysfunctional neighborhoods feel blessed to have stepped off the path that spirals downward. Their humility helps them appreciate opportunities and relationships with good people. Their humble beginnings and good character seem to serve as a checks-and-balances system that helps them avoid the traps of ego and self-destruction.

My great-aunt Clarisse Dunn was such a person. She lived in one the toughest parts of South Central L.A., on 83rd and Normandy. Worried for her safety because of gang violence and drug activity, members of the family tried to convince Aunt Clarisse to move to a safer part of town as she aged. She refused. Aunt Clarisse had this extraordinary love affair with her 'hood and its people, and a lifelong umbilical cord connected her to the needy souls of the community and all five of the grandchildren she raised.

Everybody—drug dealers, gangsters, and crackheads alike—called Aunt Clarisse "Momma," and they knew she'd always have a little food to eat or big hug available for whoever knocked on her back door, which was always unlocked. When I think of humility, I think of my aunt Clarisse—and I think most of all of her great kindness.

It's all about humanity, humility, and integrity.

— Debra Wilson

Kindness is a key component of humility. It means you're compassionate and aware of others. But it also means you're kind and forgiving to yourself. You consciously seek ways to not ignore your shortcomings but forgive yourself for them, the way I did when working at the Marriott. Kindness connects you with humanity —yours and that of others inside and outside your circles.

Kindness like Aunt Clarisse's is something you're born with, no question. That said, the hustlepreneur can cultivate a humble spirit through some simple practices of putting other people first. It doesn't have to be as dramatic as leaving your door open to welcome and feed whoever comes knocking; you can start by investing your thought and energy in other people's success as well as, or even above, your own. When people around you do something that's worthy of praise, don't hold back because you're afraid their light will put you in the shadow. Give them their due, and let others see and hear you do it. Don't be in a hurry to take credit if the credit should be shared—or, sometimes, even if it truly is your due.

Alicia Rodriguez, a nurse in a big-city hospital, was understandably proud of herself when she came up with a new way to organize patients' charts that saved the charge nurse valuable time and made it easier for all the staff members to find the information they needed. Even the patients benefited directly as their care became swifter and more streamlined. Alicia's supervisor applauded her and enthusiastically helped put the new system in place.

But at the same time, Alicia knew that her boss was on the hot seat with the higher-ups: she'd been the subject of some patient complaints (which Alicia considered unfair). Worse, her boss had recently been involved with treating a patient who had died, and the family was asking for an investigation. So when the director of nursing singled out the department to praise the new charting system, Alicia subtly let her boss know that she should take the credit. She knew the other woman needed the boost to her reputation. "Anyway," Alicia said when her boss resisted, "I wouldn't have come up with that if I hadn't been watching and learning from you." Alicia was humble enough to forgo the praise she could have received for the sake of supporting her mentor, and she didn't let her ego get in the way.

You may not be in a position to pass up credit for something important you've done, but there are lots of other ways to put others first. It can be as simple as *literally* putting them first: when you're squeezing through a crowded restaurant door, make it a point to go in last. Hold doors for people, and don't let it annoy you if they don't say "Thank you." Find some way to serve others every day, no matter how small; the opportunities are all around you. You know the proverb "The last shall be first"; as you get in the practice of *not* always putting yourself ahead, you'll be building the habit of street-smart humility that will set you up for success when the time is right. Even as a drug dealer, I put many of my co-dealers first by making sure they were taken care of, many times before my own needs were met. Though my activities were criminal during that time, I still understood the value of service and humility.

The Confidence to Be Humble

So does being humble mean you can't feel positive about who you are and what you do? No way! That would go against a lot of what we've been talking about in this book—like identifying and using your strengths—and it wouldn't help you at all in your quest to achieve your goals and realize your vision.

This is where you need to really understand the difference between confidence and arrogance. Arrogance is the direct opposite of humility, and most of the time it doesn't come from healthy self-esteem, it comes from an almost subconscious fear that you *aren't* good enough—that someone else is going to steal your shine and show you up and make you look weak.

There's a huge difference between confidence and arrogance in the business world. With confidence, you can creatively introduce a new idea or service into the marketplace. With arrogance, you try to force an idea without ever taking the time to see if it's needed or wanted by consumers or clients or embraced by co-workers. Your motivations and actions are self-centered and shortsighted and mostly driven by the bottom line. But you can't see this because arrogance is attached to your eyes like blinders. If you're confident, on the other hand, you have a sense of security that lets you be humble because you don't need to trumpet your accomplishments and aren't attached to looking good.

I'll say it again: being humble doesn't mean you have to beat yourself down. But let's be real about this subject; you're going to have your times when you feel like #%#%@. The key is to never let yourself have a pity party. Turn to the people around you for support. My wife, Stacy, always makes me feel good about myself. She does this by taking me back to the day I walked out of prison. She reminds me how blessed I am to have achieved all that I have in spite of being a Black man raised in poverty and a felon who was prison educated. When she takes me back, I start to come around, realizing that I'm here against the odds and living my own version of the American dream.

Humility is the solid foundation of all virtues.

— Confucius

When I get frustrated about business or some company or person who refuses to do business with me because of my record, Stacy gives me the pump-up: "Look, honey, you were the first Black executive chef at the Bellagio; you had your own show on the Food Network; you have three published books; you own a beautiful home with a swimming pool; and you have a strong, loving family." By the time she finishes, I'm asking myself, "What the hell was I complaining about? Suck it up, man, stay focused. Be grateful!"

We all feel doubt, fear, or insecurity at some point in our lives, no matter who we are. Yet as important as it is to have some cheerleaders on your team, you need to make sure you're not just surrounded by yes-men. When I see executives surrounded by workers who won't do anything but suck up to them, I just don't get it. That's got to pump their egos up—and a hustlepreneur knows that if your head gets too big, you can't even fit through doors of opportunity when they open for you. You'll never be as successful as you can be—you'll never get those chances to humbly learn and grow—if you don't have people around you who will spot the uncomfortable truth and tell you no when that's what you need to hear.

Let's go over this one more time. Arrogance is the cocky belief that no one and nothing can ever take you down. Humility reinforced by confidence means you expect life's unexpected curveballs and you prepare yourself to swing differently each time you step to the plate. Arrogance is a form of false pride, putting yourself out there as something you aren't—a human being without flaws, the smartest guy or girl in the room, never in doubt. This kind of pride isn't honest; it's not the kind of pride you earn. True humility means you know who you are, the good right along with the bad, and you don't pretend to be what you're not. And it allows room for *true* pride when you've earned it through your talents and accomplishments. In other words, it's honest. I became arrogant in my younger drug-dealing days, thinking I was untouchable and above the law, floating around in my Mercedes-Benz, sporting high-end ornaments around my neck, while paying no taxes. What happened? I got busted and wound up losing all my ill-gotten gains—the money, vehicles, clothing, jewelry, women, the bad-ass house, and my street status.

Today, I can honestly say that my status is one that makes my mother, father, wife, children, and community *truly* proud. The respect I get from young people and adults in schools and prisons across this country far outweighs any material thing I lost. Because I am humble and grateful for this round of opportunity to serve, I am a far richer man today than I was in my darker days.

Pride Goeth Before Destruction

Many people misquote this famous line from the book of Proverbs. You've heard them say it: "Pride goeth before a fall." The correct version is even tougher talk: "Pride goeth before destruction, and an haughty spirit before a fall." Now, this doesn't mean the kind of positive pride you might feel in a job well done; it's pride in the old-fashioned sense, that is to say, the false pride we just talked about. What this often-quoted passage is saying is that hustlepreneurs need to watch out when ego starts to take the wheel in their life, and that can easily happen when success comes fast and furious.

Things can go very wrong, very fast, when the ego's left in charge. Just ask the former undisputed heavyweight champion of the world, Mike Tyson. Prior to entering the ring, the Brooklyn, New York, native lived a dysfunctional life. Reportedly, Tyson's father abandoned the family when he was just two years old. Tyson's mother, Lorna Smith Tyson, cared for Tyson and his brother and sister until she died when he was 16. An emotionally scarred teenage Tyson was raised in a boxing gym under the care of Constantine "Cus" D'Amato, his manager, trainer, and eventual legal guardian. Early in his career, he was a first-round knockout king, and by the tender age of 20, he held the record as the youngest boxer to win the WBC, WBA, and IBF heavyweight titles.

Tyson wasn't prepared for success and fame at such an early age. He probably thought he knew it all, and the truth is that, as we discussed, he didn't even know what he didn't know. Soon, his personal problems overshadowed his victories in the ring. His media-grabbing marriage to actress Robin Givens in 1988 lasted one year. Rumors of drug use started to circulate, and his critics accused Tyson of replacing his grueling workout routine with parties and woman chasing. After being arrested and charged with the rape of 18-year-old Desiree Washington, Miss Black Rhode Island, in 1991, Tyson was sentenced to six years in prison. Some would argue that an action like that arises from arrogance at its worst—a sense of entitlement that leads you to take what you want with no thought for others and no sense that your actions have consequences. But some would also say that the low point for Tyson came later, a couple of years after his release, when, during a bout with Evander Holyfield, he bit a chunk out of the other fighter's ear. This action had consequences for sure: a $3 million fine and a lifetime ban from boxing (which was, however, lifted after a year).

In an interview with *Details* magazine, Tyson talked about his early days as a multimillionaire brute and the outsized ego that drove him: "'Greatest man on the planet'—I wasn't half the man I thought I was." I'm not using his story as a wonderful "turn-around" example. I use him because I've heard him express how life has humbled him and put him on a new path. "I try desperately hard to be humble," Tyson told late-night talk-show host Jimmy Kimmel in 2009. "Because I'm humble doesn't mean I'm weak by any means. I'm still a man. But I try, because I know when my ego and my being self-absorbed, I know where that will take me, it will take me to a very dark place. I'm really not willing to go there anymore."

I expect all of you who are reading this book to be faced with hard choices in your lives, and as you gain power and access on your hustlepreneur path to success, the choices are just going to get harder. The basic choice is going to be this: Are you going to let your ego run the show, or are you going to see that you're not just here to have everything be all about you? Don't make the mistake of thinking that you don't have to worry about this just because you don't have an opportunity to bite someone's ear off on national television. The choices you make every day—right now, today—are going to set you up for the choices you'll make down the road. Make them in a spirit of humility and gratitude, and you'll be more likely to stay on the straight path.

Gratitude is also something Tyson acknowledged. During a 2010 guest appearance on *The View,* he talked about the vast fortune he wasted, his marriage in 2009, and how he happily lived paycheck to paycheck: "I'm totally destitute and broke. But I have an awesome life. . . . I'm very grateful. I don't deserve to have the wife that I have; I don't deserve the kids that I have, but I do, and I'm very grateful."

Like Tyson, I am grateful for my second chances: my wife, my children, and my life. After leaving Gadsby, I was a bit overly confident and believed my string of good fortune would continue without any attitude or behavioral adjustments. Humility helped me regain my cutting edge, define my niche, and retool my approach. I learned to listen more, open my ears, and close my mouth at the right times. I started appreciating setbacks and challenges with the understanding that they were really life lessons. With fresh, humble eyes I now see so-called enemies as teachers who can make me stronger and wiser. With an ingrained sense of gratitude, I acknowledge the small blessings that I previously ignored and I understand that I am blessed to be in the game at all. Humility mixed with confidence (not arrogance) allows me to learn from others and appreciate their gifts and contributions. Because I am authentically humble and sincerely invested in helping others transform their lives, powerful people tend to want to hang around me and help me achieve this goal.

I'm also aware that—even with all the positives in my life—I won't be a true success unless I continue to repay the huge debt to humanity that I owe for the destruction I sowed in my earlier life. People talk about having a compass, sometimes a "moral compass," to guide you in life. But you can't use a compass if you don't know which way north is—and an out-of-control ego ruins your sense of direction. Because I now have a working compass, I've been able to set my course to repay this debt.

> **You can't use a moral compass if you don't know which way north is.**

This is the kind of humility in action that we should all strive to achieve. It is that balancer that separates the true hustlepreneur from the people who are just out to get theirs. It is more than just a worthy endeavor—it's a way of life.

Street-Smart Challenges for:

The Last-in-Liner

☆ **Stretch yourself.** Give yourself a task or project in an area that's new to you and discover how much you don't know.

☆ **Learn what you have to learn.** Ask someone—your boss, a co-worker, a friend, or family member—to give you an honest critique of your strengths and weaknesses in a particular area. Thank him sincerely, whether you like what you hear or not—he's doing you a real service.

☆ **Ask for help.** Go to someone at work or in your personal life and say, "I don't know how to do this. Can you show me?"

☆ **Put others first.** Volunteer one hour a week at a homeless shelter, soup kitchen, or community-outreach program.

☆ **Don't take the credit.** For one week, make it a point not to call attention to things you've done, even if they're small—"Hey, I fixed the copier" or "I went and bought milk." Let everyone wonder how the copier got fixed!

☆ **Be proud when you've earned it.** In your See It, Be It journal, write down something you've done that you're proud of. *Today, I signed up for a class. Today, I rewrote my resume. Today, I let somebody else go first.*

The No-Strings Giver

The strategy of
selfless service

> *Truly successful people know*
> *it's not enough just to get yours.*
>
> — Chef Jeff

Afew chapters back I told you about how I got the chance to appear on *The Oprah Winfrey Show*. That was a life-changing experience and an incredible honor—as well as a profound dose of inspiration when she told me I was "a role model to little Black boys everywhere." Getting on *Oprah* once was amazing enough; can you imagine how I felt going on *a second time*? But that's exactly what happened in 2011 when Oprah featured my story on her show *Oprah's Lifeclass* on her network, OWN.

"It's never too late to have a wake-up call," Oprah told the camera. Then she flashed back to the story and images of my early life, my days on the streets, and my time behind bars. In footage from our earlier interview, we talked about how that experience was what finally brought about a change in me and—this is no exaggeration—saved my life. "What is the most important thing you think you learned about yourself in prison?" she asked.

"That I am somebody," I said simply.

On *Lifeclass*, Oprah used that conversation as an example and a starting point to talk about how we're all evolving toward our own moment of transformation when we discover the power that's within all of us. "All life is about growing to be who you were most meant to be," she said, "the best version of yourself."

It's my sincere hope that that's what this book is helping you to do: grow to be the best possible you. Living a good life doesn't just mean taking and enjoying the good things that come your way. It also means giving something back out of the riches you receive—not just money, but whatever you have in your power to give.

Sure, you can be a success by simply following everything you've read in this book. If you "picture-power" your dream; discover and develop your natural strengths and talents; commit to your vision, your goals, and your action plan; and use your street-smart

> **Truly successful individuals find ways to pass the good along.**

survival recipes to perfect your dish—you can indeed become a success. Maybe you'll have that fancy crib and luxury car, travel the world and have all the material gadgets and trinkets you desire. But if you keep it all for yourself, you'll be missing the extra ingredient that will add value to your vision and extra passion to your action plan. This is the seed from your garden that you must plant for the next generation. In this chapter, we'll look at what it means to give back with no strings attached.

Service and Success

These days, it's no longer enough just to get yours. "Yours" isn't all yours anyway. Truly successful individuals know this and find ways to pass the good along, whether it's by donating money, doing good works, or giving of their time and talents in some other way. Colleges and universities are paying more and more attention to volunteer work as part of a student's credentials for admission; when they have to find some way to distinguish one extremely highly qualified applicant from another, service to others has proven to be a good measure of whether someone is headed down the road to success.

My way of serving is to engage, inspire, and empower, not only "little Black boys," as Oprah put it, but any individual who has ever been beaten down by life or life's circumstance. My vision is to use my life story to reach those on the verge of giving up and to convince them that they were born with the right stuff. Although this moment may seem like the end, when you use your power to choose, it can be a new beginning. As a life transformation coach, it's my job to use my experiences to inspire people to rise above the obstacles, tap into their hidden talents, and take responsibility for changing their lives—*today!*

It is an awesome responsibility, but one I cling to with unshakable passion. You see, I know I'm not supposed to be here in this powerful space. I played a dangerous game back in the day and caused a lot of pain in pursuit of material gain. I owe a huge debt to society that a prison sentence can never totally repay.

It was at Pen University—prison—that I was first inspired by the power of giving back. It all started while finishing up my last three years. A group of inmates and I approached Warden Morton, Captain Washington, and Officer Torrance about bringing the national Bureau of Prisons' Teenage Awareness Program (TAP) to the prison, and we launched the program to great success, reaching out to high school students while on lockdown. Kids were bused in to the prison, where we schooled them about choices, prison life, and how education is the only way to really get ahead. Occasionally, the warden bused us out, shackled up, to local high schools to bring the message right to the neighborhood.

I saw that light of hope begin to flicker in the eyes of the kids I was blessed to engage with. Even with that prison tag, I was empowered with the knowledge that I could save a young life or inspire someone with crushed dreams.

So I know I'm here for a reason. I know my success is directly linked to my give-back. There are hundreds of thousands of young people who believe that my former criminal lifestyle is the only option for making money. There are others who've bought into the idea that their upbringings have slammed the door of opportunity on their future. There are even more who have no idea that they have the right to be happy, prosperous, and successful.

Today, I'm working to launch the Chef Jeff Foundation, designed to help at-risk youth get those lessons so they can prosper personally and professionally and live healthier lives, through a books-for-boys program and unique education workshops. Whenever I can, I make it a point to visit juvenile detention centers, prisons, and alternative high schools during my travels to different cities. When I'm engaged to do a corporate presentation in a particular city, I almost always add on a free presentation for young people in difficult circumstances, or those working toward careers in the culinary arts. During these talks, I show photographs of myself as a livin'-large drug dealer; as a convict in federal prison; and as a newly released inmate with no guarantee of making a decent living or providing for his family upon his release. I want young people, at-risk people, and no-hope people to look at those pictures and say to themselves, *Hey, he's just a regular dude, parts of his story are my story. He puts his pants on one leg at a time and has made mistakes in life, just like me. Hell, if he can do it, so can I!*

I want them to feel the life-transforming power of a second chance. My wish is that all of them discover their unique gifts and achieve their personal version of the American dream.

I wish you big-time success, too, but there's a catch. Because it serves as the foundation for my success, I insist that on every step of your road to success, you include the practice of giving back.

Paying It Forward

Many of us remember the movie *Pay It Forward*, where a little school kid inspired thousands of people to make the world a better place by passing the favors given to them along to at least three new people. It was more than just paying back a debt; it was paying a blessing forward.

In an October 2006 show, Oprah Winfrey played out the movie's theme in real life. Oprah and her crew decided to give the 300 or so audience members the opportunity to experience what she called "truly the best gift"—the gift of giving back. Each person received $1,000 in the form of a debit card, along with a video camera. They were also given a mandate: they had one week to donate the money to a charitable cause of their choice.

Within a week, Oprah received more than 300 videos that documented random acts of kindness all over the country. One Centralia, Illinois, woman went to her community and turned her $1,000 gift into a $70,000 donation to a struggling father of nine who had a deadly brain tumor. Thanks to this selfless act, the father could buy groceries for his family, pay on his mounting hospital bills, and send his oldest son to college.

Other audience members purchased airline tickets for parents who couldn't afford to visit their sick children in out-of-state hospitals; provided new sneakers for 425 students at a Pittsburgh elementary school; helped a woman who had been shot in the face by an abusive boyfriend pay for reconstructive surgery; bought a car for a bus-riding, hardworking single mom with four kids; and more. The incredible thing about the gestures of the 300 people is that once they articulated their desire to help, the generosity spread. Strangers, friends, family, companies, and organizations chipped in to grow the gifts.

Each of us has something
to contribute to the life of this nation.

— Michelle Obama

And Oprah didn't stop there. In 2008, she launched a new show called *Oprah's Big Give,* in which ten contestants were given the name of a person in need, along with a sum of money and a mission to use it to better that person's life. Contestants traveled across the country and met people all over who were making a difference in their communities and in the wider world. The winner, Stephen Paletta, was awarded $1,000,000 to do still more good. He donated it to causes he supported, close to home and far away—but *he* didn't stop there, either. Paletta started a foundation that makes it possible for people to start their *own* "foundations"—accounts managed by Paletta's organization. Members can accumulate more funds in a lot of cool ways through benefit programs with corporate partners, and they can give their money away to any charity in the United States. The name of Paletta's brainchild? GiveBack.

Giving Large

The giving-back movement has kept on gathering steam at every level. At one end of the spectrum, there's Warren Buffett—a guy who isn't exactly hurting for money and has no need to prove anything. Not only does Buffett invest in ideas that will make the world cleaner and safer, he's led the charge to get other billionaires to donate their fortunes to worthy charities. In 2010, Buffett announced that he had gotten 10 percent of the wealthiest Americans on the Forbes 400 list to commit at least half of their entire net worth to charitable causes. The Giving Pledge, which Buffett kicked off with the Bill and Melinda Gates Foundation, attracted the richest of the rich, such as New York mayor Michael Bloomberg; hotel magnate Barron Hilton; investor Ronald Perelman; and Paul Allen, co-founder of Microsoft.

When asked how he got the first 40 *Fortune* 400 billionaires to sign on to the pledge, Buffett said, "It was a very soft sell." I imagine the rich philanthropists reacted in the same way as those who helped Oprah's audience with their charitable causes. When Buffet articulated the need and put his own money behind his passions, other influential individuals recognized their ability to do likewise. A powerful give-back movement has spread thanks to one act of generosity.

Now, before you start thinking that giving is only for the rich and famous, think about this: the average American donates about 3 percent of his or her salary to charity, but low-income workers give more than any other group—an average of 4.5 percent. And consider that sometimes the most meaningful gifts come from those who have less to give but give their all.

That's what Oseola McCarty of Hattiesburg, Mississippi, did. After leaving school in the sixth grade to care for sick relatives, McCarty lived just about the most retiring life you can imagine, taking in washing to earn a living and rarely venturing far from home. All that time, though, she was saving up the small amounts of money she earned—and in 1995, at 87 years old, she made headlines and history with a stunning gift. She donated $150,000, the bulk of her life savings, to the University of Southern Mississippi to fund scholarships for Black students.

I have found that among its other benefits,
giving liberates the soul of the giver.

— Maya Angelou

McCarty's generosity touched a nerve in her community: businesses in Hattiesburg came together to match her donation and double the size of the Oseola McCarty Scholarship Fund right off the bat. People from around the world began to donate, too. "This is the first time I've experienced anything like this from an individual who simply was not affluent," marveled Bill Pace, the executive director of the university's foundation. "She gave almost everything she had." And all she asked in return was to attend the graduation ceremony of a student who finished college on her scholarship. McCarty didn't even keep the many gifts she received from people who were moved and inspired by her story; saying she loved them all but didn't have room for them, she gave them to the school as well.

Giving of Yourself

I'll admit that Oseola McCarty sets the bar pretty high. Most of us aren't in a position to give everything we have to charity, no matter how good the cause. But the real lesson of her story is that everyone has something to give—and it doesn't have to make headlines.

In this time of economic turmoil, so many people are asking for help in some form. So if you have a little money to give away and you're unsure where to give it, there are lots of ways to find out. You might check out Stephen Paletta's GiveBack and set up your own account. Or visit a Website such as CharityNavigator .org, a guide to aid organizations across the United States that evaluates charities in a number of areas—from the environment to education—to help you figure out where your dollars will do the most good. If you belong to a church or civic group, start there, or find a group that's fighting hunger or building housing in your city or town.

But here's what's really important for you to know: giving doesn't have to be counted in dollars. Giving money is great, no question. But giving of yourself—your time, talents, knowledge, and energy—can be even more personal and meaningful. If you did the work in Part I of this book, you should be really clear by now on what your gifts and strengths are. That's what you can best pay forward: the core essence of who you are. Doesn't matter who you used to be; you're working with who you are *right now,* and that is bound to be a great gift to someone.

Do you have a talent for cooking or baking? Make a dish to take to someone on your block who's sick or down. Stay and talk awhile if you can; that's as nourishing as the food for someone who's in a low place. Are you handy with a wrench or a paintbrush? Volunteer with an organization that builds housing for people in need, such as Habitat for Humanity, or just lend your services to someone you know who needs a hand. You can offer child care, transportation to a doctor's appointment, or coaching in any area you know well—from sports to schoolwork to personal growth—and you don't need to sign up anywhere to do it. Just giving simple kindness—a smile, a laugh, or a gentle word—can transform someone's day, and likely yours as well. Pope Francis recently told a group of teens in a Roman detention center, "Among us the one who is highest up must be at the service of others." To put it another way, you don't need to worry that anything is beneath you if it helps lift someone else up.

If you do want to work within the structure of an organization, where you can be confident you'll be matched with people who need what you have to offer, there's no shortage of opportunities. In fact, it seems like there's a volunteer organization for just about every skill. I'm reminded of a group called Open Heart Magic that sends volunteer "hospital magicians" into Chicago-area hospitals to engage and energize seriously ill children. The healing power of wonder and laughter comes into play as these individuals—who aren't professional performers—engage the children one-on-one in interactive performances to bring smiles to faces that haven't smiled in a while.

Service organizations often have a need for people power in areas you might not expect. The Lions Club supports an eye bank in Washington State and Idaho, and there's a whole roster of volunteers on call to pick up donated corneas when they arrive via bus or train and get them to the hospital. One Lions Eye Bank employee tells the story of a volunteer who had signed up to work afternoons and evenings, and only in good weather. When the phone rang at 1 A.M. on a snowy night, he protested—but the program coordinator had nowhere else to turn. "I'll do it just this once," he said, "but please don't ever call me again."

With his 13-year-old son (who wanted to help Dad "run an errand" and keep him company), the man drove through the snow to the bus station, picked up the package, and drove it to the hospital. On the way home, the boy asked what had been in the package. When he learned that it was tissue from the eyes of someone who had died, which would in turn help someone else to see again, he took a minute to think that over. Then he said, "Wow! Dad, I never knew you did such important things!" The very next day, the man called the program coordinator and put himself back on the list.

Selfless Service

It's proven that giving makes us feel good: the very act of doing something for someone else gives us a kind of rush, releasing positive brain chemicals like serotonin and dopamine. (Scientists have a name for this: the warm-glow effect.) People who do charitable work have been shown to have lower rates of depression and higher self-esteem. And then, of course, there's the approval and applause we get from others—that sure feels good! But I think it's safe to say that that eye bank volunteer didn't have a change of heart because his young son praised him; I think it's more likely that he realized the true value of what he was doing for the person on the receiving end.

> *The giving of love is an education in itself.*
>
> — Eleanor Roosevelt

Thinking about the *other person:* that's the real definition of self-less service, the highest form of giving there is. It means giving because it's good for someone else, not because it makes *you* feel good. It means giving without any thought of self or expectation of anything in return. And that means that you have to put yourself and your motives under the microscope. It's fine that you cleaned out your closet and gave a bunch of clothes you don't want to Goodwill, but who is that really helping most directly? Probably you, because now you have a clean closet. It's great that you covered for your co-worker when she was sick, but are you secretly (or not so secretly) expecting that she'll do the same for you? Maybe she will, but giving shouldn't come with strings attached; it has to go beyond "I'll scratch your back if you scratch mine."

Selfless giving means that you're giving others what they really need, not what you think they need or ought to get. Don't be the person who's always jumping in with solutions to people's problems if all they want is a sympathetic ear. Don't go visit residents in a nursing home and spend the whole time feeling like the noble helper, or like you're suffering through a really unpleasant task, instead of truly being present and connecting with them, and even acknowledging your nervousness or discomfort if that's what you're feeling. They can tell the difference, and you aren't doing them any favors if you act like you're under some obligation. That's the kind of toxic giving most people would choose not to receive.

Selfless giving also means you can't give in a spirit of superiority to people who are less fortunate than you: *Look, I'm feeding the poor starving children in Africa!* Feed the children by all means, but be sure you're doing it for the right reasons. One really good reason is gratitude for all the good things that you yourself have—because until you demonstrate your gratitude in your actions, "thank you" is just a couple of words.

More Than Just Words

You probably won't hear the name Lester Dixon spoken by many success coaches or motivational speakers. Yet Lester truly fits the description of someone who has achieved massive success. Dixon is not rich by any means. He isn't on the cover of any Who's Who magazines, but he lives a fortunate, rich life—a life of supreme giving in action, infinitely beyond "just words."

One of my boys shared Lester's story with me after seeing his profile on WTVD-TV News out of Raleigh-Durham, North Carolina. Raised in Houston, Lester and his three brothers, Tyreese, Demetrius, and Audreece, grew up with two passions in their lives—church and sports. Their single mother, who is legally blind, raised the boys and made sure they studied hard in school. They got by on the meager wages she made playing the organ at a local church.

The boys grew up with NFL dreams and all earned sports scholarships. Demetrius went to West Point, Tyreese to the University of Texas, Audreece to Los Angeles City College, and Lester won a scholarship to Sul Ross State University. His on-the-field record was so impressive that Lester was invited to the National Football League Scouting Combine to showcase his skills in front of NFL coaches, general managers, and scouts.

Lester rejected the invitation and quit college. He was needed at home. His younger brother, Tyreese, had been paralyzed from the waist down after being struck by a drunk driver on his way home from a UT football game. Lester has few regrets about his decision: "I had the talent to make it, but God needed me to be somewhere else," he said during his WTVD-TV interview. "I needed to be there for my children, my mom, and the family."

Lester, who spends most of his time tending to his children's, brother's, and mother's needs, also works as the maintenance engineer for Woodland United Methodist Church of Rock Hill, South Carolina. His sacrifice has not been ignored by his co-workers, bosses, and church members, as Minister Rob Renfore attests: "People have this incredible ability to rise above their circumstances and live lives that are noble, and Lester does that."

According to Lester, he is simply doing what his faith demands:

"I always remain patient, put others before me, and treat others how you want to be treated, and go with that in life."

Lester's story touches me. His giving is the truly selfless kind. It's a supreme surrender of possible rewards for himself in the service of someone else's real needs, done out of caring and love.

> It's not about who you were, it's about who you are now.

In my life, I always try to give back out of love and caring for the people around me. I'm not patting myself on the back, I'm just keeping it real so I can help you do the same. And this book is an important part of my "give back." It is my way of sharing the lessons of a homeboy on a path to doom who miraculously turned his life around and is now living his dream. Most of you have not lost years of your lives to prison. You are in a much better position than I was to make that change today, and maybe to help other people change their lives, too.

When I speak before audiences in the criminal justice, educational, or employment fields, I hit hard on the fact that they have the unique ability to create future Jeff Hendersons, Mark Wahlbergs, or Jay-Zs. With my story as a guide, I can get them to see the potential of the disregarded or dismissed individuals they interact with on a daily basis. I put them in the place of the scholarly inmates who educated me, of Robert Gadsby who mentored me, and of Oprah Winfrey who inspired me. I try to get them to rise above the stereotypes or their biased perceptions of class and race and see how investing in these ignored and neglected individuals can create stronger workforces and contribute to a powerful nation of doers.

You may have come from a bad beginning, been a young Wahlberg or Jay-Z, but like I said earlier in this chapter, it's not about who you were, it's about who *you are now*. You've got the perspective on your life now to know who that is and to know what's truly important. I'm excited to see how you use your gifts to give back.

There's a great story that spiritual teachers Ram Dass and Paul Gorman tell in their book *How Can I Help?*, about a young Black man who's done crimes and done time. "Nobody ever treated me like I had anything to give," he tells the authors. "Just to take. So that's all I ever did." But when he gets involved with a volunteer program at a senior center—a last-chance shot at rehabilitation —he meets a little old Jewish lady who shows him different. She enjoys his attention, awakens his curiosity about other people and the world around him, and shows him that he does have something of value to offer others. And the lesson he learns about the gift of giving back is something all of us need to get. "I've done enough time," he says in the end. "I've done enough taking. Time to be free."

Street-Smart Challenges for:
The No-Strings Giver

☆ **Get inspired.** Identify someone you know, or someone you've read about, who strikes you as a truly selfless giver. What do you admire about him or her? How could you be more like that?

☆ **List your gifts.** Write down five ways that you could offer service to others starting right now.

☆ **Start a fund.** If you're able, make a commitment to put aside a certain amount of money every week for a cause you support. Even if it's just a few dollars at a time, it adds up.

☆ **Pay a visit.** Go to a nursing home, assisted-living facility, or senior center and spend at least an hour with the people there. If you don't know someone living in one of these places whom you can visit, call a facility in your area and ask if they need volunteers.

☆ **Lend a hand.** Identify at least one person in your family, workplace, or community who may need help with a practical task, such as moving. Ask how you can pitch in, and then do whatever is asked of you.

☆ **Look in the mirror.** Think of the last time you offered some kind of help or service to someone. What was your real motivation? Did you get anything in return? If not, did you think you should have?

The Shot-Caller

The strategy of
visionary leadership

When you're at the top of your game,
you're ready to show others the way.

— Chef Jeff

*O*ver the course of my career, I've had the honor of receiving a number of awards, starting in 2001 when I was named Las Vegas Chef of the Year by the American Tasting Institute. But the honors that mean the most to me by far are the ones I've received for my work helping others, like Job Train's Role Model of the Year Award. This is the work that gets me the most inspired—and the work I know I'm meant to do.

That's how I felt standing on stage at the Hyatt Regency in Chicago, in front of a room full of Chicago business leaders of all ages and races, being given the Safer Achievement Award from the Safer Foundation. This is an organization that's dedicated to helping people with criminal records reintegrate into the community, assisting them in finding jobs and providing a host of other needed services. The award is given annually to an individual with a record who has made a success of his life and given back to others as well.

When I stepped up to receive the award, I accepted it humbly on behalf of all incarcerated individuals who have given back to their communities. I said, "I would never have imagined 25 years ago when I walked into federal prison that I would have changed my life and become a success and proved all the critics, the haters, and the dream crushers wrong."

Then I got real with them. "It was my generation of the late '70s and early '80s that influenced a generation of killers and lawlessness and hopelessness," I said. "It was us that the young watched, drug dealing, gang banging, pimping, jacking, the whole nine yards." I thought they needed to hear me admit that. "But over the past 20 years I have been committed to working with young people in youth detention centers," I went on. "I have successfully hired formerly incarcerated individuals in every management position I've had. I'm extremely blessed for all the organizations, all the people like yourself here today, who see potential in people like us. I want to put out a call of action to all the formerly incarcerated that we need to step to the plate and go back into the community and fix what we broke." At that, they started to applaud. "We need to hold ourselves accountable. So I'm challenging you—we need to go back and help our young people. We need to get those blinders off them and help them to see the world through a different set of eyes."

The Mind of a Leader

At that luncheon, I was being honored as a leader in my own right, just the way the people in that room were leaders in theirs. And it was no accident that I talked about seeing the world through new eyes. Because real leadership is visionary. It's the quality that lets you see possibilities and mobilize others—as well as yourself—to make things happen for good in the world. That's what I'm trying to do when I speak to an audience, no matter if it's teens in a detention center or executives at a white-tablecloth dinner.

Leadership is the last of the street-smart strategies we're discussing, because in a real sense it's the top of the peak. You don't get it until you've understood and really worked through the other skills we've discovered together in this book. Because when you're at the top of your game, that's when you're ready to show others the way.

*The task of the leader is to get his people
from where they are to where they have not been.*

— Henry A. Kissinger

Being a leader doesn't have to mean being the actual CEO of a corporation, but you can learn a lot from the way they roll, because we are all the CEOs of our own lives and our own success, and all of us can be leaders in our families, neighborhoods, schools, places of worship—any place we come into contact with other people whom we can influence for good.

It's said that the most effective leaders don't use their positions of power to call the shots—they use their own personal power, and that's something you've been working hard to develop over the course of this book, something I know and you know that you have. At the same time, leadership itself isn't a personality trait. You've heard people say, "He's a born leader," but that's actually not accurate. Even if you possess some natural leadership abilities, on the complicated game board that we all operate on today, a successful leader is a constant work in progress. A leader's skills have to be upgraded daily because everything moves so fast. The good news is that you can cultivate the qualities of a great leader, but I want to be sure that you're straight with the most important thing—a *leader's mind*. In this chapter we will explore exactly what's on a successful leader's mind.

Shot-Callers on the Street

There aren't many college students bold enough to choose a gang leader as the subject for a dissertation. Obviously, Sudhir Venkatesh was cut from a different mold. The University of Chicago graduate student moved into the Robert Taylor Homes, one of the city's poorest housing projects on Chicago's South Side, for about seven years to develop his doctoral dissertation. He intentionally chose to hang out with and study J.T., the leader of the Black Kings, Chicago's largest and most feared crack-cocaine-dealing gang.

Somehow Venkatesh managed to befriend the gang leader, who seemed to enjoy the attention of an academic wanting to study his then-$100,000-a-year operation. Venkatesh's experiences with J.T. were first introduced in the best-selling book *Freakonomics* by Steven D. Levitt and Stephen J. Dubner. Venkatesh, however, expanded on the thesis—and the day J.T. gave him control of his enterprise—in his own book, *Gang Leader for a Day*.

J.T., a college graduate who left corporate America to pursue street capitalism, saw himself as an entrepreneur, business leader, and philanthropist. Venkatesh found it hard not to be swayed by the dope dealer's rationale. After all, J.T.'s enterprise was structured like a corporation. He had a treasurer, a security coordinator, and "directors" on the payroll who managed the lower-paid street-level workforce. As the gang's leader, J.T. had to maneuver around the competition and motivate his troops to keep selling even in the midst of deadly drug wars. Like a tobacco CEO, he had to placate those who protested his deathly deeds. He donated money and supplies to charities and neighborhood recreational centers and dispatched his security team to watch out for the elderly and deal with violent thugs, thieves, and other neighborhood predators. In some ways, J.T.'s reputation was that of an irreplaceable community asset rather than a lawbreaker.

Note that I use the past tense when I describe J.T.'s hustle. I chose it purposely because I seriously doubt he's still mastering his game, if you could ever say that he was. I shared a common flaw with J.T. We both chose lucrative but short-lived, underground careers. But looking at it from the economic perspective that Venkatesh explored, we were real-deal street CEOs. We managed and motivated people, delegated duties, and capitalized on our market based on the economic theory of supply and demand.

As she introduced me at the Safer Foundation lunch, President and CEO Diane Williams talked about this very thing—how street leadership really can translate into success in other lanes. "If you think about what it takes to run a cocaine distribution network, you've got to have a certain set of skills to do that," she said. "In the corporate arena, we talk all the time about transferring skills from one environment to another, but somehow we forget that people who make mistakes and lead businesses in the wrong arena can also do good in the right arena." In other words, the skills that make a successful "street exec" are remarkably similar to the ones that work in the CEO's corner office—and they can work for you when you step into the shoes of a leader, too. Let's break them down some more.

The Head of the Family

I've always been a fan of the movie *The Godfather*. I especially appreciate what it teaches us in the way that Vito Corleone manages the "corporate" structure of his organized-crime family. Putting the criminal angle aside, that structure is a success because it's based in the time-honored principles that make a real family work, with the Don as the head of the household, sternly but wisely managing the different personalities of all the family members—the favored son, the good-for-nothing—and all of them looking up to him like children do to a father.

In the conventional corporate model, the CEO is, in fact, something of a father figure. And even if that model seems outdated in today's diverse and changing workplace, we can still learn from the concept. A true CEO leader treats those around him (or her—women can adopt these qualities, too) as a family, which doesn't just mean the business equivalent of warm hugs. It means the CEO making rules, imposing discipline, and setting an example for the executives and employees below him. He has to walk his talk, because just like children with a parent, they're going to model their own actions on what he does much more than on what he says. He treats them with appreciation and consideration, and they return it with loyalty and respect for him and for one another.

That's how it looks when a "CEO dad" figure is operating at his best—blessed with the characteristics of a good father: fairness, firmness, integrity, and an appropriate degree of protectiveness. The reward is employees' admiration, as Carlos Fuente, Jr., told *USA Today* about his own family business. At the headquarters of A. Fuente Cigar, when patriarch Carlos, Sr. walks by, he said, all 3,000 employees look at him "like he is Vince Lombardi."

Management is about arranging and telling. Leadership is about nurturing and enhancing.

— Tom Peters

But relationships between parents and children take all sorts of forms, some more dysfunctional than others. It doesn't always pan out for a CEO to be the parent figure, if it means that he starts treating employees and high-level executives like children in a negative way—or if they start acting that way, helpless or needy or too eager to please. So when you're in this position, ask yourself: Do the people you're trying to lead fear you or do they love you? Do you inspire them or slowly take their power away? Do they admire you and your accomplishments or want to appease you because you control their livelihoods? As a leader, you must be honest about how your "family" is functioning and change things up if you need to for their success and your own.

Staying in Harmony

Just as a real family works best when there's harmony among the family members, the same is true in a corporation or in any collective endeavor—and it's up to the leader to set the tone. Because the truth is that leaders are responsible for everything— period. If the leader is weak, the team will be weak. If the leader is disorganized, self-centered, arrogant, or fearful, those distasteful attributes will reflect in his or her workforce, personal and business relationships, or whatever endeavor he or she is pursuing.

He who does not trust enough will not be trusted.

— Lao Tzu

This insight comes from some of the classiest, most prestigious hotels and restaurants where I worked in Los Angeles and Las Vegas. I was an employee of high-powered and well-paid managers, directors, VPs, and executive chefs. They seemed successful on the outside, but some of their operations were weak in various ways. This is not to say that they didn't have top-tier skills. It's that some had cultural intelligence flaws. They couldn't relate with their employee's lives, values, or backgrounds. Therefore, they had unmotivated, disgruntled workers who didn't give a shit about the big boss's vision or aspirations. They weren't giving their best in the kitchen, because management failed to get the "little people" to buy into anything that came from the top.

A real leader could make that situation better in several ways. First and foremost, he could develop a culture of trust in the workplace so that those so-called "little people" would understand that he had their best interests at heart, rather than suspecting the worst of their bosses. And trust starts to grow from the simplest gestures—like walking around the kitchen or the office, asking workers how they're doing, what they're proud of, what they need to do their jobs better, and really listening to the answers.

If and when the discontent blew up into actual conflict, a leader could step in to skillfully manage the opposing forces—while also understanding that opposition in and of itself isn't necessarily a bad thing; it can open the way for new ideas and innovations, as long as the conflict gets resolved in the end. To that end, a leader has to stay neutral—not letting personal feelings come into play—and to some extent detached; trying to force a reconciliation will only backfire. It takes patience to wait it out, but that's what a leader has to do when there's division in the rank and file. He or she is there to help the people or groups in conflict find their own common ground, not to take sides but to make space for the kind of discussion that will let the members of the "family" come back into harmony with one another.

Caring and Connection

Remember that from the leader's point of view, "family" isn't just your kin; it's the extended family you've pulled into your business, company, network, or bubble of possibilities. Out-of-touch CEOs treat those under their charge as product pushers or faceless caseloads. Too often, businesses and well-intentioned community organizations come to a crashing halt because the leader forgot about the "family's" needs.

When I'm with my actual family, we have downtime; we laugh, play, and eat together. I talk to my children about their challenges, dreams, and aspirations. I share my frustrations and my achievements, too. I try to involve them in my world so they, too, can begin to carve out their own pathways. My work family needs the same attention. In order to care about the leader, they need to know that the leader cares about them, personally. They have to feel appreciated and know deep down that their opinions and dedication matter; that they are part of the bigger picture.

Let me tell you about Tocarra Hawkins. I met this incredible young lady during a trip to New Orleans in 2005, shortly after Hurricane Katrina devastated the region. Tocarra was part of the Cafe Reconcile program—a community-based organization dedicated to taking at-risk kids off the streets and training them as cooks. But Tocarra had another disadvantage—she was born with only one arm.

When we met, I instantly honed in on her passion and desire to cook. Her bigger-than-life smile also caught my attention. Today's youngsters tend to be mean muggers, which signals anger. I tell kids that their expressions say a lot about their attitude, and I always remind them to smile during my one-on-one time with them.

Despite Tocarra's disability, she wanted to become a chef. Before leaving New Orleans, I wanted to show her how to work with her challenge. So I placed one of my hands in my pocket and kept it there while we worked side by side. I showed her how to use a pair of tongs like a second hand, and Tocarra picked up on it right away.

I was treating her with caring and appreciation, and I know she felt valued in that moment. This simple gesture and our brief time together inspired her, and she kept working her dream. The last time I checked in, Tocarra was working at the Hilton Hotel in New Orleans.

Building Community

The most successful CEOs—or leaders of any kind—foster a feeling of community within their organization, and they also look beyond their immediate "family" to extend caring and make connections in the wider community. Take Wendell Pierce, the actor already known for his roles in series such as *Treme* and *The Wire*, who's moved into community building in one of the most direct ways you can imagine. The co-founder of New Orleans–based

Sterling Farms Fresh Foods is bringing low-income, high-crime neighborhoods something that many Americans take for granted: supermarkets.

"In the Lower Ninth Ward," Pierce told NPR, "there hasn't been a decent grocery store in 20 years." Now Sterling Farms is moving into these so-called food deserts to offer quality merchandise, including plenty of fresh fruits and vegetables, to customers whose only options before were to get B and C grade products at a distant grocery or to buy unhealthy food at a convenience store. Pierce and his colleagues are partnering with other community organizations to arrange for building restoration and affordable rent; getting the word out at a local level with events like community crawfish boils; and offering customers amenities like clean restrooms and van service. And his vision is rooted in a deeply personal sense of community. "It was the memory of that Friday-night grocery trip that I used to take with my mother," he told NPR. "It was the town square, you know, men and women getting off of work and you would see them at our neighborhood grocery store. . . . I felt as though that was something that everybody should have in their neighborhood."

Community is a bit farther-flung for social entrepreneur Scott Harrison, but the sense of connection is just as strong. Harrison is the founder and chief executive of charity: water, an organization that brings clean, safe drinking water to people in developing nations (and passes 100 percent of donations straight into the field to fund water projects). A club promoter in his former life, the young CEO had his eyes opened when he went to volunteer in Africa and discovered that people were living on annual incomes roughly equivalent to the cost of a bottle of high-end vodka at one of his clubs. His model of leadership is strongly rooted in gratitude: staffers have made personalized thank-you videos for donors, dressing as bakers, for example, to thank someone who raised money for the charity by baking. It's also overwhelmingly positive; the charity publishes profiles of people whose lives have been improved by water, rather than hyping those who are suffering without it, and the photos of small boys filling cans at a well in Rwanda, smiles beaming on their faces, are irresistibly uplifting.

Passing On the Power

Scott Harrison truly knows himself: it was an unflinching examination of his former life that led him to his new vision. The best leaders have honestly examined and overcome their own shortcomings, so they are in better positions to understand those around them and help them build on their inherent strengths.

> The best leaders have honestly examined and overcome their own shortcomings.

In some of those challenging Las Vegas kitchens I described earlier, many of the shot-callers failed because they didn't know their employees—other than the fact that they were mostly uneducated, mostly minority or poor Whites, many immigrants, and some, convicted felons. They hadn't bothered to learn where they came from, how they were raised, or what challenges they had to overcome to even show up for work on time. I would argue that many of the bosses didn't know their employees because they didn't truly know themselves. Most hadn't tapped into their own potential to inspire or fire up those lower down the line.

In my leadership role I walked into those kitchens, and, right away, I knew my workers—most were homies from the neighborhood, some who had shared my past experiences. I knew where they came from because I had once walked in their shoes. Rarely, if ever, had they been given that needed pat on the back. They hadn't been acknowledged as essential members of the workforce, so, instinctively, I knew they had to be empowered.

So what did I do? I'd pull a few promising crew members into my office and say something like, "You guys are amazingly talented. We're changing the menu and I need different dishes from each of you. I'll give you three days to get back to me with your ideas for consideration." They were blown away, because no chef had ever asked for their input before.

When I needed to correct something they were doing, I followed the same playbook. Instead of saying "You need to freaking learn how to do this better," I would say, "Wow! This dish is amazing. You have so much talent." Then I'd pause, and I'd follow up: "But there are a couple of areas where I think, if you put in extra effort, you can create even a better dish, and become an even better cook than you are today." This proved so effective that now I do the same thing with my children: "You guys are amazing and smart—I'm so proud of you! And these are some of the areas Daddy wants you to focus on next year."

When you're in the position of a leader, it's worth looking at how you're using your skills to lead. Let's say you're the neighborhood block organizer or that go-to guy or girl everyone turns to to make plans for parties or the extended family. Okay, so you might be able to get people to do the things you'd rather not do—but can you motivate them to do what they're *supposed* to do? Can you help them become better mothers, fathers, role models, or hustlepreneurs in their own right?

Leadership is the capacity to translate vision into reality.

— Warren G. Bennis

At the same time as he was building his crew, Gadsby was doing me a service that would change my life—helping me do what I was supposed to do. Nowadays, I can put myself in Gadsby's shoes. I'm always on the lookout to help build up communities; I'm always on the lookout for gifted people who have yet to tap into their true potential. I usually find them in dishwashing positions, quick-service restaurants, trade schools, youth detention centers, housing projects, or prisons. If I can do a little bit to help these people improve their chances in life, without expectation of reward, my crew gets stronger and another soul finds his or her purpose.

And each of those souls is now more likely to do the same for others. That's the principle behind Girls Who Code, a program founded by former NYC deputy public advocate Reshma Saujani to train teenage girls in coding, robotics, Website development, and app making—a valuable step toward greater equality in a field where three out of four jobs are held by men. The effect Saujani hopes for is just like that old shampoo ad you may remember—*I told two friends, and they told two friends....* "The replication effect is so powerful," Saujani told *Fast Company* magazine. "Teach one girl how to code, she'll teach four."

The Servant Leader

By now it should be clear that the street-smart rule of leadership is more than just getting people to do your bidding. If that's all you want to do, call yourself something else—a manager or a boss, maybe even a bully or a tyrant—but you're not a true leader.

There's a model of leadership that I love—the concept of the "servant leader"—that takes in a lot of the traits we've been discussing, not just in this chapter but throughout this book. Though its basic principles go back as far as leadership itself, it was made popular in the modern era by the management expert Robert K. Greenleaf several decades ago, and many wise heads have played off it since then. Servant leaders are humble, empathetic, and fully accountable. They foster trust and teamwork and community, listen to others' ideas and opinions, and don't put themselves first, just the way I told you a while back that I always tried to run a "we" kitchen rather than a "me" kitchen. Above all, they are dedicated to *serving*: when they pursue opportunities, it's not just for personal gain but to make a positive difference in other people's lives. They're committed to helping the people around them step into their own best selves. I know this is the kind of leader I need to be. And it's my hope that it's the kind of leader you're learning to be, too.

My icon and spiritual mentor Bishop T. D. Jakes may be the finest example of "servant leadership" I know. Jakes is the real deal, a serious and true leader. The charismatic minister's empire includes best-selling books and films; popular television and radio programs; his own greeting-card line; Potter's House, his 30,000-member, nondenominational mega-church in Dallas, and sold-out conferences the world over. He was named "America's Best Preacher" by *Time* magazine and ranks among the "25 Most

Influential African Americans," Britain's "100 Most Influential Black People," and *Ebony*'s "Power150." He has been called on to impart wisdom to leaders around the world, and many know him for his homily at the historic 2009 Presidential Inauguration when Barack Obama took office. With more than 35 years in ministry, T. D. Jakes is still a powerful international force of inspiration and influence for millions.

But more impressive even than his many accomplishments is the strong sense of service behind them. The bishop is committed to mentoring, to serving a new generation, and to being accessible as a leader. In the true spirit of servant leadership, he's said that "real power is not at the top, but at the bottom." In 2013 he received a Keeper of the Dream Award, given by the National Action Network to honor those who keep alive the principles for which Dr. Martin Luther King, Jr., worked and gave his life. In his acceptance speech, harking back to what Dr. King called life's most urgent question—"What are you doing for others?"—he said, "To be acknowledged in the service of others is the culmination of a lifelong mission."

In one of his sermons, Jakes told it straight: "The worst thing about living and dying is to get to the end of your life, staring death in the face, and think to yourself, 'I have made *no* difference. . . .' Woe be unto you if you don't make a difference."

I thought of this recently when I read the story of a young man who's already making a difference even before he's out of his teens. Kelvin Doe, a 16-year-old from Sierra Leone, is unquestionably a servant leader in the making, a self-taught engineering whiz who builds marvels out of materials from the scrap heap. In a country where the power comes on, as he puts it, "once in a week," he made his own battery to light people's houses; then he patched together the equipment to launch a one-man radio station, along with a generator to run it. It wasn't ego that made him want to hit the airwaves, it was a desire to give a voice to his community. His latest project is to build a windmill to provide power for some of his neighbors in Sierra Leone's capital, Freetown.

In 2012, Kelvin traveled to MIT for three weeks—the first time he had ever left home—to work on engineering projects in an environment where you can pick a fuse or a capacitor out of a bin full of them, rather than out of the trash. A video of his travels shown on YouTube makes it clear he's having the time of his life, but also that he's taking in everything he sees to help him in the task of designing his country's future and inspiring other young people to join in. "It's a movement," says the MIT Ph.D. student who arranged Kelvin's trip. Kelvin himself puts it even more clearly: "Whatever I've learned here, I will share it with my friends, colleagues, and loved ones and do it as a team."

Woe be unto you if you don't make a difference.

— T. D. Jakes

I second what T. D. Jakes said: woe be unto the would-be leader who can't make a positive difference in someone else's life the way Kelvin Doe is doing already. If you want to become a street-smart leader, that's what you need to aim for. We should all aspire to be life changers for ourselves and others—to help them, as much as we are able, to see the world through a new set of eyes.

☆ **Learn from a leader—or two or three.** Think of at least one person you know who's shining as a leader in his or her lane. What is he or she doing that you can learn from and apply for yourself?

☆ **Check your family.** Did you have a model of leadership at the head of your household growing up? What about now? If the head of the household is you, how do you think you're doing?

☆ **Stop and listen.** Every day this week, make it a point to ask someone a question that doesn't have a yes-or-no answer—someone who's on your team or in your circle of community. Listen without judgment and let him know he's heard.

☆ **Resolve a conflict.** The next time people around you are going head to head, step in. Don't take sides, but encourage them to talk to each other and try to help them see where their common interests lie.

☆ **"Find the good and praise it."** This week, find at least one opportunity to give someone around you a compliment he or she deserves—followed by a suggestion for how to do something better.

☆ **Pass on the power.** This week, teach at least one person something you know how to do well. Ask him or her to pass the knowledge—and the power—along to others.

Afterword

The first move toward mastery is always inward—
learning who you really are and reconnecting with
that innate force. Knowing it with clarity, you will find
your way to the proper career path
and everything else will fall into place.
— Robert Greene, *Mastery*

While I was writing this book, I had the chance to give a presentation at Grand Rapids Community College to students in
the Secchia Institute for Culinary Education there. In a beautiful
amphitheater with a state-of-the-art kitchen, I stood behind the
stove and looked at the rows of students watching me, men and
women, not all of them young, most of them in chef's whites or
black uniforms. "What I'm gonna share with you isn't taught in
schools," I said.

"You guys know my background," I went on. "You guys know
that in my former life I was a bad guy." Then I told them my story
with the power of food woven through it, because that was our
common language. I took them on the journey you've taken with
me, from the streets to that six-burner stove I was standing behind. And I told them what they had to do to find their own road
to success. "In order to be successful in anything you do," I told
them, "there are certain traits you must have. There's a certain
level of sacrifice you have to make. There's a high level of drive
and determination needed to get there—a high level of willingness to put in the man- or woman-hours required—to reach that
level of mastery."

As we went on, I did my cooking demonstration, talking them
through every step. I chopped onions and celery, I cooked up

molasses short ribs and king crab gumbo, my granddaddy's version. Then I asked a student named Laura to come up to the front to help me pour the gumbo over hot, steamed white rice. As she reached for the pot, she was a little awkward, but something about her caught my attention, and I stopped her for a moment. "Let me tell you something about Laura," I said to the audience. "Laura is gonna make it. I don't care what that little voice says that sometimes gives her doubt inside. It doesn't matter what people in class say, or what the people who know her outside of class think. You know why she's gonna make it? Laura, hold up your hands." Embarrassed, she did. Her left hand had notes written all over it.

"Look at that," I said. "We don't have pens and paper, so she wrote on her hand." That's how much she wanted to take in and remember what she was hearing. "Tell you what, I'll e-mail you those notes," I said to Laura, handing her a towel to grasp the hot pan handle. "Now, I need you to put this in your hand and bring that pot over here." And she worked alongside me for the rest of the presentation.

I love to visit places like GRCC, because it's community colleges and trade schools like this that open their doors to everyone, no matter what their past has been. When I met some of the students after my talk, I learned that some of them came from difficult backgrounds, too. At least nine people came up to me and said that they'd been in prison or homeless, and that food had given them an avenue to hope. I just hoped that hearing what I had to say had made their long path to mastery a little smoother.

The Journey to Mastery

Let's be real. Some folks believe that a master is someone who's perfect, someone who never has to learn anything more. And the truth is that no one knows it all. You're a student for life. But there are levels of mastery that you can reach.

When I took the VIA Survey, one of my top five signature strengths was "appreciation of beauty and excellence." The drive to excellence is in my DNA, and excellence is what mastery is all about. It's not a one-time achievement; it's a lifestyle, a mind-set that sees you through your whole life as you keep on growing and learning. There are experts called masters in every field—masters in the building trades, like plumbers and electricians; masters in the arts, like film directors or orchestra conductors; masters in the kitchen and the classroom; masters in athletics, where we call them Olympians; even grandmasters in fields like chess and martial arts. And you can best believe that these masters are always learning, always striving for excellence, always perfecting their craft, whatever it may be.

Author Malcolm Gladwell, in his book *Outliers: The Story of Success,* tells us that mastery of anything takes a tremendous amount of practice: 10,000 hours, to be exact. Drawing on examples from Mozart to the Beatles, he argues that that's the "magic number" for greatness—the time it takes to become a world-class expert in anything. Ten thousand hours may sound like a lot of time to spend honing your hustle and sharpening your street smarts—but think about it: the people we think of as the best of the best have surely put at least 10,000 hours into their craft to become the best at what they do. Michael Jordan and Kobe Bryant spend their summers shooting three-pointers, not doing reality shows. Paul Allen and Bill Gates worked for free as janitors at one of the first computer labs in the nation so they could get access to the computers to become the best at what they do. Studies have shown that changes actually start to happen in the brain when you get close to the 10,000-hour mark—so when I talk about "getting your mind right," you can take it literally.

Robert Greene, who wrote *The 48 Laws of Power* and *The 50th Law,* doesn't even stop at 10,000 hours. In his book *Mastery,* he makes the case that it takes up to twice that long—20,000 hours—for the brain to undergo yet another transformation, one that allows you to make connections and process ideas at a level of thought so high it's practically beyond rational. So you see, even the people who write about mastery are always reaching for a higher level of mastery!

Back in the day, there was a time-honored system in place for logging those hours. A young worker would sign on as an apprentice to a master—say, a cobbler or a painter—then spend the next several years working alongside him, copying his techniques and learning his skills by practicing them over and over and over. If you repeat an action or task often enough, something called "muscle memory" kicks in and you're able to perform the task almost effortlessly—so before too long, the apprentices had their craft down cold and could progress to higher levels of artistry and achievement. Well, "muscle memory" applies to any capability you're exercising, not just physical actions. And even though formal apprenticeships aren't so common today, that commitment to practice is the key to excellence just like it's always been. It puts mastery within our reach, if we're willing to do the hard work.

My thousands of hours of practice started right in my makeshift cell kitchen, whipping up Top Ramen dishes for fellow prisoners. When I got into the restaurant world, I was the guy who unloaded the truck. I was the guy who broke down all the lobster claws, cut up all the mirepoix. I was the guy who cleaned all the cipollini onions, small-diced all the shallots. Many people thought they were taking advantage of me. I didn't look at it that way. Every time they had me break lobsters down or dice shallots and garlic, I got better and better and better at what I was doing. I was on my way from unconscious incompetence—when I didn't know what I didn't know—to unconscious competence, when muscle memory would take over and I would be able to deliver excellence almost without giving it a thought.

If you've done the work in this book and successfully changed your mind-set, then by now I know you're on your way down that path toward excellence, accepting what you don't know and fully appreciating what you do know. And now that we've come to the end of our journey together, I'm about to send you off to continue on your lifelong quest to reach new levels of mastery in your own life, where you're operating at full swing and employing the highest and best expression of the unique strengths and gifts that make you you.

So where are you going to get your 10,000 or 20,000 hours? Maybe you've been working at your craft for a while and already have a bunch of hours under your belt. If not, stay with me for a minute, because I'm gonna show you that you already know where to start.

Never Too Late

Robert Greene really got my attention with those 20,000 hours. And something else in his book got my attention, too—probably the best description I've read of where mastery really begins. "You possess an inner force that seeks to guide you toward . . . what you are meant to accomplish in the time that you have to live," Greene writes. "The first move toward mastery is always inward—learning who you really are and reconnecting with that innate force. Knowing it with clarity, you will find your way to the proper career path and everything else will fall into place."

Think about that for a moment. Everything else will fall into place. If you know with crystal clarity who you are and what dream drives you, you will find your way.

Greene goes on to say, "It is never too late to start this process" —and you already have! In the course of this book, you've made that move inward. You've learned a lot about who you are; you've gotten a fix on your innate strengths and drilled down on your deepest dreams. So you're already well on your way to being a certified hustlepreneur, someone who has attained a level of mastery in the 12 street smarts and is putting them to work in the world.

This is why everybody's journey to mastery, and everybody's recipe for success, is different: because your recipe is based on who you are. Some people need a little more of this and a little less of that. Some need double this and three times as much of that. Some need to slap the ingredients on a hot grill, and some need to simmer them gently in a braising pan. And even if your recipe happens to look just like somebody else's on paper, it's never going to come out exactly the same.

Think about real cooking for a second. If you and I both follow the same recipe word for word, the dishes are going to be very similar but not quite alike, because my vegetables come from California and yours may come from Connecticut or Georgia, and the different soils they grew in give those vegetables a different flavor. In your recipe for success, when you throw your street-smart secret ingredients into the mix, they're going to have a different flavor from somebody else's, and the resulting dish is going to be uniquely yours.

So I want you to remember the work you've done in this book and take it with you when you step back into your life. Remember what's uniquely yours, what you discovered about yourself on that journey inward with your VIA and E-gram profiles. Keep your vision close to your heart and your goals close at hand, where you can check back with them and check your progress often. Use your action plan to help you decide where you're directing your energy and your time every day.

Like I said, mastery isn't a one-time achievement. It's a mind-set and a way of life. So you're going to need to keep this up! Keep on checking in with you, the real self you've come to see more clearly through VIA and the E-gram—don't let your reflection in the mirror get all blurry or out of focus. Keep on updating your vision for your life as you grow and change; set new goals for yourself as you achieve the old ones; and refresh your action plan to keep you in that space where every step moves you forward. What I've given you in this book isn't just a way to get something you want in the short term, it's a set of tools you can use for the rest of your life. And it starts right now—because while it's true that it's never too late, it's also true that once you're ready, you've got no time to waste.

Over to You

When I think of you reading this page, about to close this book and move on, I see a clock sitting in front of me, and I say to myself, *The time has come.* In fact, *your* time has come. You can make this the defining moment in your life—if you make that choice.

It *is* a choice, and it's one you have to be ready to make, the way I did so many years ago. At the end of the day, this book means nothing if you're not ready—if you're not willing to accept who you are, to hold yourself accountable for where you are in life today, and then say, *I'm ready for change.*

If you can see it, you can be it. That's the truth. But you have to do the work. No one else can do it for you. No one else can help you reach a level of mastery in your own life. It's over to you now, my friend.

And I want you to believe that you can do it! Because that's what I believe. No matter who you are, no matter where you come from, whatever the color of your skin, whatever the hand you were dealt in life, whatever your story is, I believe that all of us—all of us—have the power to transform our lives.

Like Laura at Grand Rapids Community College, writing notes on her hand, you're gonna have to do whatever it takes to get yours. As I told the students in that audience, I don't care what that little voice says that sometimes gives you doubt inside. You have to tune out that voice that says, You can't do. You can't dream. You can't have. I'm here to say, You can dream. You can do. You can have.

That's what I told the students in that audience, and that's what I'm telling you right now. Straight up. *If you can see it, you can be it.* Now—are you ready?

Acknowledgments

Without a doubt, the Almighty has blessed me with the power to overcome some difficult times throughout my life. The content of this book would not be possible without his grace and hand over me. My wife, Stacy, my hero, loving confidante, and toughest critic, along with my six amazing children, have allowed me to build over the years, relentlessly in pursuit of my personal mission to become the best me so that I can help others. Thank you, Stacy, for wearing my hat at times to keep us all together.

So many influences of wise men and women have elevated me in many life-changing ways—from former prisoners to prep cooks, line cooks, chefs, CEOs, pastors, and self-help gurus—to get me to this stage in my life. It was key ordinary and extraordinary men and women in prison who planted the first seeds that helped me discover my purpose: Friendly Womack, Jr., Roy Ball the Baker, Big Roy, and the Wall Street Boys, Mr. Rosario Gambino, Mr. Alan Hershman, and so many others who kept whispering in my ear, coaching me, and respecting me for who I was.

My father and mother, Charles and June Henderson, who have stood by me no matter what trouble I got myself in, who wanted nothing but the best for my sister, Junell, and me. Mom, you gave me fight, and Dad, you gave humility. Making you two proud is my sign of appreciation to you both.

To my grandparents, Charles and Ethel Henderson, who would have been so proud of me, finally getting my life figured out. You two gave Junell and me a sense of family when my parents struggled. Thank you.

Chef Gadsby opened my first door of real opportunity after my release in 1996. His influence on my life is now shaping my own legacy that is shaping the lives of my children and others who were once like I was back in the day.

Chefs Sterling Burpee, Sarah Bowman, Gary Clauson, Jim Perillo, and Wolfgang Von Wieser opened more doors of access. Thank you, Chefs, for shaping, inspiring, and teaching me the ropes that allowed me to become Chef Jeff.

Mike Psaltis, my longtime literary agent, friend and the man who found me in the Bellagio kitchen. That one phone call changed my life forever. Thanks for your guidance and support.

A very special thanks to Tavis Smiley and the entire SmileyBooks team for the opportunity to write a book that would define "how I did it." Cheryl Woodruff, my editor, worked relentlessly on this project. Thank you for pushing me to go deep and share every personal gift I had used to become the best me.

Much appreciation to Sylvester Brown, Jr., for his creative guidance and valuable research. Special thanks to Anne Barthel for helping me put the final pieces in perfect place.

Thank you, Team Keppler, for helping me to bring my message of inspiration before thousands of people in corporations., associations, and organizations.

To all my family members who loved me unconditionally during my darkest moments, my friends who stuck by me no matter what, and my fans and believers who have followed me since *Cooked* hit the streets in 2007, I thank all of you from the depths of my heart.

If You Can See It, You Can Be It,
Chef Jeff

About the Author

Award-winning chef and author of the *New York Times* Best-seller *Cooked*, Chef Jeff Henderson discovered his passion and gift for cooking in a most unlikely place: behind bars.

Today, the former host of the Food Network's docu-reality series *The Chef Jeff Project* and the star of the nationally syndicated cooking show *Family Style with Chef Jeff* is one of the most influential African American chefs in the country. Henderson uses his redemptive journey—from drug dealer to TV celebrity chef to nationally acclaimed motivational speaker—to help others reboot their own dreams and gain a new foothold on the ladder to success.

Chef Jeff has appeared on *Oprah, Today, Good Morning America,* and CNN and been featured in *USA Today, The Wall Street Journal,* and *The Washington Post.* His inspiring life story is now in development by Sony/Columbia Pictures for a major feature film. Chef Jeff lives in Las Vegas with his wife, Stacy, and their five children.

Stay connected with Chef Jeff's latest adventures at www.chefjefflive.com and on Twitter@chefjefflive. For more information on the book visit www.chefjeffseeitbeit.com.

SmileyBooks Titles
of Related Interest

FORGIVENESS:
21 Days to Forgive Everyone for Everything
by Iyanla Vanzant

ALMOST WHITE:
Forced Confessions of a Latino in Hollywood
by Rick Najera

THE RICH AND THE REST OF US:
A Poverty Manifesto
by Tavis Smiley and Cornel West

HEALTH FIRST:
The Black Women's Wellness Guide
by Eleanor Hinton Hoytt and Hilary Beard

PEACE FROM BROKEN PIECES:
How to Get Through What You're Going Through
by Iyanla Vanzant

TOO IMPORTANT TO FAIL:
Saving America's Boys
by Tavis Smiley Reports

BRAINWASHED:
Challenging the Myth of Black Inferiority
by Tom Burrell

All of the above are available at your local or online bookstore, or may be
ordered online through Hay House, at www.hayhouse.com®

• • •

We hoped you enjoyed this SmileyBooks publication.
If you would like to receive additional information, please contact:

SMILEYBOOKS

Distributed by:
Hay House, Inc.
P.O. Box 5100
Carlsbad, CA 92018-5100
(760) 431-7695 or (800) 654-5126
(760) 431-6948 (fax) or (800) 650-5115 (fax)
www.hayhouse.com® • www.hayfoundation.org

• • •

Published and distributed in Australia by:
Hay House Australia Pty. Ltd. • 18/36 Ralph St. • Alexandria NSW 2015
Phone: 612-9669-4299 • *Fax:* 612-9669-4144 • www.hayhouse.com.au

Published and distributed in the United Kingdom by:
Hay House UK, Ltd., Astley House, 33 Notting Hill Gate, London W11 3JQ
Phone: 44-20-3675-2450 • *Fax:* 44-20-3675-2451 •www.hayhouse.co.uk

Published and distributed in the Republic of South Africa by:
Hay House SA (Pty), Ltd. • P.O. Box 990, Witkoppen 2068
Phone/Fax: 27-11-467-8904 • www.hayhouse.co.za

Published and distributed in India by:
Hay House Publishers India
Muskaan Complex, Plot No. 3, B-2, Vasant Kunj, New Delhi 110 070
Phone: 91-11-4176-1620 • *Fax:* 91-11-4176-1630 • www.hayhouse.co.in

Distributed in Canada by:
Raincoast • 9050 Shaughnessy St., Vancouver, B.C. V6P 6E5
Phone: (604) 323-7100 • *Fax:* (604) 323-2600 • www.raincoast.com
• • •